CREATING SPACE
BETWEEN
PESHAT AND *DERASH*
A COLLECTION OF STUDIES
ON TANAKH

CREATING SPACE BETWEEN
PESHAT AND *DERASH*
A COLLECTION OF STUDIES
ON TANAKH

HAYYIM J. ANGEL

KTAV Publishing House, Inc.
In Association with Sephardic Publication Foundation

Library of Congress Cataloging-in-Publication Data

Angel, Hayyim J.
  Creating space between peshat and derash : a collection of studies
on Tanakh / Hayyim J. Angel.
     p. cm.
  ISBN 978-1-60280-176-9
  1. Bible. O.T.--Criticism, interpretation, etc. I. Title.
  BS1171.3.A5445 2011
  221.6--dc22

                        2011008418

Published by
KTAV Publishing House, Inc.,
888 Newark Avenue, Suite 119
Jersey City, N.J. 07306
Email: orders@ktav.com
www.ktav.com

CONTENTS

FOREWORD

Traditional Biblical interpretation is like a high-wire act. Leaning too much in either one direction or the other will cause a loss of balance, which, if not corrected immediately, will inexorably result in a fall from a potentially dangerous height. Two principles, one Talmudic and one medieval, dictate the elements of traditional Jewish interpretation of Tanakh that need to be stabilized.

The Talmud declares that: אין מקרא יוצא מידי פשוטו; no verse can be divested of its literal, straightforward, meaning (BT *Shabbat* 63a). And Nahmanides notes: לא אמרו אין המקרא אלא כפשוטו; the Sages didn't say that Tanakh is only to be understood literally (*Sefer ha-Mitzvot*, Principle #2), meaning that non-literal interpretations are certainly in order.

The challenge that confronts interpreters who are loyal to tradition is how to preserve the balance between the literal and non-literal elements. On the one hand, they need to be aware of the linguistic and literary possibilities inherent in each and every verse, in order to circumscribe the range of legitimate interpretation. On the other hand, however, they need to beware of stretching the text beyond its linguistic and literary limits in order to accommodate their own ideas.

* * *

The interpretation of Tanakh begs two essential questions: Why? and How? Why assume that Tanakh requires interpretation and cannot be understood literally? And, if you grant the premise that interpretation is necessary, how do you distinguish between valid interpretations and invalid ones—let alone discriminate among the valid interpretations to establish an ascending order of preference? Our Sages, from the Talmud through the twentieth century, have given these questions their due and careful consideration and arrived at the conclusions that interpretation is mandated by the inherent multiplicity of meaning that reposes in Tanakh, and that validity is determined by adherence to and consistency with our venerable tradition.

On multiplicity of meaning, the Talmud states:

תלמוד בבלי מסכת שבת דף פח עמוד ב

תני דבי רבי ישמעאל: וכפטיש יפצץ סלע (ירמיהו כג,כט); מה פטיש זה נחלק לכמה ניצוצות - אף כל דיבור ודיבור שיצא מפי הקדוש ברוך הוא נחלק לשבעים לשונות.

The school of R. Yishmael taught: "As a hammer shatters a rock." Just as a hammer splinters into several pieces, so is every divine utterance divisible into seventy languages. (BT *Shabbat* 88b)[1]

תלמוד בבלי מסכת סנהדרין דף לד עמוד א

אמר אביי: דאמר קרא: אחת דבר אלהים שתים זו שמעתי כי עז לאלהים (תהלים ס"ב,יב). מקרא אחד יוצא לכמה טעמים, ואין טעם אחד יוצא מכמה מקראות.

Abbaye said: Scripture declares, "God speaks once [yet] I hear twice; strength is God's." A single verse yields several meanings [yet] a single meaning does not emerge from multiple verses. (BT *Sanhedrin* 34a)

Recognition of the preeminence of Tradition in establishing validity is evident in the pithy Talmudic story regarding Hillel and a prospective convert:

תלמוד בבלי מסכת שבת דף לא עמוד א

תנו רבנן: מעשה בנכרי אחד שבא לפני שמאי, אמר לו: כמה תורות יש לכם? אמר לו: שתים, תורה שבכתב ותורה שבעל פה. אמר לו: שבכתב - אני מאמינך, ושבעל פה - איני מאמינך. גיירני על מנת שתלמדני תורה שבכתב. גער בו והוציאו בנזיפה. בא לפני הלל - גייריה, יומא קמא אמר ליה: א"ב

ג"ד, למחר אפיך ליה. אמר ליה: והא אתמול לא אמרת לי הכי? אמר לו: לאו
עלי דידי קא סמכת? דעל פה נמי סמוך עלי!

The rabbis taught: It once happened that a gentile came before
Shammai and asked him: How many Torahs do you have? He
replied: Two; one written and one oral. He said: I trust you
regarding the written one, but not regarding the oral one; convert
me in order to teach me the written Torah. [Shammai] rebuked
him and chased him out angrily.

He came to Hillel who converted him. The first day [Hillel]
taught him *alef-bet-gimmel-dalet*; the next day he reversed them.
[The convert] asked: But yesterday you taught me otherwise?
[Hillel] replied: Have you not put your trust in me [for the
alphabet, i.e., the written Torah]? Trust me for the oral one as
well! (BT *Shabbat* 31a)

Rashi, building on the Talmudic premise, adds:

<u>רש"י שיר השירים פרק א</u>

אחת דבר אלהים שתים זו שמעתי, מקרא אחד יוצא לכמה טעמים וסוף דבר
אין לך מקרא יוצא מידי משמעו. ואף על פי שדברו הנביאים דבריהם בדוגמא
צריך ליישב הדוגמא על אופניה ועל סדרה כמו שהמקראות סדורים זה אחר זה.

"God speaks once [yet] I hear twice." A single verse yields several
meanings, yet, in the final analysis, no verse can be purged of
its literal sense. Even though the prophets spoke figuratively,
each figure of speech must be understood contextually[2] just as
each verse must be seen in its context. (Rashi, introduction to the
Song of Songs)

Rashi stipulates here that interpretation, to be effective, must
combine Scripture (אחת דבר אלה'ים), tradition (מקרא אחד יוצא לכמה),
(טעמים), and reason (צריך ליישב הדוגמה), in order to effect a valid
interpretation.

* * *

The noun *torah* derives from the verbal root *y-r-h*, which signifies instruction. *Y-r-h* is also at the root of the word *moreh*, which means teacher. In Tanakh, however, it also means an archer. Is there a connection between torah, teaching and archery? I believe there is, and I further believe that Hayyim Angel's present book epitomizes that connection.

The purpose of archery is to land an arrow as closely as possible to the exact center of the target, the bull's eye, known in Tanakh as the *matarah*. The purpose of the study of Torah is, likewise, to get as close as possible to the exact meaning of a text. Just as a skilled archer can consistently place his arrows within the center ring, an effective teacher can regularly locate his explanations within proximity to the central meaning of the text, the aforementioned *peshuto shel mikra'*. Hayyim Angel is such a teacher and his exegetical quiver holds a wide and engaging assortment of arrows.

His analyses of the biblical text are true and accurate reflections of both the propositions with which we began. He is sensitive to the multiplicity of available meanings, on which he focuses the resources of our revered tradition, which are aimed with the discernment born of his considerable classroom and pulpit experience. It was a pleasure to read the essays contained in this volume and that pleasure is now yours as well.

Moshe Sokolow

NOTES

1. Rashi's interpretation—which may actually reflect an alternative reading of the Talmudic text—is: "Just as a rock is splintered by a hammer into several pieces…" (מה פטיש - מתחלק הסלע על ידו לכמה ניצוצות).

2. The term אפניה is reminiscent of Rashi's remarks in his commentary to Genesis 3:8:

‎...‏ואני לא באתי אלא לפשוטו של מקרא ולאגדה המישבת דברי המקרא ‏"דבר דבור
‏על אופניו."

i.e., I have come only to establish the simple sense of Scripture and
[will utilize] only such Aggadah that settles the Biblical text, "like a
word fitly spoken."

The concluding phrase comprises a citation from Proverbs (25:11), on
which Rashi's own commentary is: ‏על כנו... מבוססת ומיושבת בקרבי‏ (on its
foundation... [i.e.,] well-founded and substantiated).

INTRODUCTION

Tanakh has bonded thousands of years of Jews together. Our perennial attempts at interpreting, applying the messages of Tanakh to our lives, and refining truth in our relationship to God are hallmarks of this tradition. By engaging in this pursuit, we join an age-old dialogue and experience with our greatest interpreters, from the ancient Sages of the Talmud, through the medieval period, down to the present day.

The formidable range of commentaries available to contemporary readers is breathtaking. Their enduring relevance is striking as they take us by the hand and impart their knowledge and methodology. Some commentators focus more on local interpretations of each word and verse. Others shift their attention to global patterns, literary allusions, and the meaning of entire passages.

As the adage goes, one person's *peshat* is another's *derash*. It is difficult to ascertain the boundary of what precisely was intended by the text's author and what is imagined by a given interpreter. A creative and compelling interpretation for one might be a forced reading for another. These ambiguities result in meaningful debate and refining of ideas. By creating space between *peshat* and *derash*, we can draw layers meaning from the disputes over these boundaries.

Although many interpreters have influenced me, I gravitate to medieval commentators such as Ramban and Abarbanel as well as contemporary rabbinic scholars such as Rabbis Yoel Bin-Nun, Shalom Carmy, and Elhanan Samet. They pursue both verse-by-verse commentary and global themes. Their synthesized approach encourages us to be methodical and careful in scholarship, and simultaneously allows for more imaginative and inspirational insight to enter the arena. Most important, they exemplify the bridge between scholarly excellence and deep religious experience. The growth inherent in this approach is something I have found personally meaningful and one that is valuable to share with others.

The response to my first two collections of essays on Tanakh: *Through an Opaque Lens* (Sephardic Publication Foundation, 2006) and *Revealed Texts, Hidden Meanings* (Sephardic Publication Foundation-KTAV, 2009) has been deeply gratifying. I hope this book will continue to generate discussion as did the first two.

As always, I thank my family for their constant love and support: Mom and Dad, Ronda and Dan, Elana and James, Grandma, my nephews and niece Jake, Andrew, Jonathan, Max, Charlie, Jeremy, and Kara.

The two highlights of my entire life occurred after the publication of my last book. The first is that I married Maxine. The second is that our beautiful twin daughters, Aviva Hayya and Dahlia Rachel, were born. It also has been a pleasure becoming part of Maxine's family, and I thank JoAnn and Dick, Matt Erin and Molly, Nate, Tagg, Caroline, Mimi and Papap for welcoming me into their family as my family has embraced Maxine. I also thank Maxine for her painting that graces the front cover of this book. She photographed this beautiful scene from our hotel window at Kibbutz Lavi after a rainstorm while we were on our honeymoon, and then made a painting based on that photograph.

Much gratitude goes to Rabbi Dr. Moshe Sokolow (Fanya Gottesfeld-Heller Professor of Jewish Education, Azrieli Graduate School, Yeshiva University), for reading all of these essays with an eagle's eye. He offered corrections, references, scholarly insights, and educational wisdom and guidance. He exemplifies high-level Tanakh study in scholarship as well as religious education. It is an honor that he has written the foreword to this book.

I thank my students at Congregation Shearith Israel, Yeshiva University, and beyond who have been my fellow travelers for over fifteen years and with whom the learning behind these studies was first explored.

Sixteen of these twenty essays have been published previously (most are slightly modified from their originals). Foremost, I thank my father, Rabbi Marc D. Angel, my predecessor as Rabbi of Shearith Israel and now Founder and Chairman of the Institute for Jewish Ideas and Ideals. He reads my essays and offers constructive feedback each time. I also thank him in his capacity as the publisher of *Conversations* for allowing me to reprint those articles here. Thanks also to *Tradition, the Jewish Bible Quarterly*, *Milin Havivin*, Tebah Educational Services, Daniel Z. Feldman and Stuart W. Halpern (the editors of *Mi-Tokh Ha-Ohel*), and Rafael Medoff (the editor of *Rav Chesed*) for allowing me to republish essays that first appeared in their publications. Citations are on the first page of each article. The other four essays in this collection have not previously been published.

Translations of biblical passages are taken from the New Jewish Publication Society *Tanakh*. Translations of passages from the Talmud and Midrash Rabbah are taken from Soncino.

I am deeply indebted to the dear friends who have made the publication of this book possible. I thank Elsi Levy, a lifelong family friend who has been a great supporter for many years. Thank you to John and Marjory Lewin for helping sponsor this book in memory of Milton Lewin. Thank you also to the Norman S. Benzaquen Publication Fund of the Institute for Jewish Ideas and Ideals (jewishideas.org).

A special word of thanks goes to the members of the Board of the Sephardic Publication Foundation for supporting the publication of this book. Thank you also to Bernard Scharfstein and Adam Bengal at KTAV for all of their help in publishing this book.

Hayyim J. Angel
New York City
Purim, 5771

ABARBANEL: COMMENTATOR AND TEACHER CELEBRATING 500 YEARS OF HIS INFLUENCE ON TANAKH STUDY*

On the whole, [Abrabanel's] commentaries are not of the highest calibre, and his avoidance of philological and grammatical observations, together with his prolixity, greatly limit their exegetical worth.

(Nahum M. Sarna)[1]

The fact is that of Abravanel we may say as we do of Maimonides that though his methods may be obsolete yet his spirit and his system have permanent value.

(Herbert Loewe)[2]

As an exegete, especially of the purely historical books of the Bible, both in his methods and in the nature of his commentary [Abravanel] stands alone and without equal, and it is difficult to understand the latter-day neglect of him.

(Louis Rabinowitz)[3]

Few biblical commentaries have been accorded the acclaim and popularity enjoyed by Don Isaac Abarbanel's commentary on the Pentateuch.

(Sid Z. Leiman)[4]

---

* This article appeared originally in *Tradition* 42:3 (Fall 2009), pp. 9–26. Reprinted here with minor modifications, with permission from the editors.

INTRODUCTION

The above-cited evaluations of the works of Don Yitzhak Abarbanel[5] (1437–1508) demonstrate the strikingly different reactions to his commentaries. Is his work mediocre or of extraordinary value? Are his commentaries obsolete or relevant? Why do scholars arrive at such disparate views of Abarbanel's work?

The appreciation of Abarbanel's exegesis is impeded by at least three factors: (1) the widespread tendency to relativize his comments to his historical setting and personal life; (2) his balance of creativity and traditionalism; (3) the preference of some scholars for a "scientific" approach to Tanakh, grounded in philology and grammar. In this essay we will consider salient examples of Abarbanel's work in light of what he was trying to achieve and will note how he continues to influence contemporary Tanakh study.

ABARBANEL'S HISTORICAL SETTING AND PERSONAL LIFE

A significant feature of *parshanut* scholarship is the inclination to relativize interpretation to historical context, that is, to argue that a commentator's setting motivated him to read a text in a certain way.[6] This tendency is greatly exacerbated in Abarbanel scholarship, since Abarbanel frequently refers to his historical setting and personal life. Consequently, several of Abarbanel's interpreters fail to recognize that his primary agenda is to explain *peshat* in biblical texts.

A. MONARCHY

If, after you have entered the land that the Lord your God has assigned to you, and taken possession of it and settled in it, you decide, "I will set a king over me, as do all the nations about me," you shall be free to set a king over yourself, one chosen by the Lord your God. Be sure to set as king over yourself one of your own people; you must not set a foreigner over you, one who is not your kinsman. (Deut. 17:14–15)

Samuel was displeased that they said "Give us a king to govern us." Samuel prayed to the Lord, and the Lord replied to Samuel, "Heed the demand of the people in everything they say to you. For it is not you that they have rejected; it is Me they have rejected as their king. Like everything else they have done ever since I brought them out of Egypt to this day—forsaking Me and worshiping other gods—so they are doing to you." (I Sam. 8:6-8)

The *tannaim* debate whether the Torah commands monarchy or whether it only permits it. R. Yehudah (*Sanhedrin* 20b) considers monarchy a positive commandment. R. Nehorai maintains that it is permitted yet frowned upon. In *Sifrei Devarim* 156, R. Nehorai asserts that monarchy is shameful for Israel, citing I Samuel 8:7, where God views the people's request to be a rejection of divine rule. R. Yehudah retorts that monarchy is a commandment but that the people sinned by requesting a king inappropriately.

Rambam rules like R. Yehudah, that monarchy is a positive commandment (*Hilkhot Melakhim* 1:1–2). Many commentators and codifiers adopted this position. Abarbanel,[7] however, dissents and critiques Rambam's view. God and Samuel were incensed at the people's very asking for a king, rather than at the formulation or timing of their request.[8] If the Torah commands monarchy, why did Joshua and his successors fail to appoint a king? When Samuel rebuked the people, why did they not respond that they wanted to fulfill a Torah commandment?

Abarbanel adopts R. Nehorai's view that while monarchy is permitted if requested, it is negative. Abarbanel likens monarchy to the laws of the "beautiful captive" (Deut. 21:10–14) as another case where the Torah permits certain less-than-ideal actions to forestall worse eventualities. He invokes the talmudic principle, "the Torah states this in consideration of the evil inclination" (*Kiddushin* 21b). Abarbanel further observes that biblical history corroborates his hypothesis. Joshua, the judges, and Samuel successfully guided their nation religiously, whereas many kings caused more religious harm than good. Abarbanel's excursus on monarchy is an outstanding specimen of his approach to Tanakh. He considers each facet of the textual evidence, methodically evaluates the opinions of his predecessors, and advances a comprehensive hypothesis that he believes best addresses all the questions.

Some scholars, however, have been sidetracked by Abarbanel's historical setting and by his rebuttal of Aristotle's claim that all nations need monarchy to govern them. They posit that Abarbanel opposed monarchy because of his negative experiences with monarchy and his favorable view of republics.[9] For that matter, some relativize the views of Rambam and his followers as well. For example, Aviezer Ravitsky suggests that Ran, who shared Rambam's positive view of monarchy, lived in a time of Jewish prosperity, whereas Abarbanel was adversely affected by the vicious Spanish monarchy of his day.[10]

These arguments suffer from a fundamental methodological flaw: Jewish life in medieval Spain notwithstanding, the Torah has to mean *something*. The unusual legal formulation in Deuteronomy and God's frustration at the people's request for a king in the Book of Samuel need to be explained. Long before the medieval debate, Hazal already were divided over this issue.[11]

There is no doubt that Abarbanel's experiences informed his teachings on the monarchy. However, that fact does not necessarily mean that these experiences are what *caused* him to explain the texts in the manner he did. It is just as reasonable to maintain that once Abarbanel reached his conclusions based on text analysis, he then buttressed his opinion in rational and historical terms. Perhaps his government familiarity even gave him an interpretive advantage over his rabbinic predecessors for understanding biblical political theory.[12]

Abarbanel had sound rabbinic precedents for his position. Aside from R. Nehorai's talmudic opinion, R. Sa'adyah Gaon, Ibn Ezra, and R. Meyuhas (twelfth-century Greece) also argued that the Torah does not command the establishment of a monarchy. Thus the argument that Abarbanel's assessment of monarchy derived from his experiences in late fifteenth-century Spain is beside the point.[13] The textual evidence convinced interpreters centuries before him and centuries after him as well.[14]

In evaluating the comments of the *mefarshim*, one always must begin by searching for text motivations. It is reasonable that Abarbanel and other commentators believed that good *peshat* also contributed to the religious and educational needs of their time. Only in cases where a *pashtan* does violence to the text, or when consistent exegetical patterns can be demonstrated, should one look elsewhere for possible motivations, and these must be evaluated on a case-by-case basis. Stated differently, there certainly is a correlation between Abarbanel's interpretation and historical setting in this instance—one that Abarbanel made explicit—but not necessarily a causal relationship whereby his historical setting distorted fair text interpretation.

B. MESSIANISM[15]

When [Abarbanel] composed [his commentary on Isaiah] in 1498, he was entirely predisposed to messianic influence... which was pronounced at the end of his life, greatly weakening his critical sense. (Meyer Waxman)[16]

Shortly after the Expulsion, Abarbanel composed his messianic trilogy: *Ma'ayanei ha-Yeshu'a*, a commentary on the Book of Daniel; *Yeshu'ot Meshiho*, an explanation of rabbinic statements about the Messiah; and *Mashmia Yeshu'a*, a commentary on passages of redemption in the Prophets and Psalms which he later incorporated into his commentaries to the Prophets. Together, they comprise the largest corpus of messianic thought ever produced by a Jewish author.[17]

Given the despair of Spanish Jewry after the Expulsion, it is little wonder that Abarbanel devoted record-setting attention to messianism. However, there are several reasons to exercise caution before concluding that Abarbanel lost his critical sense as a result of a post-Expulsion messianic bias. First, Eric Lawee observes that Abarbanel's commentary on the Book of Kings, written immediately following the Expulsion, begins and ends with stirring accounts of events surrounding the Expulsion. The body of that commentary, however, reads like a natural continuation of the commentaries on Joshua, Judges, and Samuel that Abarbanel composed in Spain in 1483. Similarly, messianic thought is almost entirely absent from Abarbanel's commentary on the Torah, which he wrote at the end of his life. Lawee concludes: "While, then, much ink has been spilled now for decades on Abarbanel's messianism, no one has explained—or, it would seem, barely even stopped to notice—the near-total absence of messianic concerns in the works of his last half-decade of life, including his monumental Torah commentaries."[18]

We may add that Abarbanel's messianic interpretations generally have precedent in earlier *parshanut*, militating against the argument that Abarbanel's post-Expulsion setting is what caused him to interpret certain prophecies as messianic. In his commentary on Isaiah 11, for example, Abarbanel repeatedly notes that most of the predictions in this chapter were not fulfilled in Hezekiah's time or in the Second Temple period. The prophecy, therefore, must refer to the messianic age.[19] Abarbanel was preceded in this messianic reading by a number of commentators, including Rashi, Kara, Radak, R. Eliezer of Beaugency, and R. Yeshaya D'Trani. Others, including R. Moshe ibn Gikatilah, R. Yosef ibn Caspi, and a hesitant Ibn Ezra, maintained that the context of this chapter indicates that Hezekiah is the intended subject of the prophecy. The utopian predictions therefore must be understood as poetic exaggeration, or as events that occurred but were not recorded in Tanakh.

One might safely attribute Abarbanel's caustic tone toward such attempts to historicize such prophecies—such as referring to them as "heretical"[20]—to his context of giving encouragement to despairing Iberian Jewish exiles and deflating Christological interpretations.[21] Similarly, Abarbanel's acceptance of the Gemara (*Sanhedrin* 39b) that identifies the prophet Obadiah with Ahab's attendant as a received tradition may be readily associated with his theological agenda to identify Edom with Rome-Christianity. By doing so, he attempted to refute Ibn Gikatilah and Ibn Ezra, who maintained that Edom refers to the biblical nation southeast of Israel.[22] However, the interpretations he advances on the passages in question represent well-established positions in medieval *parshanut*.[23]

Thus the relativizing of Abarbanel's commentaries has caused damage in at least two ways. First, this approach misrepresents Abarbanel, who rightly casts himself as a *pashtan*.[24] More important, those who are quick to suggest that nontextual factors are what triggered Abarbanel's interpretations frequently overlook the textual arguments in his discussions.

Because his interpretations are often overly relativized, Abarbanel's works are branded as being exegetically obsolete, having only biographical and historical significance. Moshe Z. Segal's assessment epitomizes this misunderstanding: "Abarbanel approached Tanakh from a subjective vantage point, which evaluates verses not from the outlook of the authors of Tanakh, but rather from the outlook of the interpreter. Such explanations necessarily vanish from the world along with the fleeting outlook of the interpreter."[25]

It is symptomatic of much Abarbanel scholarship that the title of Benzion Netanyahu's outstanding biography[26] defines Abarbanel as a "Statesman and Philosopher" rather than as a commentator and teacher of Tanakh (as well as *Pirkei Avot*, the *Haggadah*, and Rambam's *Guide*[27]).[28] In contrast, one who reads Abarbanel as a commentator and teacher immediately recognizes the enduring value of his analyses and methodology in Tanakh study.

C. ECHOES OF ABARBANEL
IN HIS UNDERSTANDING OF PROPHECY

The Masoretic text does not arrange the biblical books as prescribed in *Bava Batra* 14b: Jeremiah, Ezekiel, and then Isaiah. Abarbanel advances five reasons why he prefers the Masoretic ordering: (1) The Books of Isaiah, Jeremiah, and Ezekiel now are arranged in chronological order. (2) Isaiah was born into the royal family[29] and received a superior education, which explains his beautiful writing style and courage to criticize kings. (3) Isaiah was the greatest prophet other than Moses, as is suggested by several midrashim.[30] (4) The Book of Isaiah contains more prophecies of comfort and more aspects of redemption than any other prophetic book. (5) The Book of Isaiah contains more principles on the attainment of afterlife than any other prophetic book.[31]

Through this analysis, Abarbanel seems to identify himself as the quintessential student of Isaiah. He was raised in a noble family descended from King David, worked with royalty, prided himself on his writing style, and placed great emphasis on messianic redemption and religious teachings. As Eric Lawee observes, "as elsewhere in Abarbanel's commentaries, autobiographical reverberations are readily discerned."[32]

Another echo of Abarbanel's personality may be reflected in his analysis of shared formulations by the prophets. Isaiah 2:2–4 is nearly identical to Micah 4:1–4, and the same is true for Jeremiah 49:7–17 and Obadiah 1:1–8. Abarbanel explains that in such cases both prophets received similar visions. The earlier prophet articulated the vision, and the later prophet borrowed his predecessor's formulation. There always were variations between the two, "or else [the later prophet] would be a plagiarist."[33]

That analysis may shed light on the issue of Abarbanel's own "unacknowledged borrowings." Already in Abarbanel's time, R. Meir Arama charged that Abarbanel plagiarized his father, R. Yitzhak Arama (*Akedat Yitzhak*). Writing from the perspective of his father, he wrote that Abarbanel "composed works and authored compilations…that he called original, sweet, profound, and subtle but the words were mine."[34] In a recent article, Yair Hass defends Abarbanel against this accusation. Abarbanel had an exceptional memory, loved R. Yitzhak Arama's style, and did not co-opt excerpts verbatim.[35] Eric Lawee also notes that plagiarism did not carry the stigma it does today.[36] Finally, Abarbanel explicitly defends the practice of borrowing ideas without attribution: "even though authors of books will learn and take comments from their predecessors as though they are plagiarists, there is nothing shameful in their gathering wisdom, as all emanates from one Shepherd, i.e., God."[37]

ABARBANEL'S CREATIVITY AND TRADITIONALISM

As already noted, Don Yitzhak Abarbanel was not an original thinker. (Meyer Waxman)[38]

Abravanel prides himself upon his originality, and it is a pride for which a study of his works provides a complete justification. (Louis Rabinowitz)[39]

Given the staggering breadth of Abarbanel's reading, there is little wonder that many of his interpretations find precedent in earlier writings. At the same time, Abarbanel's penetrating questions, literary observations, and psychological insights contribute meaningfully to Tanakh study. Even where he fails to persuade, he succeeds in forcing the reader to re-evaluate the text evidence. In controversial matters, Abarbanel preferred to find rabbinic precedent to bolster his claims. In specifically textual discussions, Abarbanel was remarkably creative, particularly with his questions[40] and in straddling the boundaries of *peshat* and *derash* to answer them.

A. JUDGING BIBLICAL HEROES FAVORABLY

"[Better to] judge the prophets and wise men favorably…as the divine Torah commanded and the rabbinic sages instructed…as Maimonides wrote in the introduction to his book [the *Guide*]." (Abarbanel)[41]

Eric Lawee lists Abarbanel's critique of David first among Abarbanel's most "surprising" and "untraditional" claims.[42] According to

Abarbanel, David committed five sins: adultery; being prepared to abandon his biological child by asking Uriah to return to Bathsheba; having Uriah—a most loyal subject—killed; having Uriah killed specifically by enemies; and insensitively marrying Bathsheba soon after Uriah's demise.

Following his assessment, Abarbanel cites the celebrated Gemara: "whoever says that David sinned is merely erring" (*Shabbat* 56a). However, retorts Abarbanel, the textual proofs adduced in David's defense are uncompelling, whereas Nathan explicitly accuses David of sinning and David confesses and repents. Morever, Rav, the leading disciple of R. Yehudah ha-Nasi (= Rabbi), dismisses his teacher's defense of David on the spot: "Rabbi, who is descended from David, seeks to defend him and expounds [the verse] in David's favor." Therefore, "these words of our Sages are the ways of *derash* and I have no need to respond to them....I prefer to say that [David] sinned greatly and confessed greatly and repented fully and accepted his punishment and in this manner he attained atonement for his sins."[43]

Eric Lawee praises Abarbanel's interpretive independence: "Abarbanel could all at once criticize the conduct of a divinely appointed biblical hero, reject a midrashic absolution of him, and depart from medieval readings grounded in this rabbinic exculpation." And, "Abarbanel's critique of King David breaks with rabbinic and medieval Jewish tradition."[44] However, one modification must be introduced to Lawee's stark formulations. Though Abarbanel does present himself as an independent *pashtan* in this instance, he has not broken with rabbinic tradition. A number of rabbinic sources do not exonerate David. For example, there are opinions that Bathsheba was possibly a married woman or certainly a married woman[45]; that Bat Sheva's consent still might be viewed halakhically as a form of rape of a married woman since she was not in a position to decline[46]; that David is culpable for the death of Uriah[47]; that Joab bears guilt for failing to defy David's immoral orders regarding Uriah.[48] The unambiguous text evidence against David, including his own admission of guilt and wholehearted repentance, seems to have convinced Abarbanel that it was unnecessary to cite additional sources beyond Rav's dismissal of his teacher's defense of David.[49]

Abarbanel's responses to the other biblical figures defended in *Shabbat* 55b–56b illustrate his willingness to find fault with them when the biblical evidence is unambiguous, though he prefers to find rabbinic precedents to bolster his critiques. When there are even minor textual irregularities, he adopts the more conservative position that judges biblical characters favorably.[50]

Abarbanel remains undecided whether Reuben really "lay with Bilhah" (Gen. 35:22), since Jacob did not expel Reuben from the family.[51] Eli's sons did "lay with the women who performed tasks at the entrance of the Tent of Meeting" (I Sam. 2:22), and Samuel's sons "accepted bribes, and subverted justice" (I Sam. 8:3), since both texts are unambiguous. In both instances, Abarbanel cites rabbinic precedents.[52]

Finally, Abarbanel maintains that Solomon was not guilty of actual idol worship.[53] Dissatisfied with the talmudic defense, however, Abarbanel works harder than his predecessors at identifying further potential text ambiguities:

> At that time, Solomon built a shrine for Chemosh the abomination of Moab on the hill near Jerusalem, and one for Molech the abomination of the Ammonites. And he did the same for all his foreign wives who offered and sacrificed to their gods. (I Kings 11:7–8)

> For they have forsaken Me; they have worshiped Ashtoreth the goddess of the Phoenicians, Chemosh the god of Moab, and Milcom the god of the Ammonites; they have not walked in My ways, or done what is pleasing to Me, or [kept] My laws and rules, as his father David did. (I Kings 11:33)

Why would vv. 7–8 stress that Solomon built shrines for his wives instead of highlighting the greater crime of worshipping idols himself? Additionally, v. 33 focuses on the nation, not Solomon. While not a compelling case by any means, these texts coupled with the talmudic arguments sufficed for Abarbanel to conclude that a reasonable doubt exists.[54]

B. THE WATERS OF MERIBAH

Numbers 20 is famously cryptic as to the nature of the sin that prevented Moses and Aaron from entering the Promised Land. Several commentators also express concern that so small a sin—whatever it was—resulted in so great a punishment. Abarbanel[55] systematically critiques ten views of his predecessors, concluding, "you have now seen with your eyes all the opinions and how far from the truth they are. Now your heart will be drawn to my view."

Abarbanel proceeds to unfold a revolutionary hypothesis: Moses was barred from Israel because of his role in the Spies episode, and Aaron for his role in the Golden Calf episode. Both had noble intentions, but each unwittingly bore responsibility for the nation's two greatest failures in the desert. Moses erred by adding a military agenda to the spies' mission, thereby requiring them to report on those findings. This report led to the demoralization of the nation. While Aaron had pure intentions in fashioning the Calf, he facilitated the nation's failure as well. To protect the honor of Moses and Aaron and to dissociate them from these disasters, the Torah covers up their errors by attributing their nonentry into Israel to a trivial matter: they struck a rock instead of speaking to it.

To support his novel hypothesis,[56] Abarbanel adduces twelve proofs. Several are unconvincing, such as that Aaron died before Moses because the sin of the Calf preceded the sin of the Spies. Others, however, are textually grounded, even if alternative interpretations exist. When recounting the Spies episode in Deuteronomy, Moses included himself in the decree: "Because of you the Lord was incensed with me too, and He said: You shall not enter it either" (Deut. 1:37). Additionally, in the original decree, God says, "not one shall enter the land in which I swore to settle you—save Caleb son of Jephunneh and Joshua son of Nun" (Num. 14:30). Moses and Aaron were not mentioned, since Aaron already was excluded because of the Calf and Moses because of the Spies.

Marshaling rabbinic precedent for the idea of a cover-up by the Torah, Abarbanel cites midrashim that ascribe the deaths of Nadab and Abihu to causes other than the Torah's explicit reference to their bringing alien fire. Thus, Hazal also were willing to accept the notion that the Torah does not always fully disclose the true reasons for a punishment.

Abarbanel then confronts the Torah's refrain that Moses and Aaron did not enter the Land as a result of the Waters of Meribah episode (Num. 20:23–24; 27:13–14; Deut. 32:50–51). He strains mightily to reinterpret these verses, yet emerges completely persuaded by his interpretation: "This is what I wanted to say on this matter, and I believe that it is the entire truth."

Abarbanel may fail to convince in this instance, but he has elucidated every major and minor issue that needs to be considered. He provides a model lesson on how to evaluate opinions methodically in light of the text evidence. Moreover, his discussion pertains to Deuteronomy and its relationship to the other books of the Torah, a favorite subject in Abarbanel's repertoire.[57] Though we may not arrive at a satisfying solution, Abarbanel has given us a full appreciation of the magnitude of the question and its underlying issues.

BETWEEN STRICT *PESHAT* AND STRICT *DERASH*: LITERARY READINGS

> It is evil and bitter to me that Rashi was content in interpreting most of Scripture based on what the Sages expounded. And R. Avraham ibn Ezra [was content in explaining] grammar and the surface meaning, and consequently his commentaries are shorter than the actual verses. (Abarbanel)[58]

A prominent feature of Abarbanel's commentaries is his exploration of the vast field between strict *peshat* and nontextual *derash*.

Abarbanel exploits literary elements in the text and applies psychological insights to bind the broader narratives together.

> Moses went back to his father-in-law Jether and said to him, "Let me go back to my kinsmen in Egypt and see how they are faring." And Jethro said to Moses, "Go in peace." The Lord said to Moses in Midian, "Go back to Egypt, for all the men who sought to kill you are dead." (Exod. 4:18–19)

Moses already had conceded that he would go to Egypt. Now that he had received his father-in-law's permission, why would God command him again? Abarbanel suggests that Jethro's response, "go in peace," contains meaning beyond simple permission. Jethro remembered that before Moses had arrived in Midian, he killed an Egyptian and then meddled in an Israelite scuffle. Jethro feared that Moses, upon his return, would encounter his old adversaries and get dragged into further confrontations. Therefore, Jethro subtly hinted to Moses: "go in peace," that is, do not get into trouble as you did last time. Already insecure about returning to Egypt, Moses was demoralized by Jethro's subtle allusion to past setbacks. God therefore commanded him to go again and told him that he was safe from his past enemies. Through a textual redundancy, Abarbanel employs a psychological twist to highlight Moses' insecurities.[59]

Abarbanel combines psychology and his keen understanding of politics to explain God's choosing Aaron to bring the first three plagues and then Moses for the remaining seven. God wanted to protect Moses' honor. Knowing that the magicians would challenge the first three plagues by attempting to replicate them, God commanded Aaron to bring those plagues so that Moses' authority would not be opposed directly. Only after the magicians conceded defeat did God transfer the responsibility to Moses.[60]

Through these and so many related readings, Abarbanel offers interpretations that straddle the boundaries of *peshat* and *derash*. His creative insights are triggered by genuine text issues, though many would not pass muster in the realm of strict philological *peshat*.

CONCLUSION: IN PRAISE OF ABARBANEL'S PROLIXITY

[Abarbanel] did not recognize the spirit of his reader for whom he composed....These characteristics, which so make it greatly burdensome for us to learn his works and which drive away readers, served the opposite purpose to win the hearts of those who heard his words orally in his lectures. (Moshe Z. Segal)[61]

[Brevity] demonstrates deficient comprehension of the verses; do they not realize that there are seventy faces to the Torah?... Not so with me! In places where it is valuable to be lengthy I am not permitted to write briefly. (Abarbanel)[62]

While some have judged Abarbanel's writings to be overly wordy, Abarbanel prided himself on his style. Joseph Sarachek aptly remarked: "[Abravanel's commentaries] seem at times actually to bulge out, to be overweighted with information; not that his many works are wordy or repetitious but that he has laid plans for a large edifice and has built on a deep and broad foundation. So many aspects of bible study entered into his commentary that it had to reach its colossal size."[63]

Additionally, the second half of Segal's observation cited above remains valid: Abarbanel was a premier educator. Rabbi Joseph B. Soloveitchik's stirring portrayal of his living dialogue with the great Talmudists readily comes to mind.[64] However, the Rav was the Rav, capable of learning *with* the Torah giants of previous generations. For those of us more likely to learn *from* those Torah giants, Abarbanel's commentaries invite us to sit at his unabridged lectures and learn from his masterly presentations.

There is no need for a supercommentary on Abarbanel. One who patiently reads through his writings can generally ascertain what he means. "[I write] explicitly and will not test you with riddles as do Ibn Ezra and Ramban."[65]

Abarbanel often is inspiring. Tanakh is the bridge between the objective world of the Divine and our subjective worlds. Abarbanel injects his personality and historical setting into his writings, thereby modeling the direct link between Tanakh and real life.

For those who insist that good interpretation is limited to philology, Abarbanel contributes little and expressly intended to contribute little: "For the sake of brevity, I have omitted grammatical discussions, since they already appear in earlier commentaries—consult them."[66] For those who relativize his major interpretations to historical circumstances and personal life, Abarbanel is a fascinating historical figure but obsolete as a commentator.

But for those who wish to appreciate Tanakh with its seventy facets, who want to explore every layer between the realms of narrow *peshat* and the broader world of *derash*, who constantly question in order to reevaluate evidence and attain deeper insight, who yearn to experience Tanakh as the living word of God—they will appreciate the magnitude of Abarbanel's achievements. In the words of one of Abarbanel's most illustrious students:

> I have studied the commentators who wrote after Radak...and nobody succeeded in breathing a living spirit into the text according to the way of *peshat*, with the exception of our teacher Rabbi Yitzhak Abarbanel and a few of his contemporaries. (Malbim, introduction to Joshua)

NOTES

1. "Hebrew and Bible Studies in Medieval Spain," in *The Sephardi Heritage*, vol. 1, ed. R.D. Barnett (New York: Ktav, 1971), pp. 357–358.
2. "Isaac Abravanel and His Age," in *Isaac Abravanel: Six Lectures*, J.B. Trend & H. Loewe (eds.) (Cambridge: At the University Press, 1937), p. xxvi. Cf. the recent assessment of Abraham Melamed and Menachem Kellner: "Those future generations of historians who wonder why Abravanel has currently fallen so much out of fashion may find in this some food for thought," in "Introduction to the Special Issue of *Jewish History* Marking the 500th Anniversary of Isaac Abravanel's Death," *Jewish History* 23 (2009), p. 221.

3. "Abravanel as Exegete," in *Isaac Abravanel: Six Lectures*, p. 80.

4. "Abarbanel and the Censor," *Journal of Jewish Studies* 19 (1968), p. 49. For an extensive list of traditional scholars influenced by Abarbanel, see Eric Lawee, "Isaac Abarbanel's Intellectual Achievement and Literary Legacy in Modern Scholarship: A Retrospective and Opportunity," in *Studies in Medieval Jewish History and Literature III*, Isadore Twersky and Jay M. Harris (eds.) (Cambridge: Harvard University Press, 2000), p. 231.

5. For the preference of this spelling of Abarbanel's last name, see Sid Z. Leiman, "Abarbanel and the Censor," p. 49 n. 1. When citing writers who used other spellings, I have retained their preferences.

6. For further discussion, see Hayyim Angel, "The Paradox of *Parshanut*: Are Our Eyes on the Text, or on the Commentators, Review Essay of *Pirkei Nehama: Nehama Leibowitz Memorial Volume*," *Tradition* 38:4 (Winter 2004), pp. 112–128; reprinted in Angel, *Through an Opaque Lens* (New York: Sephardic Publication Foundation, 2006), pp. 56–76.

7. Deuteronomy, 163–171; Samuel, 202–209. References to Abarbanel's commentaries on Tanakh refer to the pages in the Commentaries on the Torah (3 vols. Jerusalem: Benei Arabel, 1964); Commentaries on the Former Prophets (Jerusalem: Torah va-Da'at, 1955); Commentaries on Isaiah, Jeremiah, Ezekiel (Jerusalem: Benei Arabel, 1979); Commentaries on the Twelve Prophets (Tel-Aviv: Sefarim Abarbanel, 1961).

8. Cf. I Sam. 10:19; 12:17.

9. See, e.g., Yitzhak Baer, "Don Yitzhak Abarbanel and His Relationship to Problems of History and Politics" (Hebrew), *Tarbiz* 8 (1937), pp. 241–259; David Polish, "Some Medieval Thinkers on the Jewish King," *Judaism* 20 (1971), pp. 323–329. In their introduction to a special issue of *Jewish History* commemmorating the 500th anniversary of Abarbanel's passing, Abraham Melamed and Menachem Kellner state that Abarbanel "does not seem to have realized…just how untraditional was his political anti-monarchism…" ("Introduction to the Special Issue of *Jewish History* Marking the 500th anniversary of Isaac Abravanel's Death," *Jewish History* 23 [2009], p. 220). Ephraim E. Urbach ("The State in the Eyes of Don Isaac Abarbanel" [Hebrew], in *Mehkarim be-Mada'ei Yahadut*, vol. 1, Moshe D. Herr and Yonah Frankel [eds.] [Jerusalem: Magnes Press, 1998], pp. 462–469) presents a more balanced approach by developing

Abarbanel's text analysis first before asserting that the biblical evidence alone cannot fully explain Abarbanel's strong political opposition to the institution of monarchy.

10. "Kings and Laws in Late Medieval Jewish Thought: Nissim of Gerona vs. Isaac Abrabanel," in *Scholars and Scholarship: The Interaction between Judaism and Other Cultures*, ed. Leo Landman (New York: Yeshiva University Press, 1990), pp. 67–90.

11. Gerald J. Blidstein ("The Monarchic Imperative in Rabbinic Perspective," *AJS Review* 7–8 [1982–1983], pp. 15–39) suggests that the tannaitic debate was sparked by rabbinic understandings of the Bar Kochba rebellion. He admits, though, that his discussion is speculative.

12. See, e.g., Louis Rabinowitz: "But perhaps the greatest excellence of his commentary is the direct result of the exalted positions which he held in the service of the various courts. All previous commentators had been too far removed from worldly events to enable them to possess a proper evaluation and estimate of the historical and social background of Scripture" ("Abravanel as Exegete," in *Isaac Abravanel: Six Lectures*, p. 82).

13. It also is noteworthy that not all Abarbanel's experiences with kings were negative. He writes glowingly of Afonso V of Portugal, under whom he served (Joshua, 2).

14. R. Meyuhas also likened monarchy to the "beautiful captive" as concessions to the evil inclination. See Gerald Blidstein, *Political Principles in Rambam's Thought* (Hebrew), 2nd expanded ed. (Ramat-Gan: Bar-Ilan University Press, 2001), pp. 21–25, for a fuller survey of opinions of Hazal, Geonim, and Rishonim. See Gerald Blidstein, "Halakha and Democracy," *Tradition* 32:1 (Fall 1997), pp. 11–12 for a roster of twentieth-century thinkers who agree that monarchy is not mandatory. For other critiques of the over-relativizing of Abarbanel's view of the monarchy, see David Polish, "Isaac Abravanel (1437–1509)," in *Gevuroth Haromah: Jewish Studies Offered at the Eightieth Birthday of Rabbi Moses Cyrus Weiler*, ed. Ze'ev W. Falk (Jerusalem: Mesharim Publishers, 1987), pp. xxxiii–lxv; Reuven Kimmelman, "Abravanel and the Jewish Republican Ethos," in *Commandment and Community: New Essays in Jewish Legal and Political Philosophy*, ed. Daniel H. Frank (New York: SUNY Press, 1995), pp. 195–216.

15. For a review of the current state of scholarship on this issue, see Eric

Lawee, "The Messianism of Isaac Abarbanel, 'Father of the (Jewish) Messianic Movements of the Sixteenth and Seventeenth Centuries,'" in *Millenarianism and Messianism in Early Modern European Culture, Volume I: Jewish Messianism in the Early Modern World*, Matt D. Goldish and Richard H. Popkin (eds.) (Dordrecht/Boston/London: Kluwer Academic Publications, 2001), pp. 1–39.

16. "Don Yitzhak Abarbanel" (Hebrew), *The American Jewish Year Book* 3 (1938), p. 80.

17. Eric Lawee, "The Messianism of Isaac Abarbanel," p. 9.

18. "The Messianism of Isaac Abarbanel," pp. 9–12. For demonstration that Abarbanel's post-Expulsion writings generally have antecedents in his thought while he was still in Portugal (and therefore should not casually be attributed to post-Expulsion circumstances), see Eric Lawee, "Yitzhak Abarbanel's Intellectual Biography in Light of His Portuguese Writings" (Hebrew), in *Yahadut Portugal be-Mifneh ha-Idan he-Hadash*, ed. Yom-Tov Assis (Jerusalem: Dinur Center, 2009), pp. 103–125.

19. Isaiah, 89–94.

20. E.g., when he explains Joel 3–4 as messianic and expresses outrage at Ibn Gikatila and Ibn Ezra for arguing that these prophecies were fulfilled in the time of Jehoshaphat (Joel, 71–72). See further discussion in Avraham Lipshitz, "The Exegetical Approaches of R. Avraham ibn Ezra and R. Yitzhak Abarbanel Regarding Future Prophecies" (Hebrew), *The Sixth World Congress of Jewish Studies (1973)*, vol. 1 (Jerusalem: World Organization of Jewish Studies, 1977), pp. 133–139.

21. See further discussion in Eric Lawee, *Isaac Abarbanel's Stance Toward Tradition: Defense Dissent, and Dialogue* (New York: SUNY Press, 2001), pp. 127–134.

22. Obadiah, 111. Eric Lawee observes that when Abarbanel avers that a midrash reflects a received tradition rooted in prophetic authority, there likely is a sensitive theological argument nearby (*Isaac Abarbanel's Stance Toward Tradition*, p. 104). For discussions of the origins of the Edom-Rome-Christianity link in Jewish literature, see Gerson Cohen, "Esau as Symbol in Early Medieval Thought," in *Jewish Medieval and Renaissance Studies*, ed. Alexander Altmann (Cambridge: Harvard University Press, 1967), pp. 19–48; Yair Hoffmann, "Edom as a Symbol of Wickedness in Prophetic Literature" (Hebrew), in *Ha-Mikra ve-Toledot*

Yisrael (Festschrift Yaakov Liver), ed. Binyamin Uffenheimer (Tel-Aviv: Tel-Aviv University Press, 1972), pp. 76–89; Solomon Zeitlin, "The Origin of the Term Edom for Rome and the Roman Church," *JQR* 60 (1970), pp. 262–263.

23. For further analysis, see Hayyim Angel, "Prophecy as Potential: The Consolations of Isaiah 1–12 in Context," *Jewish Bible Quarterly* 37:1 (2009), pp. 3–10; reprinted in Angel, *Revealed Texts, Hidden Meanings: Finding the Religious Significance in Tanakh* (Jersey City, NJ: KTAV-Sephardic Publication Foundation, 2009), pp. 117–126.

24. Cf. Eric Lawee (*Isaac Abarbanel's Stance Toward Tradition*, p. 254 n. 13), who criticizes scholars who fail to recognize Abarbanel as a *pashtan*.

25. "R. Yitzhak Abarbanel as a Biblical Exegete" (Hebrew), *Tarbiz* 8 (1937), p. 289.

26. *Don Isaac Abravanel: Statesman and Philosopher* (Ithaca and London: Cornell University Press, first edition 1953).

27. For a review of the current state of scholarship on Abarbanel's relationship to Rambam's teachings, see Eric Lawee, "'The Good We Accept and the Bad We Do Not': Aspects of Isaac Abarbanel's Stance toward Maimonides," in *Be'erot Yitzhak: Studies in Memory of Isadore Twersky*, ed. Jay M. Harris (Cambridge; London: Harvard University Press, 2005), pp. 119–160.

28. Of course, Abarbanel also was a statesman and philosopher. In addition to the growing body of scholarship on Abarbanel's exegetical work, it is encouraging to see the increased attention to Abarbanel's philosophical teachings. See recently Alfredo F. Borodowski, *Isaac Abravanel on Miracles, Creation, Prophecy, and Evil: The Tension between Medieval Jewish Philosophy and Biblical Commentary* (New York: Peter Lang, 2003); Seymour Feldman, *Philosophy in a Time of Crisis: Don Isaac Abravanel: Defender of the Faith* (London/New York: RoutledgeCurzon, 2003). See also the review of these two books and Eric Lawee's *Isaac Abarbanel's Stance Toward Tradition* by James T. Robinson, "Review Essay: Three Recent Books on Isaac Abarbanel/Abravanel (1437–1508/9)," *AJS Review* 28 (2004), pp. 341–349. Several books and monographs by Menachem Kellner also give Abarbanel's philosophical teachings abundant coverage. For an updated bibliography of works on Abarbanel, see Jolene Kellner, "Academic Studies on and New Editions of Works by Isaac Abravanel: 2000–2008," *Jewish History* 23 (2009), pp. 313–317.

29. Following the midrashic tradition that Isaiah's father Amoz and King Amaziah were brothers (e.g., *Megillah* 10b).

30. See, e.g., *Deut. Rabbah* 2:4; *Midrash Tehillim* 90:4.

31. Isaiah, 3–12. Much has been written on Abarbanel's introductions to the biblical books. See especially Eric Lawee, *Isaac Abarbanel's Stance toward Tradition*, pp. 169–186; and Eric Lawee, "Don Isaac Abarbanel: Who Wrote the Books of the Bible?" *Tradition* 30:2 (Winter 1996), pp. 65–73. For a survey and analysis of the antecedents of Abarbanel's style of critical introduction, see Eric Lawee, "Introducing Scripture: The *Accessus ad Auctores* in Hebrew Exegetical Literature from the Thirteenth through the Fifteenth Centuries," in *With Reverence for the Word: Medieval Scriptural Exegesis in Judaism, Christianity, and Islam*, Jane Dammen McAuliffe, Barry D. Walfish, and Joseph W. Greenberg (eds.) (Oxford University Press, 2003), pp. 157–179. For a study of the historical-autobiographical material in Abarbanel's introductions, see Cedric Cohen Skalli, "Discovering Isaac Abravanel's Humanistic Rhetoric," *JQR* 97 (2007), pp. 67–99.

32. *Isaac Abarbanel's Stance Toward Tradition*, p. 49.

33. Obadiah, 112; cf. Isaiah, 26; Micah, 140.

34. Translation in Eric Lawee, "Isaac Abarbanel's Intellectual Achievement and Literary Legacy in Modern Scholarship," p. 227.

35. "Regarding the Problem of the Occurrence of the Words of R. Yitzhak Arama in the Writings of R. Yitzhak Abarbanel" (Hebrew), *Sinai* 134 (2005), pp. 154–159.

36. "Isaac Abarbanel's Intellectual Achievement and Literary Legacy in Modern Scholarship," pp. 227–229.

37. Jeremiah, 297. Abarbanel is expounding on Ecc. 12:11–12.

38. "Don Yitzhak Abarbanel," p. 101.

39. "Abravanel as Exegete," in *Isaac Abravanel: Six Lectures*, p. 80.

40. For a survey and analysis of the antecedents of Abarbanel's method of asking a series of questions and then answering them, see Marc Saperstein, "The Method of Doubts: Problematizing the Bible in Late Medieval Jewish Exegesis," in *With Reverence for the Word,* McAuliffe, Walfish, and Greenberg (eds.), pp. 133–156. Eric Lawee considers the length and involved nature of Abarbanel's questions as having achieved a level beyond that of his predecessors. See his "Isaac Abarbanel: From Medieval to Renaissance Jewish Biblical Scholarship," in *Hebrew Bible/Old Tes-*

tament: The History of Its Interpretation. Vol. 2: From the Renaissance to the Enlightenment (1300–1800), ed. Magne Saebo (Gottingen: Vanderhoeck & Ruprecht, 2008), pp. 190–214.

41. *Ateret Zekenim*, 2 (trans. in Eric Lawee, *Isaac Abarbanel's Stance Toward Tradition*, p. 62).

42. *Isaac Abarbanel's Stance Toward Tradition*, p. 6.

43. Samuel, 342–343.

44. *Isaac Abarbanel's Stance Toward Tradition*, p. 119; p. 261 n. 140.

45. *Bava Metzia* 59a; *Sanhedrin* 107a.

46. *Ketuvot* 9a.

47. *Yoma* 22b; *Kiddushin* 43a.

48. *Sanhedrin* 49a.

49. Abarbanel was not the first medieval interpreter to assert David's guilt either. R. Yehuda bar Natan (Rashi's son-in-law, in *Teshuvot Hakhmei Provencia*, vol. 1 #71), R. Yeshaya D'Trani (on Ps. 51:1; but see his remarks on II Sam. 12:4, where he adopts the view in *Shabbat* 56a that Uriah had given Bathsheba a *get*), and Ibn Caspi (on II Sam. 11:6) preceded him. For a survey of rabbinic sources, see R. Yaakov Medan, *David and Bathsheba* (Hebrew) (Alon Shevut: Tevunot, 2002), especially pp. 7–26. I have not seen anyone address one anomaly in Abarbanel's assessment of the Bathsheba episode: In his commentary to I Kings 15:5, "David had done what was pleasing to the Lord and never turned throughout his life from all that He had commanded him, except in the matter of Uriah the Hittite," Abarbanel (Kings, 568) explains that "the matter of Uriah" indicates that the Bathsheba affair was *not* considered a sin, since Bathsheba "was predestined for David from the six days of Creation, but that she came to him with sorrow" (*Sanhedrin* 107a).

50. It is noteworthy that Abarbanel's first work, *Ateret Zekenim*, was dedicated to defending the elders in Exodus 24. By adopting this conservative approach, Abarbanel established his interpretive independence from midrashim and earlier medieval commentators who had been critical of those elders. See discussion in Eric Lawee, *Isaac Abarbanel's Stance Toward Tradition*, pp. 59-82.

51. Genesis, 357. Radak and Bekhor Shor maintain that Reuben perpetrated the act with Bilhah as literally described.

52. Regarding Eli's sons, Abarbanel quotes *Yoma* 9a in support of his posi-

tion (Samuel, 180), though the continuation of that Gemara (9b) remains consistent with the passage in *Shabbat* 55b. *Midrash Shoher Tov* 53:1, Rashi, and Radak accept the literal reading of the biblical passage. Regarding Samuel's sons, Abarbanel states "and a few of our Sages agreed" without citing sources (Samuel, 202). Again, Radak preceded Abarbanel.

53. Kings, 545–550.

54. For discussion of Abarbanel's view of Solomon in the context of medieval thought, see David Berger, "'The Wisest of All Men': Solomon's Wisdom in Medieval Jewish Commentaries on the Book of Kings," in *Hazon Nahum: Studies in Jewish Law, Thought, and History Presented to Dr. Norman Lamm on the Occasion of His Seventieth Birthday*, Yaakov Elman and Jeffrey S. Gurock (eds.), (New York: Yeshiva University Press, 1997), pp. 93–114.

55. Numbers, 100–105; Deuteronomy, 21–26.

56. Avraham Gross ("R. Yosef Hayyun and R. Yitzhak Abarbanel: Intellectual Relationships" [Hebrew], *Mikhael* 11 [1989], p. 29), states that Hayyun—Abarbanel's probable teacher in Lisbon—similarly proposed that Moses may have been barred from entering Israel as a result of the Spies episode. Gross suggests that either commentator could have learned the idea from the other, or perhaps it was an idea current in learned circles in Lisbon at that time. Regardless, Hayyun accepts that they were precluded from entering Israel because of their sin at the Waters of Meribah. For the full text of Hayyun's monograph, see Avraham Gross, *R. Yosef b. Avraham Hayyun: Leader of the Lisbon Community and His Works* (Hebrew) (Ramat-Gan: Bar-Ilan University Press, 1993), pp. 216–230. Eric Lawee (*Isaac Abarbanel's Stance Toward Tradition*, p. 31) believes that Abarbanel wrote a longer monograph while still in Portugal. Abarbanel refers to this earlier monograph, stating that his commentary is a synopsis of that earlier work (Deuteronomy, 23).

57. See further in Yaakov Elman, "The Book of Deuteronomy as Revelation: Nahmanides and Abarbanel," in *Hazon Nahum: Studies Presented to Dr. Norman Lamm,* Elman and Gurock (eds.), pp. 229–250.

58. Joshua, 13.

59. Exodus, 42.

60. Exodus, 68.

61. "R. Yitzhak Abarbanel as a Biblical Exegete," pp. 264–265.

62. Joshua, 13.

63. *Don Isaac Abravanel* (New York: Bloch Publishing Co., 1938), p. 69.

64. See *Ish ha-Halakhah—Galui ve-Nistar* (Jerusalem: The World Zionist Organization—Dept. for Torah Education and Culture in the Diaspora, 1989), p. 232; cf. *Al ha-Teshuvah* (Jerusalem: The World Zionist Organization—Dept. for Torah Education and Culture in the Diaspora, 1978), p. 296.

65. Joshua, 13.

66. Joshua, 13. Moshe Segal observes that *no* commentator after Radak contributed substantially in the area of philology ("R. Yitzhak Abarbanel as a Biblical Exegete," p. 262).

"THE CHOSEN PEOPLE": AN ETHICAL CHALLENGE*

The concept of the Chosen People is fraught with difficulties. Historically, it has brought much grief upon the Jewish people. It also has led some Jews to develop chauvinistic attitudes toward non-Jews. Nonetheless, it is a central axiom in the Torah and rabbinic tradition, and we therefore have a responsibility to approach the subject forthrightly. In this essay we will briefly consider the biblical and rabbinic evidence.

THE BOOK OF GENESIS

A major theme of the Book of Genesis is the refining process of the Chosen People. The Torah begins its narrative of humanity with Adam and Eve, created in the Image of God. The Torah's understanding of humanity includes a state of potential given to every person to connect to God, and an expectation that living a moral life necessarily flows from that relationship with God.

Cain and Abel, the generation of Enosh, Noah, and the Patriarchs spontaneously brought offerings and prayed without any divine commandments to do so. God likewise held people responsible for their immoral acts without having warned them against such behaviors. Cain and the generation of the Flood could not appeal to the fact that they never received explicit divine commandments. They naturally should have known such conduct was unacceptable and punishable.

* This article appeared originally in *Conversations* 8 (Institute for Jewish Ideas and Ideals, Fall 2010), pp. 52-60. Reprinted here with minor modifications, with permission from the editor.

Adam and Eve failed by eating of the Tree of Knowledge but were not completely rejected by God, only exiled. Cain murdered his brother, and he too was exiled. Their descendants became corrupt to the point where the entire human race was overwhelmed by immorality.

At this point, God rejected most of humanity and restarted human history with Noah, the "second Adam." After the Flood, God explicitly commanded certain moral laws (Genesis 9), which the Talmud understands as the "Seven Noahide Laws" (ethical monotheism). Noah should have taught these principles to all his descendants. Instead, the only recorded story of Noah's final 350 years relates that he got drunk and cursed his grandson Canaan. Although Noah was a righteous man, he did not transmit his values to succeeding generations.

The only narrative spanning the ten generations between Noah and Abraham, the story of the Tower of Babel represents a societal break from God. It marked the beginnings of paganism and unbridled human arrogance. At this point, God appears to have given up on having the entire world perfected and instead chose Abraham— the "third Adam"—and his descendants to model ethical monotheism and teach it to all humanity.

This synopsis of the first twelve chapters of Genesis is encapsulated by Rabbi Ovadiah Seforno (sixteenth-century Italy). Only after these three failures did God select Abraham's family, but this was not God's ideal plan:

> It then teaches that when hope for the return of all humanity was removed, as it had successfully destroyed God's constructive intent three times already, God selected the most pious of the species and chose Abraham and his descendants to achieve His desired purpose for all humanity. (Seforno, introduction to Genesis)

There was no genetic superiority ascribed to Abraham and his descendants. To the contrary, the common descent of all humanity

from Adam and Eve precludes any racial differentiation, as understood by the Mishnah:

Furthermore, [Adam was created alone] for the sake of peace
among men, that one might not say to his fellow, my father was
greater than yours. (*Sanhedrin* 37a)

Abraham and his descendants thus became the Chosen People—a
nation expected to do and teach what *all* nations ideally should have
been doing. Indeed, Abraham is singled out in the Torah as the first
teacher of these values:

The Lord said, Shall I hide from Abraham that thing which I do,
seeing that Abraham shall surely become a great and mighty nation, and all the nations of the earth shall be blessed in him? For I
know him, that he will command his children and his household
after him, and they shall keep the way of the Lord, to do justice and judgment; that the Lord may bring upon Abraham that
which he has spoken of him. (Gen. 18:17–19)

The remainder of the Book of Genesis revolves around the selection process within Abraham's family. Not all branches would
ultimately become Abraham's spiritual heirs. By the end of Genesis,
it is evident that the Chosen People is comprised specifically of all
Jacob's sons and their future generations.

Although the Book of Genesis specifies the role and identity of the
Chosen People, two difficult questions remain. (1) Once Israel was
chosen, was this chosenness guaranteed forever, or was it contingent
on the religious-ethical behavior of later generations? Could a sinful Israel be rejected as were the builders of the Tower of Babel?
(2) Since the Tower of Babel, is chosenness exclusively limited to
Israel (either biological descendants or converts), or can non-Jews
again become chosen by becoming ethical monotheists (either on an
individual or national level)?

ISRAEL'S ETERNAL CHOSENNESS

God addressed the first question as He was giving the Torah to Israel:

Now therefore, if you will obey My voice indeed, and keep My covenant, then you shall be My own treasure among all peoples; for all the earth is Mine; And you shall be to Me a kingdom of priests, and a holy nation. These are the words which you shall speak to the people of Israel. (Exod. 19:5–6)

Thus God's covenant with Israel is a reciprocal agreement. If Israel does not uphold her side, it appears that she would cease to be God's treasure. It is remarkable that the very beginning of Israel's national covenantal identity is defined as conditional rather than absolute.

Later prophets stress this message as well. Amos states that Israel's chosenness adds an element of responsibility and accountability. Infidelity to the covenant makes chosenness more dangerous than beneficial:

Hear this word that the Lord has spoken against you, O people of Israel, against the whole family which I brought up from the land of Egypt, saying: Only you have I known of all the families of the earth; therefore I will punish you for all your iniquities. (Amos 3:1–2)

Amos's contemporary, Hosea, employed marriage imagery to demonstrate that Israel's special relationship with God is contingent on her faithfulness to the covenant. As the Israelites were unfaithful in his time, God rejected them:

She conceived and bore a son. Then He said, "Name him "*Lo-ammi*," for you are not My people, and I will not be your God. (Hos. 1:8–9)

However, this was not a permanent rejection from this eternal covenant. Rather, the alienation would approximate a separation for the sake of rehabilitating the marriage rather than being a permanent divorce. The ongoing prophecy in the Book of Hosea makes clear that God perpetually longs for Israel's return to an ideal restored marriage:

And I will espouse you forever: I will espouse you with righteousness and justice, and with goodness and mercy, and I will espouse you with faithfulness; then you shall be devoted to the Lord. (Hos. 2:21–22)

The Book of Isaiah makes the point even more explicit: there was no bill of divorce:

Thus says the Lord, Where is the bill of your mother's divorcement, with which I have put her away? Or which of My creditors is it to whom I have sold you? Behold, for your iniquities have you sold yourselves, and for your transgressions your mother was put away. (Isa. 50:1)

At the time of the destruction of the Temple, Jeremiah took this imagery to a new level. There *was* a divorce, yet God still would take Israel back:

It is said, If a man sends away his wife, and she goes from him, and becomes another man's, shall he return to her again? Shall not that land be greatly polluted? You have played the harlot with many lovers; yet return to me! says the Lord. (Jer. 3:1)

Jeremiah elsewhere stressed the eternality of the God–Israel relationship:

Thus said the Lord, Who established the sun for light by day, the laws of moon and stars for light by night, Who stirs up the sea into roaring waves, Whose name is Lord of Hosts: If these laws should ever be annulled by Me—declares the Lord —only then would the offspring of Israel cease to be a nation before Me for all time. (Jer. 31:5–6)

To summarize, Israel's chosenness is conditional on faithfulness to the covenant. However, failure to abide by God's covenant leads to separation rather than divorce, and the door always remains open for Israel to return to God. The special relationship between God and Israel is eternal.

RIGHTEOUS GENTILES CAN BE CHOSEN

Let us now turn to the second question, pertaining to God's rejection of the other nations after the Tower of Babel. Can these nations be chosen again by reaccepting ethical monotheism? The answer is a resounding "yes." Prophets look to an ideal future when *all* nations can again become chosen:

> In that day five cities in the land of Egypt shall speak the language of Canaan, and swear by the Lord of hosts; one shall be called, The city of destruction. In that day there shall be an altar to the Lord in the midst of the land of Egypt, and a pillar at its border to the Lord.... In that day shall Israel be the third with Egypt and with Assyria, a blessing in the midst of the land; Whom the Lord of hosts shall bless, saying, Blessed be Egypt My people, and Assyria the work of My hands, and Israel My inheritance. (Isa. 19:18–25)

Similarly, Zephaniah envisions a time when all nations will speak "a clear language," thereby undoing the damage of the Tower of Babel:

> For then I will convert the peoples to a clear language, that they may all call upon the name of the Lord, to serve Him with one accord. (Zeph. 3:9)

Thus God's rejection of the nations at the time of the Tower of Babel similarly was a separation for rehabilitation, not a permanent divorce. Were the nations to reaccept ethical monotheism, they too would be chosen. Perhaps the most dramatic example of this phenomenon in Tanakh is the descent of King David from Ruth (Moabite) and Tamar (Canaanite) as well as Judah.

In halakhic terminology, non-Jews who practice ethical monotheism are called "Righteous Gentiles" and have a share in the world to come (see *Hullin* 92a). According to Rambam, they must accept the divine imperative for the seven Noahide laws to qualify as Righteous Gentiles. If they act morally without accepting this divine imperative, they should instead be considered "Wise Gentiles":

> [Non-Jews] who accept the seven [Noahide] commandments are considered Righteous Gentiles and have a share in the World to Come. This is on condition that they observe these commandments because God commanded them in the Torah.... But if they observe them because of reason, they are not called Righteous Gentiles, but rather, *elah* (printed editions: and not even, *ve-lo*) Wise Gentiles. (Rambam, *Laws of Kings*, 8:11)[1]

To summarize, then, one is chosen *if one chooses God*. For a Jew, that means commitment to the Torah and its commandments; for a non-Jew, that means commitment to the seven Noahide laws (see *Mishnat Rabbi Eliezer* 6, quoted in Moshe Greenberg, pp. 375–376). Non-Jews who are Righteous Gentiles are chosen without needing to convert to Judaism. God longs for the return of all humanity, and the messianic visions of the prophets constantly reiterate that aspiration.

ISRAEL AS A NATION OF PRIESTS

Although the door remains open for all descendants of Adam and Eve to choose God and therefore be chosen, Israel occupies a unique role in this discussion. Israel was the *first* people to recognize God in this way. God calls Israel His "firstborn" (Exod. 4:22). Using the marriage imagery, Israel is God's wife, a status that carries with it a special relationship.

Perhaps the most fitting analogy that summarizes the evidence is Non-Jew : Jew :: Jew : Priest. God employs this terminology at the Revelation at Sinai:

Now therefore, if you will obey My voice indeed, and keep My covenant, then you shall be My own treasure among all peoples; for all the earth is Mine; and you shall be to Me a kingdom of priests, and a holy nation. These are the words which you shall speak to the people of Israel. (Exod. 19:5–6)

Commenting on these verses, Seforno remarks:

And you shall be to Me a kingdom of priests: and in this manner you will be a treasure, for you will be a kingdom of priests to teach the entire human race to call in God's Name and to serve Him alike. As it is written "you shall be called God's priests," and as it is written, "for Torah will come from Zion."

Being Jewish and being a priest both are genetic. A priest also is a bridge between the people and God and serves in the Temple on behalf of the people. Similarly, Israel is expected to guard the Temple and teach the word of God. Just as priests have more commandments than most Israelites, Israelites have more commandments than the nations of the world. The one critical distinction is that a non-Jew may convert to Judaism and is then viewed as though he or she were born into the nation. Nobody can convert to become a priest (though a nazirite bears certain resemblances to the priesthood).

When dedicating the first Temple, King Solomon understood that the Temple was intended for all who seek God, and not only Israelites:

Or if a foreigner who is not of Your people Israel comes from a distant land for the sake of Your name—for they shall hear about Your great name and Your mighty hand and Your outstretched arm—when he comes to pray toward this House, oh, hear in Your heavenly abode and grant all that the foreigner asks You for. Thus all the peoples of the earth will know Your name and revere You, as does Your people Israel; and they will recognize that Your name is attached to this House that I have built. (I Kings 8:41–43)

In their messianic visions, the prophets similarly envisioned that Israel would occupy a central role in worship and in teaching the nations. All are invited to serve God at the Temple:

In the days to come, the Mount of the Lord's House shall stand firm above the mountains and tower above the hills; and all the nations shall gaze on it with joy. And the many peoples shall go and say: "Come, let us go up to the Mount of the Lord, to the House of the God of Jacob; that He may instruct us in His ways, and that we may walk in His paths." For instruction shall come forth from Zion, the word of the Lord from Jerusalem. (Isa. 2:2–3)

Rather than serving primarily as an ethnic description, the Chosen People concept is deeply rooted in religious ethics. It is a constant prod to faithfulness to God and the Torah, and it contains a universalistic message that belongs to the community of nations. All are descendants from Adam and Eve, created in God's Image. God waits with open arms to choose all those who choose to pursue that sacred relationship with Him.

Dr. Norman Lamm observes that "a truly religious Jew, devoted to his own people in keen attachment to both their physical and spiritual welfare, must at the same time be deeply concerned with all human beings. Paradoxically, the more particularistic a Jew is, the more universal must be his concerns" (*Shema*, p. 35).

For further study, see:
- Elijah Benamozegh, *Israel and Humanity*, trans. Maxwell Luria (New York: Paulist Press, 1995).
- Alan Brill, *Judaism and Other Religions: Models of Understanding* (New York: Palgrave Macmillan, 2010).
- Moshe Greenberg, "Mankind, Israel, and the Nations in the Hebraic Heritage," in *Studies in the Bible and Jewish Thought* (Philadelphia: Jewish Publication Society, 1995), pp. 369–393.
- Rabbi Hayyim David Halevi, *Asei Lekha Rav* 8:69.

- Menachem Kellner, "On Universalism and Particularism in Judaism," *Da'at* 36 (1996), pp. v–xv.
- Jon D. Levenson, "The Universal Horizon of Biblical Particularism," in *Ethnicity and the Bible*, ed. Mark G. Brett (Boston: Brill, 1996), pp. 143–169.
- Rabbi Jonathan Sacks, "Jewish Identity: The Concept of a Chosen People," at www.chiefrabbi.org/ReadArtical.aspx?id=454.
- Symposium on "You Have Chosen Us from Amongst the Nations," *Jewish Action* 65:1 (Fall 2004), especially the articles of Rabbis Chaim Eisen and Norman Lamm.
- Symposium on "The State of Jewish Belief," *Commentary* 42:2 (August 1966), pp. 71–160, especially the articles of Rabbis Eliezer Berkovits, Marvin Fox, Immanuel Jacobovits, Norman Lamm, and Aharon Lichtenstein.

NOTES

1. Regarding those printed editions that say *ve-lo* instead of *elah*: this appears to be a faulty text, and Rambam intended *elah*, that is, that they are indeed Wise Gentiles. See Rabbi Hayyim David Halevi, *Asei Lekha Rav* 1:53, p. 158; Rabbi Joseph Soloveitchik, *Abraham's Journey: Reflections on the Life of the Founding Patriarch*, David Shatz et al. eds. (Jersey City, New Jersey: KTAV, 2008), pp. 172–173; Rabbi Abraham Isaac Kook (*Iggerot Ha-Ra'ayah* 89, vol. 1, pp. 99–100, quoted in Shalom Rosenberg, *In the Footsteps of the Kuzari: An Introduction to Jewish Philosophy* [New York: Yashar Books, 2007], vol. 1 p. 161.)

HUR AND PHARAOH'S DAUGHTER:
MIDRASHIC READINGS OF SILENT HEROES*

INTRODUCTION

Certain characters in Tanakh receive significant attention, riveting readers of all ages. Other characters, however, are relatively minor, leaving little impression on casual readers. Hur and Pharaoh's daughter are two such characters in the Book of Exodus. Both play significant enough roles to warrant mention, but neither is developed and both vanish shortly after they appear. Various midrashim explore and exploit the sparse biblical evidence about them to create more comprehensive portraits.

In his recent book-length midrashic reading of Moses, Rabbi Mosheh Lichtenstein sets out a working definition of *peshat* and *derash*. *Peshat* explicates the text itself, whereas *derash* explains dimensions beneath or beyond the simple meaning of the text. While *peshat* looks for correspondence to the text, *derash* seeks internal coherence that does not contradict the text.[1]

In Midrash Aggadah, there exists a blurred boundary between: the Sages as interpreters reading beneath the text; the Sages as transmitters of received oral traditions; and the Sages as *darshanim*, teaching their own lessons (*derekh ha-derash*) without impacting on the *peshat* in Tanakh. This essay will focus on strands of what the Sages may be attempting to teach regardless of whether they derived their

---

* This article appeared originally in *Mitokh Ha-Ohel: Essays on the Weekly Parashah from the Rabbis and Professors of Yeshiva University*, Daniel Z. Feldman and Stuart W. Halpern (eds.) (New York: Yeshiva University Press, 2010), pp. 205-213. Reprinted here with minor modifications, with permission from the editors.

particular readings from the text, based it on tradition, or were using their own creativity.

HUR

From the beginning of Moses' tenure as Israel's leader, three people stood by his side: his brother Aaron, his disciple Joshua, and Hur. Who was Hur? From the Torah's scant evidence, Ibn Ezra (short commentary on Exod. 24:14) aptly remarks that "we do not know who he is."

First, let us consider the explicit references to Hur in the Torah. During Israel's battle against Amalek, Moses ordered Joshua to lead the troops. Moses, Aaron, and Hur ascended the hill, and Aaron and Hur ultimately supported Moses' tiring arms:

Joshua did as Moses told him and fought with Amalek, while Moses, Aaron, and Hur went up to the top of the hill. Then, whenever Moses held up his hand, Israel prevailed; but whenever he let down his hand, Amalek prevailed. But Moses' hands grew heavy; so they took a stone and put it under him and he sat on it, while Aaron and Hur, one on each side, supported his hands; thus his hands remained steady until the sun set. (Exod. 17:10–12)

Hur never is given a "proper" introduction but clearly is counted among the highest echelons of the nation's leadership.

This impression is confirmed as Moses ascended Mount Sinai to receive the Torah. Again, his three associates occupied important positions. Joshua waited for his master at the base of the mountain while Moses delegated the leadership to Aaron and Hur:

To the elders he had said, "Wait here for us until we return to you. You have Aaron and Hur with you; let anyone who has a legal matter approach them." (Exod. 24:14)

It is surprising, then, that when the people despaired of Moses' return from Sinai they clamored only to Aaron and built the Golden Calf:

When the people saw that Moses was so long in coming down from the mountain, the people gathered against Aaron and said to him, "Come, make us a god who shall go before us, for that man Moses, who brought us from the land of Egypt—we do not know what has happened to him." (Exod. 32:1)

Similarly, Moses found Joshua at the base of the mountain, right where he had been waiting (Exod. 32:17–18). Mysteriously, though, Hur disappears from the narrative, and we never hear about him again. Where did he go? On the textual level, we never will know.

We are left to the world of midrash, which capitalizes on any information it can glean from Tanakh. The portrait of Hur may be developed in different layers.

[During the episode of the Golden Calf,] Hur arose and rebuked them: You brainless fools! Have you forgotten the miracles God performed for you? Whereupon they rose against him and killed him. They then came to Aaron…and said to him: We will do to you what we have done to this man. When Aaron saw the state of affairs, he was afraid. (*Exod. Rabbah* 41:7)

This midrash casts Hur as a religious martyr. His sudden disappearance in the text lends itself to this interpretation.[2] This reading helps explain Aaron's willingness to build the Calf, and also provides *someone* in the camp who opposed the Calf while Moses was atop the mountain.

The next layer of Hur's midrashic portrait derives from the construction of the Mishkan. God designated Bezalel as the chief artisan in the construction:

See, I have singled out by name Bezalel son of Uri son of Hur, of the tribe of Judah. (Exod. 31:2)

Why would the Torah trace Bezalel back to his grandfather Hur? One midrash states that since Hur martyred himself during the Calf episode, God rewarded him by choosing his grandson Bezalel as the chief artisan:

Why is Hur mentioned here? Because when Israel were about to serve idols, he jeopardized his life on God's behalf and would not allow them to do so, with the result that they slew him. Whereupon the Holy One, blessed be He, said: I assure you that I will repay you for this. (*Exod. Rabbah* 48:3)[3]

In Chronicles, the Sages found another clue. In the genealogy of the tribe of Judah, Caleb son of Hezron married Ephrath, who gave birth to Hur:

Caleb son of Hezron had children by his wife Azubah, and by Jerioth; these were her sons: Jesher, Shobab, and Ardon. When Azubah died, Caleb married Ephrath, who bore him Hur. Hur begot Uri, and Uri begot Bezalel. (I Chron. 2:19–20)

Whether this Caleb son of Hezron (a son of Perez son of Judah) should be identified with Caleb son of Jephunneh on the level of *peshat* is dubious (see Ibn Ezra's short commentary on Exod. 24:14). However, several midrashim identify them at the level of *derash*. Caleb son of Jephunneh was the most heroic spy during that disaster, stalwartly opposing his collegues and the entire nation and demanding that they have faith in God. The nation threatened to stone him (Num. 13:30; 14:6–10). Perhaps the midrashim that depict Hur's heroic martyrdom during the Calf episode derive in part from the story of Caleb. By creating this conceptual father-son relationship, the midrashic story of Hur's martyrdom becomes even more poignant. Caleb and Hur are cast as the two courageous men of faith who opposed everyone else during Israel's two greatest desert sins. Caleb was almost killed by the mob, whereas Hur was killed.

One final layer of *derash* interpretation exists. Who was Ephrath, Hur's mother (from I Chron. 2:19–20)? A midrash identifies her with Miriam:

The king of Egypt spoke to the Hebrew midwives (Exod. 1:15): Rav and Shemuel [differ in their interpretation]; one said they were...Jochebed and Miriam; and [the other said] they were Jochebed and Elisheba (Aaron's wife, see Exod. 6:23)....

And because the midwives feared God, He established households for them (Exod. 1:21): Rav and Shemuel [differ in their interpretation]; one said they are the priestly and Levitical houses, and the other said they are the royal houses. One who says they are the priestly and Levitical houses: Aaron and Moses; and one who says they are the royal houses: for also David descended from Miriam, as it is written: When Azubah died, Caleb married Ephrath, who bore him Hur. Hur begot Uri, and Uri begot Bezalel (I Chron. 2:19), and it is written: Now David was the son of that Ephrathite etc. (I Sam. 17:12). (*Sotah* 11b)

In the Torah, Miriam watched over baby Moses' ark. The associations of the midwives Shiphrah and Puah with Jochebed and Miriam (or Elisheba) in this talmudic passage further underscore the midrashic characterization of Miriam as a risk-taker as she heroically defied Pharaoh's murderous decrees.

By having Hur's midrashic parents as Caleb son of Jephunneh and Miriam, both his parents put their lives on the line for God and their people. As a bonus, these associations would make Hur into Moses' nephew. The two individuals supporting Moses' tired arms in the battle against Amalek would be Moses' brother and his sister's son.

The texts in Exodus and Chronicles give us precious few hints to Hur's character, despite his being so prominent a leader at the time of the Exodus. At the level of *peshat*, Hur was from the tribe of Judah (I Chron. 2:19–20) and was the grandfather of the artisan Bezalel (Exod. 31:2). The various midrashim we have considered expand him into a religious hero and martyr, son of the elite of the desert generation: Caleb and Miriam. Hur thereby is brought to life through these midrashic expansions.

PHARAOH'S DAUGHTER

The daughter of Pharaoh came down to bathe in the Nile, while her maidens walked along the Nile. She spied the basket among the reeds and sent her slave girl to fetch it. When she opened it, she saw that it was a child, a boy crying. She took pity on it and said, "This must be a Hebrew child." Then his sister said to Pharaoh's daughter, "Shall I go and get you a Hebrew nurse to suckle the child for you?" And Pharaoh's daughter answered, "Yes." So the girl went and called the child's mother. And Pharaoh's daughter said to her, "Take this child and nurse it for me, and I will pay your wages." So the woman took the child and nursed it. When the child grew up, she brought him to Pharaoh's daughter, who made him her son. She named him Moses, explaining, "I drew him out of the water." (Exod. 2:5–10)

The story of Pharaoh's daughter seems simple enough. Pharaoh's daughter knew Moses was an Israelite either because he was circumcised or because mothers do not normally float their babies down a river. There also is something delightfully ironic about Miriam's getting Pharaoh's daughter to pay Moses' mother Jochebed to nurse Moses.

Perhaps the most curious element in the *peshat* is that Pharaoh's daughter names the baby "Moses," since "I drew him out of the water" (*ki min ha-mayim meshitihu*). How did Pharaoh's daughter know Hebrew to make such a wordplay? Hizkuni and Abarbanel were so bothered by this question that they espoused a forced reading that Moses' mother named him. A more likely interpretation, adopted by Shadal and Netziv, is that "Moses" was an Egyptian name, meaning "son." The Torah makes a "*derashah*" on this Egyptian word into a Hebrew wordplay. At the level of *peshat*, then, Pharaoh's daughter serves as an agent of Moses' rescue and adoptive mother and then disappears from the narrative.

Midrashim, however, exploit several details in this brief account that would not have bearing in *peshat*. For example, one midrash asks why Pharaoh's daughter would go to the river to bathe. Were there no baths in the palace? Its answer: Pharaoh's daughter was using the river as a *mikveh* in order to banish paganism from herself, essentially converting (*Sotah* 12a).

The Torah reports that "*she* spied the basket among the reeds." Were there not also maidservants present? Perhaps the Torah should have said that *they* spied the basket. One midrash concludes that of course everyone physically saw the basket. However, the Torah distinguishes between the mindset of Pharaoh's daughter and that of her maidservants. When Pharaoh's daughter wanted to save Moses, her maidservants critically reminded her that her own father had made the decree (*Sotah* 12b)!

A third example: the Torah notes that Pharaoh's daughter "made him her son." Why add this seemingly superfluous phrase? One midrash concludes that Pharaoh's daughter hugged and kissed Moses as though he really was her own child (*Exod. Rabbah* 1:31).

The aforementioned questions and responses are not likely to be raised by *pashtanim*, but they still may have bearing on the textual account of Pharaoh's daughter. There is something remarkable in the courage of Pharaoh's daughter, who defied her own father and her society. In addition, several midrashim assume that Pharaoh's daughter must have learned Hebrew in order to name Moses using a Hebrew etymology. Midrashically, this combination points to some form of "conversion" from the paganism and immorality of her father, associates, and entire society.

On a different plane, the Torah reports that a grown Moses left the palace endowed with an incredible moral sense. In short order he killed an Egyptian taskmaster, intervened in an Israelite quarrel, and stepped into a struggle among Midianites at the well. Where did this moral fortitude come from? Seemingly, it derived at least partially from Pharaoh's daughter. Moses' defiance of Pharaoh and society parallels the heroism of his adoptive mother. Moses also instantly identified with his brethren, the Israelites. Perhaps Pharaoh's daughter, who could have raised him as an Egyptian, reminded him who he really was.[4]

Since Moses left the palace as a young adult, Pharaoh's daughter forever lost her beloved adopted son whom she had raised as her own. She likely was heartbroken, but also incredibly proud. She had raised a child who shared her vision of looking beyond the pagan immorality that characterized Egyptian society.

From the Torah we will never know who Pharaoh's daughter was or even her name. But her moral courage in rescuing Moses against her father's orders and in the presence of her maidservants, and her nurturing his moral and Israelite identity, changed the world by her rescuing and then raising the greatest individual who ever lived. We may view Pharaoh's daughter's break from Egyptian immorality as a form of "conversion" from all Egyptian society from Pharaoh down to the maidservants.

Turning to Chronicles, we find a named daughter of Pharaoh in the Judahite genealogy: "These were the sons of Bithiah daughter of Pharaoh, whom Mered married" (I Chron. 4:18).[5] Midrashically, this woman is identified with Moses' rescuer. The name Bithiah is understood as "*bat Ya-h*," or "the daughter of God." One midrash remarks, "God told Pharaoh's daughter: Moses was not your child, yet you treated him as you would your own son. Even though you are not My daughter, I will call you My daughter" (*Lev. Rabbah* 1:3).

People often act heroically though they might be forgotten from conscious memory. However, their impact can transform individuals and change the world. The silent yet powerful impact of Hur and Pharaoh's daughter in the Torah, fleshed out by various midrashic traditions, represents this type of greatness.

NOTES

1. Rabbi Mosheh Lichtenstein, *Moses: Envoy of God, Envoy of His People* (KTAV-Yeshivat Har Etzion, 2008, pp. 221–227). See also my review of his book "A Modern Midrash Moshe: Methodological Considerations,"

Tradition 41:4 (Winter 2008), pp. 73–86; reprinted in Angel, *Revealed Texts, Hidden Meanings: Finding the Religious Significance in Tanakh* (Jersey City, NJ: KTAV-Sephardic Publication Foundation, 2009), pp. 48–64.

2. *Tanhuma Tetzavveh* 10 spells out the textual derivation from Hur's mention in Exodus 24:14 and subsequent absence in the Golden Calf narrative. Cf. *Sanhedrin* 7a.

3. This midrash assumes that God commanded the building of the Tabernacle after the Golden Calf episode, rather than simultaneous to it.

4. Offering an alternative possibility, Joseph H. Hertz surmises that Moses' formative years nursing with his mother enabled Jochebed to teach Moses about his Israelite identity (*The Pentateuch and Haftorahs*, [London: Soncino Press, 1968], p. 210).

5. Cf. *Megillah* 13a: "These are the sons of Bithya whom Mered took" (I Chron. 4:18): Was Mered his name? Was not Caleb his name? The Holy One, blessed be He, said: Let Caleb who rebelled [*marad*] against the plan of the spies come and take the daughter of Pharaoh who rebelled against the idols of her father's house." In this midrashic identification, Moses and Hur would now be half-stepbrothers.

WHY DID MOSES NOT APOLOGIZE
AFTER HIS SIN AT MERIBAH?

But the Lord said to Moses and Aaron, "Because you did not trust Me enough to affirm My sanctity in the sight of the Israelite people, therefore you shall not lead this congregation into the land that I have given them." Those are the Waters of Meribah— meaning that the Israelites quarrelled with the Lord—through which He affirmed His sanctity. (Num. 20:12–13)

Being one of the most cryptic narratives in the Torah, Numbers 20 has received much exegetical attention. What was Moses' actual sin that led to his forfeiture of entering the Land? Why did Aaron deserve punishment? These enigmas never have received compelling explanations despite a millennium of efforts by the greatest commentators. In the fifteenth century, Rabbi Yitzhak Arama concluded that none of the suggestions proposed by our rabbis were convincing.[1] Some 500 years later, Meshullam Margaliot still could preface his study of this narrative by observing that "the passages describing the event at Mei Meribah have so far not been satisfactorily explained."[2]

Rashi's classical interpretation—that Moses and Aaron should have spoken to the rock instead of striking it—is beset with many objections raised by later commentators. For example, Ramban notes that God commanded Moses to take a staff. This demand could reasonably have been taken to mean that Moses should strike the rock as on the earlier occasion when he struck a rock to produce water (Exod. 17:1–7). Additionally, striking a rock to provide water is a great miracle, and the nation had not heard God command Moses to do anything else. Why would God consider striking the rock as a failure in sanctifying God's Name?

Ramban adopts the view of R. Hananel and R. Yosef Bekhor Shor, that the sin of Moses and Aaron was in saying, "Shall *we* get water for you out of this rock?" (Num. 20:10). Though of course they intended for God to produce the water, the people misunderstood the ambiguity in their rhetorical question, concluding that Moses and Aaron themselves had the powers to generate water.[3]

Other commentators suggest that the sin lay in aspects of their anger (Rambam, Maharal), failed leadership (Ibn Ezra, Albo),[4] or other alternatives with greater or lesser textual support. Abarbanel surveys ten opinions of his predecessors, rejecting each of them. Though he concludes that Rashi's interpretation is the most textually sound, Abarbanel suggests that the Torah actually is concealing a different reality. Moses was denied entry because of his role in the sin of the Spies, and Aaron was denied entry because of his role in the sin of the Calf. Though Abarbanel's reading is truly innovative, it hardly is compelling and only serves to highlight the difficulty of finding a satisfying answer in the text.[5]

In the nineteenth cenutry, Samuel David Luzzatto observed that each novel suggestion imputes blame onto Moses and Aaron for yet another thing they may not have done wrong. Ultimately, Luzzatto also concludes that Rashi has the smoothest reading.

Rather than attempt yet another solution to this age-old conundrum, I will approach this passage from a different angle. The Torah blames Moses for "lacking faith." What constituted that lack of faith, and why did he lack faith? This line of questioning may shed light on the passage without having to resolve what precisely he did wrong.

At the very beginning of his prophetic calling, Moses stalled at the burning bush. After he claimed that he was slow of speech, God responded that He always would be there to help him speak:

And the Lord said to him, "Who gives man speech? Who makes him dumb or deaf, seeing or blind? Is it not I, the Lord? Now go, and I will be with you as you speak and will instruct you what to say." (Exod. 4:11–12)

Within Rashi's reading of Numbers 20, one might suggest that Moses did not have faith that God would instruct him what to say. Instead, Moses struck the rock. This reading connects Moses' rebellion in the fortieth year to his insecurities from the beginning of his career.[6] However, the question remains: why would Moses lack faith in God after forty years of steady guidance?

Moses' reaction at Meribah appears to parallel an earlier crisis in Numbers 11. When the people complained regarding meat:

Moses heard the people weeping, every clan apart, each person at the entrance of his tent. The Lord was very angry, and Moses was distressed. (Num. 11:10)

When "Moses was distressed," at whom was he distressed? From the parallel with the first half of the verse, "the Lord was very angry," it would appear that Moses also was angered with the people for their unwarranted complaint. However, his ensuing outburst indicates that Moses was distressed with God as well:

And Moses said to the Lord, "Why have You dealt ill with Your servant, and why have I not enjoyed Your favor, that You have laid the burden of all this people upon me? Did I conceive all this people, did I bear them, that You should say to me, 'Carry them in your bosom as a nurse carries an infant,' to the land that You have promised on oath to their fathers? Where am I to get meat to give to all this people, when they whine before me and say, 'Give us meat to eat!' I cannot carry all this people by myself, for it is too much for me. If You would deal thus with me, kill me rather, I beg You, and let me see no more of my wretchedness!" (Num. 11:11–15)

Moses complained that God had set him up for failure. How could he care for this nation and supply all their needs? Returning to his primal fears from the burning bush, Moses was prepared to resign and even die rather than remain in a situation where God appeared to be failing him.

This reading is strengthened by a literary parallel to Exodus 5:22, immediately following Moses' first disappointment. Pharaoh denied Moses' request for three days of worship and also deprived the Israelites of straw for their brickmaking. Moses protested, *lamah hare'ota la-am ha-zeh* (O Lord, why did You bring harm upon this people?). In Numbers 11:11 he complained *lamah hare'ota le-avdekha* (Why have You brought harm upon Your servant?).

God solved the crisis in Exodus 5 by beginning the plagues and exodus; He did so in Numbers 11 by supplying meat and appointing leaders to help Moses. Yet Moses appears to have been wounded by God's allowing him to fail—if only temporarily. In the fortieth year, when the people again complained about water, Moses again felt abandoned by God. Though God had promised that He would always instruct Moses what to say (Exod. 4:12), Moses had a brief lapse of faith in God's support. Therefore, Moses struck the rock instead of speaking.

We may offer a symbolic interpretation to Moses' striking the rock *twice* (Num. 20:11). Parallel to his negative experience in chapter 11, Moses now was frustrated with the people and with God. Moses consequently struck the rock twice as a sign of his double distress.

This discussion elucidates a question seldom raised by our commentators: Whatever Moses' sin may have been at Meribah, why did he never apologize to God? He did not repent immediately following God's stark decree, and God offered him no fewer than three further opportunities to repent by reiterating the sin. The first appears when it was time for Aaron to die:

> Let Aaron be gathered to his kin: he is not to enter the land that I have assigned to the Israelite people, because you disobeyed my command about the waters of Meribah. (Num. 20:24)

The second occasion was when God told Moses that he would see the Land but not enter:

> The Lord said to Moses, "Ascend these heights of Abarim and view the land that I have given to the Israelite people. When you have seen it, you too shall be gathered to your kin, just as your brother Aaron was. For, in the wilderness of Zin, when the community was contentious, you disobeyed My command to uphold My sanctity in their sight by means of the water." Those are the Waters of Meribath-kadesh, in the wilderness of Zin. (Num. 27:12–14)

And finally there was a third instance immediately prior to Moses' death:

> Ascend these heights of Abarim to Mount Nebo, which is in the land of Moab facing Jericho, and view the land of Canaan, which I am giving the Israelites as their holding. You shall die on the mountain that you are about to ascend, and shall be gathered to your kin, as your brother Aaron died on Mount Hor and was gathered to his kin; for you both broke faith with Me among the Israelite people, at the waters of Meribath-kadesh in the wilderness of Zin, by failing to uphold My sanctity among the Israelite people. You may view the land from a distance, but you shall not enter it—the land that I am giving to the Israelite people. (Deut. 32:49–52)

In all three cases, Moses listened obediently but never expressed remorse.

Even more remarkably, though God always blamed Moses for his lack of faith at Meribah, Moses repeatedly transferred blame to the people when reviewing the nation's history in Deuteronomy:

> *Because of you* the Lord was incensed with me too, and He said: You shall not enter it either. (Deut. 1:37)

Now the Lord was angry with me *on your account* and swore that I should not cross the Jordan and enter the good land that the Lord your God is assigning you as a heritage. (Deut. 4:21)

It appears that there was a debate between God and Moses over whose fault the sin at Meribah was![7]

The divergence between the views of God and Moses may relate to our previous discussion. Moses believed that God had failed him during his initial encounter with Pharaoh (Exod. 5), with the meat (Num. 11), and again at Meribah. In contrast, God maintained at Meribah that Moses let Him down. This was a battle over principle. Of course, God wins all battles over principle. Moses was punished, and God did not reprimand the people for their complaints.

However, the Torah affords Moses a sympathetic view as well:

I pleaded with the Lord at that time, saying…Let me, I pray, cross over and see the good land on the other side of the Jordan, that good hill country, and the Lebanon. But the Lord was wrathful with me *on your account* and would not listen to me. The Lord said to me, "Enough! Never speak to Me of this matter again! (Deut. 3:23–26)

In this heart-wrenching plea, Moses again blamed the people and again did not apologize. Instead, he asked God to allow him into the Land as a personal favor. He did not express remorse, because he did not feel himself guilty. Moses went to his grave after looking at his nation's Promised Land, not convinced that he should be left out, but obediently following God's command to the end.

This story often is used to illustrate the principle that even the greatest human being is not perfect. It also teaches that God does not necessarily respond affirmatively to prayer—not even to Moses. We have explored the possibility that also included in this series of messages is the fact that even the greatest person has a blind spot in seeing his own mistakes. There is much that one can learn from these central lessons.

NOTES

1. *Akedat Yitzhak, Hukkat* chapter 80.

2. Meshullam Margaliot, "The Transgression of Moses and Aaron—Num. 20:1–13," *JQR* 74 (1983), p. 196.

3. For recent expansions and modifications of this view, see Meshullam Margaliot, "The Transgression of Moses and Aaron—Num. 20:1–13," pp. 196–228; Jacob Milgrom, "Magic Monotheism, and the Sin of Moses," in *The JPS Torah Commentary: Numbers* (Philadelphia: The Jewish Publication Society, 1990), pp. 448–456.

4. Nathaniel Helfgot ("'And Moses Struck the Rock': Numbers 20 and the Leadership of Moses," *Tradition* 27:3 [1993], pp. 51–58) suggests that Moses' striking the rock instead of speaking to it (following Rashi's reading) demonstrates a failure in leadership rather than mere deviation from the divine command. Moses mistakenly believed that the second generation still needed to be threatened rather than spoken to as adults. By his failing to perceive the educational needs of the new generation, it became evident that new leadership was necessary. See also Jacob J. Schacter, "*Teshuvah*, Punishment, and the Leadership of Moshe," in *Mitokh Ha-Ohel: Essays on the Weekly Parashah from the Rabbis and Professors of Yeshiva University*, Daniel Z. Feldman and Stuart W. Halpern (eds.) (New York: Yeshiva University Press, 2010), pp. 477–482.

5. See further discussion of Abarbanel's view in Hayyim Angel, "Abarbanel: Commentator and Teacher: Celebrating 500 Years of His Influence on Tanakh Study," *Tradition* 42:3 (Fall 2009), pp. 22–23; reprinted in this volume.

6. Though commentators generally assume that the sin of Meribah occurred in the 40th year, that dating is not made explicit in the Torah. See Ibn Ezra, Yehiel Moskowitz (*Da'at Mikra: Numbers* [Hebrew], [Jerusalem: Mossad ha-Rav Kook, 1988], p. 230).

7. Some psalmists ascribe the underlying blame to the people when recounting this episode: They provoked wrath at the waters of Meribah, and Moses suffered on their account, because they rebelled against Him and he spoke rashly (Ps. 106:32–33); Do not be stubborn as at Meribah, as on the day of Massah, in the wilderness, when your fathers put Me to the test, tried Me, though they had seen My deeds (Ps. 95:8–9). Cf. Ps. 81:8:

In distress you called and I rescued you; I answered you from the secret place of thunder; I tested you at the waters of Meribah.

However, these Psalms include exhortations to later generations not to emulate the rebellious behaviors of earlier generations. Therefore, it is difficult to view these Psalms as taking an interpretive stance on the account in the Torah. Rather, the psalmists select elements from the Torah that suit their own didactic purposes.

See also the praises of God producing water from rocks in the wilderness in Isa. 43:20; 48:21; Ps. 78:15–16, 20; 105:41; 114:8; Neh. 9:15.

WHERE THE RULES OF
PESHAT AND *PESAK* COLLIDE:
DEUTERONOMY AND PROPHETIC NARRATIVES

INTRODUCTION

To a large degree, Tanakh and halakhah operate on different planes. Biblical commentators concern themselves with the meaning of Tanakh, whereas legal decisors work primarily with the Talmud and later authoritative halakhic codes and rulings. In halakhah, talmudic passages are intended as literal and are generally accepted as binding by later rabbinic authorities. In aggadah, talmudic passages often are intended as allegorical. Even when they are understood literally, later commentators generally reserve the right to disagree with them.[1]

This distinction is self-evident to R. Yom Tov Lipmann Heller (1579–1654), who extends the argument to the arena of theoretical halakhah, that is, situations when there are no practical consequences (I have added several clarifying points in brackets):

Rambam wrote ... even though the Gemara did not interpret [the Mishnah] in that manner. Since there is no practical legal difference, permission is granted to interpret [the Mishnah in a manner different from the Gemara's interpretation]. I see no difference between interpreting Mishnah and interpreting Scripture. Regarding Scripture, permission is granted to interpret [differently from how the Gemara interprets] as our own eyes see in the commentaries written since the time of the Gemara. However, we must not make any halakhic ruling that contradicts the Gemara. (*Tosafot Yom Tov* commentary on *Nazir* 5:5)

There are occasions, however, where halakhic rulings are based primarily on *peshat* readings of biblical verses outside of the Torah, rather than on normative rabbinic halakhic texts. This difference creates the unusual situation where *pashtanim* may clash with halakhists on *peshat* grounds. This essay will consider three such occasions as a means of exploring different aspects of the conflict between the two sets of rules.

THE TEST OF A FALSE PROPHET

And should you ask yourselves, "How can we know that the oracle was not spoken by the Lord?"—if the prophet speaks in the name of the Lord and the oracle does not come true, that oracle was not spoken by the Lord; the prophet has uttered it presumptuously: do not stand in dread of him. (Deut. 18:21–22)

There does not appear to be any ambiguity in this law. Anyone claiming prophecy whose predictions fail to come true must be a false prophet and is executed in court.

However, these verses are not easily taken at face value. Jonah and Isaiah both were true prophets. Nevertheless, Jonah's prediction of the destruction of Nineveh did not occur (Jon. 3:4–10), nor did Isaiah's prediction of Hezekiah's imminent death (II Kings 20:1–11~Isa. 38:1–8).

Rambam turns to the Book of Jeremiah for clarification. During his conflict with the false prophet Hananiah son of Azzur, Jeremiah stated:

The prophets who lived before you and me from ancient times prophesied war, disaster, and pestilence against many lands and great kingdoms. So if a prophet prophesies good fortune, then only when the word of the prophet comes true can it be known that the Lord really sent him. (Jer. 28:8–9)

Rambam understands Jeremiah's challenge to Hananiah as a modification of Deuteronomy 18:21–22. He therefore rules that if one prophesies something negative, the decree can be abrogated by repentance. However, if one prophesies something positive, the prediction must come true in full or else the person is executed as a false prophet:

> Regarding prophecies of doom...if they do not occur, his prophetic standing is not contradicted...it is possible that they repented and God forgave them as in the case of the people of Nineveh; or that retribution was deferred as in the case of Hezekiah. However, if he promised that good would occur...and it did not, then it is known for certain that he is a false prophet. Any good decree from God, even if it is provisional, is not retracted...as we learn in Tractate *Shabbat* (55a).[2] We learn from this principle that a prophet may be tested only through his positive prophecies. This is what Jeremiah told Hananiah son of Azzur.... (Rambam, *Hil. Yesodei ha-Torah* 10:4)[3]

From the perspective of Jeremiah's audience, the sudden downfall of Babylonia was indeed a favorable prophecy. Thus, were Babylonia not to fall in two years as Hananiah had predicted, Hananiah certainly would be a false prophet. On the other hand, if Babylonia were to fall after two years, Jeremiah could not be convicted as a false prophet since he would be able to claim that the people repented and therefore averted the decree of destruction he had been proclaiming.

Abarbanel challenges Rambam's reading of Jeremiah 28:8–9. Without going into the technical points here, the different interpretations may be summarized in this manner:

"You know the prophets who lived in the past and prophesied doom?"

Rambam: "It was only when one of them would prophesy good fortune and the prophecy came true that it would be known for sure that the Lord really sent him."

Abarbanel: "When a prophet would prophesy good fortune in opposition to those prophets of the past, only if the prophecy came true would it be known for sure that the Lord really sent him."

Abarbanel views Hananiah as vulnerable because of his opposition to a long prophetic tradition, not because he made a positive prediction.

Aside from Abarbanel's objections to Rambam's reading of Jeremiah 28:8–9, other verses in Jeremiah appear to contradict Rambam's ruling outright:

At one moment I may decree that a nation or a kingdom shall be uprooted and pulled down and destroyed; but if that nation against which I made the decree turns back from its wickedness, I change My mind concerning the punishment I planned to bring on it. At another moment I may decree that a nation or a kingdom shall be built and planted; but if it does what is displeasing to Me and does not obey Me, then I change My mind concerning the good I planned to bestow upon it. (Jer. 18:7–10)

This passage suggests that *all* prophecies are contingent on human behavior. If people repent after a negative prophecy, the decree may be annulled. Conversely, if people do evil, a favorable prophecy may be repealed. Not only does this passage challenge Rambam's ruling, but it appears to be antithetical to Deuteronomy 18:21–22. The Torah indicates that all prophetic predictions must occur or else one may be executed as a false prophet. Jeremiah 18:7–10 indicates that all prophecies are contingent on the behavior of an individual or nation and therefore the outcomes may not match the predictions.

Rambam addresses this conflict in chapter 2 of his *Introduction to the Commentary of the Mishnah*. Jeremiah 28 is generally correct. When a prophet announces evil tidings and they do not occur, we may assume that the people repented and God forgave them. If, however, a prophet predicts something positive, then his prediction must occur to verify him as a prophet. Jeremiah 18, on the other hand, discusses only cases where the prophet never announced the good tidings in public; such positive prophecies are vulnerable to changes in behavior. Rambam cites Jacob as an example: he feared that his sins might have cancelled the good future which God had privately promised him.[4]

Ralbag, R. Yitzhak Arama, and Abarbanel challenge Rambam, deeming it unlikely that God would keep His word when the prophet announced the prophecy in public, whereas He would be willing to retract a good decree if nobody else knew of it. Further, Jeremiah 18:7–10 does not distinguish between public and private prophecies. Nathan prophesied that David's enemies no longer would oppress him (II Sam. 7:10). This announced prophecy did not come true, since David lived a life filled with warfare against other nations and his own son. Rambam does not have an adequate resolution of the verses.[5]

R. Yitzhak Arama (*Akedat Yitzhak, sha'ar* 96) asserts that prophecy generally is contingent on consistent behavior by the recipients as per Jeremiah 18.[6] Deuteronomy 18:21–22 deals with the limited case where two unproven prophets present conflicting predictions— as in the case of Jeremiah vs. Hananiah. In such instances, how could people determine which one is telling the truth? Whichever one of those prophecies is not fulfilled is false.[7]

To summarize: Rambam rules that if a prophet predicts a good occurrence and it does not come true in entirety, we would execute the prophet in court. According to Ralbag, R. Yitzhak Arama, and Abarbanel, we would not execute him, since it is possible that the negative behavior of an individual or nation would have abrogated, mitigated, or delayed the fulfillment of that prediction. There are no halakhic sources in Talmud or midrash that govern this case. These halakhic positions are rooted in a *peshat* debate over how best to reconcile Deuteronomy 18:21–22 with Jeremiah 18:7–10 and 28:8–9.

According to the rules of learning *peshat* in Tanakh, this is a debate among rabbinic commentators, and their different views must be evaluated against the textual evidence. According to the rules of *pesak*, however, not all commentators are equal. Were this halakhic possibility to exist today, would Rambam carry more weight because he was a great halakhist whereas the others were not in his league? Or could/should a *posek* learn the verses and at least possibly decide that the reading of Ralbag, R. Yitzhak Arama, and Abarbanel is more likely and therefore not execute someone who prophesies something positive that does not occur?

MONARCHY

If, after you have entered the land that the Lord your God has assigned to you, and taken possession of it and settled in it, you decide, "I will set a king over me, as do all the nations about me," you shall be free to set a king over yourself, one chosen by the Lord your God. Be sure to set as king over yourself one of your own people; you must not set a foreigner over you, one who is not your kinsman. (Deut. 17:14–15)

Samuel was displeased that they said "Give us a king to govern us." Samuel prayed to the Lord, and the Lord replied to Samuel, "Heed the demand of the people in everything they say to you. For it is not you that they have rejected; it is Me they have rejected as their king." (I Sam. 8:6–7)

Surprisingly, the Torah's formulation legislates monarchy only in the second verse of the passage. This, coupled with Samuel's vigorous opposition to the people's request, led to a talmudic debate whether the Torah commands monarchy or whether it permits and governs it when the people request a king. R. Yehudah (*Sanhedrin* 20b) considers monarchy a positive commandment. R. Nehorai maintains that it is permitted yet frowned upon. In *Sifrei Devarim*

156, R. Nehorai asserts that monarchy is shameful for Israel. He cites I Samuel 8:7, where God deems the people's request to be a rejection of divine rule. R. Yehudah retorts that monarchy is a commandment but that the people sinned in Samuel's time by requesting a king inappropriately.

Rambam rules like R. Yehudah, that monarchy is a positive commandment and that Samuel opposed the manner in which the people asked for a king (*Hil. Melakhim* 1:1–2). Many later commentators and codifiers adopted this position.

Abarbanel dissents and offers a thorough critique of Rambam's view.[8] God and Samuel were incensed at the people's very asking for a king, rather than at the specific formulation or timing of their request (cf. I Sam. 10:19; 12:19). If the Torah commands monarchy, why did Joshua and his successors fail to appoint a king? When Samuel rebuked the people, why did they not respond that they simply wanted to fulfill a Torah commandment?

Abarbanel adopts R. Nehorai's view that while the Torah permits monarchy if requested, the institution is fundamentally negative. Abarbanel likens monarchy to the laws of the "beautiful captive" (Deut. 21:10–14) as another case where the Torah permits certain less-than-ideal actions to forestall worse eventualities (cf. *Kiddushin* 21b).[9]

To summarize: in this instance, the Talmud and halakhic midrashim present an unresolved disagreement over how to reconcile the biblical verses. Rambam and Abarbanel take opposite sides of this debate at least partially, if not primarily, as a result of their analysis of *peshat* in the biblical verses.

Again we may ask: were this halakhic possibility to exist today, would Rambam carry more weight because he was a great halakhist while Abarbanel was not at his level? Or could/should a *posek* learn the verse and at least possibly decide that Abarbanel's reading is more likely and therefore not insist on a monarchy if people do not want one?

Although we do not have actual monarchy today, the laws of monarchy in the Torah formed the basis of many contemporary discussions regarding the halakhic authority of the elected government of the State of Israel. In an Orthodox Forum volume, R. Aharon Lichtenstein and Professor Gerald Blidstein discuss monarchy as a precedent for the authority of Israel's civil government. R. Lichtenstein quotes Ibn Ezra (who also believes that monarchy is permitted and not commanded) and Abarbanel alongside Rambam, but he adds the caveat that they are "admittedly of far lesser status as *baalei halakhah* [halakhic authorities]." Professor Blidstein, on the other hand, cites all three equally as prominent medieval rabbinic authorities on the subject.[10]

SOLOMON'S MARRIAGE TO AN EGYPTIAN WOMAN

You shall not abhor an Edomite, for he is your kinsman. You shall not abhor an Egyptian, for you were a stranger in his land. Children born to them may be admitted into the congregation of the Lord in the third generation. (Deut. 23:8–9)

Solomon allied himself by marriage with Pharaoh king of Egypt. He married Pharaoh's daughter and brought her to the City of David [to live there] until he had finished building his palace, and the House of the Lord, and the walls around Jerusalem. The people, however, continued to offer sacrifices at the open shrines, because up to that time no house had been built for the name of the Lord. And Solomon, though he loved the Lord and followed the practices of his father David, also sacrificed and offered at the shrines. (I Kings 3:1–3)

In the two aforementioned cases, medieval rabbis debated halakhic issues. While Rambam is a classical halakhic decisor whereas Ibn Ezra, Ralbag, R. Yitzhak Arama, and Abarbanel are not, nobody disputed a final talmudic legal ruling. In the case of Solomon's marriage to Pharaoh's daughter, however, a final talmudic legal ruling is at stake.

The Mishnah (*Yevamot* 76b) debates whether Egyptian women are included in the Torah's prohibition against Egyptians in Deuteronomy 23:8–9. The majority view prohibits both men and women until the third generation after they convert, while R. Shimon permits Egyptian women who convert to marry Israelites immediately. Though R. Shimon claims a received tradition, the Talmud rules like the majority opinion.

Despite this clear talmudic ruling, however, Radak and Abarbanel puzzle over the fact that the Book of Kings does not condemn Solomon for marrying Pharaoh's daughter, reserving its criticism for when his wives led his heart astray at the end of his life (I Kings 11). According to the talmudic ruling, however, Solomon was guilty of violating the Torah's prohibition against intermarriage with an Egyptian, even if she had converted beforehand.

Radak suggests that the neutral tone of the Kings narrative in chapter 3 indicates that in fact R. Shimon's rejected view must have been in force in Solomon's time, that is, that Egyptian women were permitted to convert and marry Israelites:

> In truth, it appears that [Solomon] converted her to the Jewish religion[11] even though she was prohibited to him as a first- generation Egyptian. There was a Sage who believed that she was permitted to him.… And even though the law is not like this Sage despite his claim of a received tradition, his ruling appears correct. We do not find in the verses condemnation of Solomon for marrying Pharaoh's daughter. (Radak on I Kings 3:3)

The talmudic ruling now is purely theoretical, that is, the halakhic category of "Egyptian" prohibited by the Torah no longer exists. Therefore, Radak is arguing over historical circumstances rather than disputing a ruling of the Talmud that has practical ramifications today. What Radak would think if there were halakhic Egyptians today is a matter of speculation, but it lies at the heart of this conflict between the sets of rules governing *peshat* and *pesak*.

In his analysis, Abarbanel first proposes several hypothetical alternative readings of Deuteronomy 23:8–9. (1) Perhaps being "admitted into the congregation" does not refer to marriage, as is commonly assumed. (2) Perhaps, as per R. Shimon and Radak, Egyptian women were excluded from the prohibition. (3) Perhaps the Torah intended this law to apply exclusively to the first three generations of Egyptians from the time of the exodus, since only they enslaved the Israelites; after that initial prohibition, however, Egyptians who converted could marry Israelites immediately.

After those theoretical suggestions, however, Abarbanel submits to the halakhic understanding of the verse: that it does apply to marriage to Egyptians even in Solomon's time, and the prohibition includes Egyptian women as well as men. Confronted by what he perceives as an irresolvable tension, Abarbanel concludes that Solomon erred in his understanding of Torah law. He was young and it was good diplomacy to marry the Egyptian princess, so God did not punish or even criticize him for the marriage. Solomon even received prophecy in the following narrative (I Kings 3:4–15).[12] Unlike Radak, Abarbanel resigns himself to reconciling the perspectives of *peshat* and *pesak* in this instance, leading him to the remarkable conclusion that Solomon was ignorant of the halakhah governing his marriage.[13]

To summarize: though the Talmud reached a halakhic ruling in this instance, Radak believes that the rejected minority opinion in fact is historically correct based on the Book of Kings. Abarbanel, in contrast, ultimately resigns himself to the authoritative halakhic ruling of the Talmud.

CONCLUSION

In the case of ascertaining false prophets, Rambam bases a halakhic ruling on a *peshat* analysis of the apparent conflicts between

Deuteronomy 18:21–22, Jeremiah 18:7–10, and Jeremiah 28:8–9. Several *pashtanim* challenge Rambam's reading of those biblical texts and with it his ruling on a capital case. Similarly, Rambam's halakhic ruling on the institution of monarchy is rooted at least partially in *peshat* readings of the apparent conflict between the laws in Deuteronomy 17:14–15 and the narratives in I Samuel 8–12. Abarbanel challenges Rambam's reading of *peshat* and with it his halakhic decision. In a third instance, Radak and Abarbanel confront the talmudic ruling that female Egyptians as well as their male counterparts cannot marry Israelites even after conversion (based on Deut. 23:8–9). However, they wonder if that ruling in fact was practiced in Solomon's time, given that the Book of Kings does not criticize Solomon's marriage to Pharaoh's daughter (I Kings 3:1–3).

These tensions are inherent to the system. It is important to recognize how each set of rules can yield different results within a traditional learning framework.

NOTES

1. See, e.g., R. Marc D. Angel, "Authority and Dissent: A Discussion of Boundaries," *Tradition* 25:2 (Winter 1990), pp. 18–27; R. Hayyim David Halevi, *Aseh Lekha Rav*, vol. 5, resp. #49 (pp. 304–307); R. Chaim Eisen, "Maharal's *Be'er ha-Golah* and His Revolution in Aggadic Scholarship— in Their Context and on His Terms," *Hakirah* 4 (Winter 2007), pp. 137– 194; R. Michael Rosensweig, "*Elu va-Elu Divre Elokim Hayyim*: Halakhic Pluralism and Theories of Controversy," *Tradition* 26:3 (Spring 1992), pp. 4–23; Marc Saperstein, *Decoding the Rabbis: A Thirteenth-Century Commentary on the Aggadah* (Cambridge MA: Harvard University Press, 1980), pp. 1–20.

2. In his cogent critique of Rambam's position, Isaac S. D. Sassoon observes that *Shabbat* 55a refers to an exceptional case, where sins *preceding* a decree helped overturn it (*Destination Torah: Notes and Reflections on Selected Verses from the Weekly Torah Readings* [Hoboken, NJ: KTAV, 2001], p. 66). The present study will remain focused on the biblical analyses of Rambam and his critics.

3. Translation (with minor modifications) from R. Eliyahu Touger, *Mishneh Torah* (NY-Jerusalem: Moznaim Publishing, 1989).

4. See Gen. 28:15, where God promised Jacob that He will protect him wherever he goes, and 32:8, where Jacob was frightened nevertheless. Cf. *Berakhot* 4a.

5. See Abarbanel, commentary on Deuteronomy, pp. 176–184.

6. As the Tosafists stated centuries earlier, "Prophets do not prophesy except what should occur if there is no sin" (Tosafot *Yevamot* 50a, s.v. *teda*). See further discussion of this position in Hayyim Angel, "Prophecy as Potential: The Consolations of Isaiah 1–12 in Context," *Jewish Bible Quarterly* 37:1 (2009), pp. 3–10; reprinted in Angel, *Revealed Texts, Hidden Meanings: Finding the Religious Significance in Tanakh* (Jersey City, NJ: KTAV-Sephardic Publication Foundation, 2009), pp. 117–126.

7. According to this line of interpretation, however, one must wonder whether if there were such a prophetic conflict, would God insist on proving the true prophet's veracity even if people were to change their behavior. In our case, for example, were the people to have repented fully, would God have allowed the Babylonians to destroy Jerusalem and the Temple simply to prove Jeremiah right?

8. Commentary on Deuteronomy, pp. 163–171; commentary on Samuel, pp. 202–209.

9. For a survey and analysis of scholarly positions on the debate between Rambam and Abarbanel regarding monarchy, see Hayyim Angel, "Abarbanel: Commentator and Teacher: Celebrating 500 Years of His Influence on Tanakh Study," *Tradition* 42:3 (Fall 2009), pp. 9–26; reprinted in this volume.

10. R. Aharon Lichtenstein, "Communal Governance, Lay and Rabbinic: An Overview," pp. 19–52, esp. pp. 21–26; Prof. Gerald Blidstein, "On Lay Legislation in Halakhah: The King as Instance," pp. 1–17, in *Rabbinic and Lay Communal Authority*, ed. Suzanne Last Stone (New York: Yeshiva University Press, 2006).

11. Cf. Rambam, *Hil. Issurei Bi'ah* 13:14, who also assumes that King Solomon must have converted Pharaoh's daughter before marrying her.

12. Commentary on Kings, pp. 458–460.

13. For a different approach to the lack of criticism of Solomon until chapter 11, see Hayyim Angel, "Reading the Bible Forward and Backward: The Sins of David and Solomon," printed in this volume.

MOONLIT LEADERSHIP:
A MIDRASHIC READING OF
JOSHUA'S SUCCESS*

INTRODUCTION

The Book of Joshua represents one of Israel's ideal eras: "Israel served the Lord during the lifetime of Joshua and the lifetime of the elders who lived on after Joshua, and who had experienced all the deeds that the Lord had wrought for Israel" (Josh. 24:31). Given the nation's propensity toward complaint and rebellion throughout Moses' tenure, it is striking that Israel remained loyal to God and to Joshua. Only one man—Achan—sinned, and the people never complained to Joshua, even after their demoralizing loss at Ai.

This study will consider Joshua's characterization in the Torah and in the Book of Joshua. With a careful survey of the narratives in which Joshua appears, several rabbinic statements serve as catalysts in explaining the roots of his phenomenal success as a leader.

THE BATTLE AGAINST AMALEK

Amalek came and fought with Israel at Rephidim. Moses said to Joshua, "Pick some men for us, and go out and do battle with Amalek. Tomorrow I will station myself on the top of the hill, with the rod of God in my hand." Joshua did as Moses told him and fought with Amalek, while Moses, Aaron, and Hur went up to the top of the hill....Then the Lord said to Moses, "Inscribe

* This article appeared originally in the *Jewish Bible Quarterly* 37:3 (2009), pp. 144–152. Reprinted here with minor modifications, with permission from the *Jewish Bible Quarterly*, POB 29002, Jerusalem, Israel; www.jewishbible.org.

this in a document as a reminder, and read it aloud to Joshua: I will utterly blot out the memory of Amalek from under heaven!" (Exod. 17:8–14)

The first time Joshua is mentioned in the Torah, he appears without introduction. The reader is not told who Joshua is or why Moses chose him to serve as military commander in the battle against Amalek. Curiously, the Book of Chronicles reports that Joshua was the grandson of Elishama son of Ammihud, the chieftain of the tribe of Ephraim at the time of the Exodus (I Chr. 7:26–27, cf. Num. 1:10). The omission of this information in the Torah and in the Book of Joshua implies that his noble pedigree was not a significant factor in his being chosen. Clearly, Moses had detected some outstanding qualities in his disciple.[1]

ATTENDANT OF MOSES

Joshua is first introduced as a military general and then begins to appear as a close spiritual disciple of Moses. When Moses ascended Mount Sinai to receive the Torah, he left the people in the care of Aaron and Hur (Exod. 24:14). Joshua, however, separated himself from the people and faithfully waited for his master at the base of the mountain (24:13). When Moses later descended to confront the Golden Calf, he encountered his disciple:

When Joshua heard the sound of the people in its boisterousness, he said to Moses, "There is a cry of war in the camp." But he answered, "It is not the sound of the tune of triumph, or the sound of the tune of defeat; it is the sound of song that I hear!" (Exod. 32:17–18)

The first time Joshua is quoted in the Torah, Moses had to correct him.

Joshua then disappeared from the scene for the duration of the Calf narrative, confining himself to the Tent of Meeting: "The Lord would speak to Moses face to face, as one man speaks to another.

And he would then return to the camp; but his attendant, Joshua son of Nun, a youth, would not stir out of the Tent" (Exod. 33:11).

ELDAD AND MEDAD
When Eldad and Medad prophesied in the camp during Moses' leadership crisis in Numbers 11, Joshua again responded incorrectly:
A youth ran out and told Moses, saying, "Eldad and Medad are acting the prophet in the camp!" And Joshua son of Nun, Moses' attendant from his youth, spoke up and said, "My lord Moses, restrain them!" But Moses said to him, "Are you wrought up on my account? Would that all the Lord's people were prophets, that the Lord put His spirit upon them!" (Num. 11:27–29)

Detecting this surprising pattern, one midrash expresses concern with Joshua's future role as the nation's leader:
There were two statements of Joshua which Moses did not find favorable. One was [regarding] the appointment of elders, and the other was at the Golden Calf. . . . Regarding the Golden Calf . . . Moses said, "Joshua, who will one day lead 600,000 people, is unable to distinguish between different types of voices!" (*Ecc. Rabbah* 9:11)

THE SPIES
During the debacle with the spies, Joshua was one of the two faithful among them, along with Caleb. However, it is noteworthy that only Caleb spoke out in the first round of the debate (Num. 13:30), whereas Joshua joined him only after the people were irreversibly demoralized (Num. 14:6–10). Why was Joshua initially silent? Perhaps, since he had been mistaken twice before in his judgment, he now waited for Moses to act. Perhaps he believed that the people would not listen to him anyway, since he was Moses' disciple.

Perhaps more germane to the issue, the episode of the spies is prefaced by a reference to Joshua's change of name: "Those were the names of the men whom Moses sent to scout the land; but Moses changed the name of Hosea son of Nun to Joshua" (Num. 13:16). When did this renaming occur—at the time of the spies, or prior to the battle against Amalek, where Joshua already is called by his new name?[2] Ramban (on Exod. 17:9) assumes that Moses must have changed Joshua's name before the battle against Amalek, demonstrated by the occurrence of the name Joshua in the Amalek narrative. If so, the literary inclusion of his renaming with the later spies episode is particularly significant.

Following these textual cues, the Talmud states: "['Moses changed the name of Hosea son of Nun to Joshua, saying,'] 'May God save you from the [wicked] counsel of the [bad] spies [*Yah yoshiakha me-atzat meraglim*]'" (*Sotah* 34b). Did Moses worry about the faith of his disciple? Did he suspect that Joshua would succumb to the counsel of the majority? Perhaps he (or the Talmud) recognized that Joshua may have partially shared the fears of the other spies. This feeling would explain his initial silence, though he eventually did join with Caleb.

It appears that Joshua's ambivalence during the episode of the spies is indicative of an unusual personality that subsumed both sides of a seemingly irreconcilable debate. He had internalized Moses' resolute faith in entering the Land, but also the people's fears and insecurities about the formidable dangers ahead.

MOSES' SUCCESSOR

When God informed Moses that he would not bring the people into the Promised Land, Moses pleaded for a new leader. God responded:

Single out Joshua son of Nun, an inspired man, and lay your hand upon him. Have him stand before Eleazar the priest and before the whole community, and commission him in their sight. Invest him with some of your authority, so that the whole Israelite community may obey. (Num. 27:18–20)

Of course, Joshua was the natural successor by virtue of his being Moses' disciple, but until now he had spoken twice incorrectly (Calf and Eldad-Medad) and had remained silent when it may have been appropriate to speak (Spies). Capturing this negativity, the Sages express further concern with Joshua's upcoming leadership: "'Invest him with *some* of your authority'—but not *all* of your authority. The elders of that generation said, 'Moses' face is like the sun and Joshua's like the moon. Alas, for such shame! Alas for such reproach'" (*Bava Batra* 75a).

BE STRONG AND RESOLUTE!

The growing uncertainties over Joshua's leadership spiral in Deuteronomy. God ordered Moses to encourage Joshua, and Moses obeyed. The result is an outpouring of encouragement, yielding the impression that Joshua sorely needed it:

Joshua son of Nun, who attends you, he shall enter it. *Imbue him with strength*, for he shall allot it to Israel. (Deut. 1:38)

Give Joshua his instructions, and imbue him with *strength and courage*, for he shall go across at the head of this people, and he shall allot to them the land that you may only see. (3:28)

Then Moses called Joshua and said to him in the sight of all Israel: "*Be strong and resolute*, for it is you who shall go with this people into the land that the Lord swore to their fathers to give them, and it is you who shall apportion it to them." (31:7)

And He charged Joshua son of Nun: "*Be strong and resolute*: for you shall bring the Israelites into the land that I promised them on oath, and I will be with you." (31:23)

These fears are carried over into the Book of Joshua. After Moses died, God encouraged Joshua to be strong and resolute three times in four verses:

Be strong and resolute, for you shall apportion to this people the land that I swore to their fathers to assign to them. But you must be *very strong and resolute* to observe faithfully all the Teaching that My servant Moses enjoined upon you . . . . I charge you: *Be strong and resolute;* do not be terrified or dismayed, for the Lord your God is with you wherever you go. (Josh. 1:6–9)

Even more remarkably, the leaders of the eastern tribes echoed this sentiment: "Any man who flouts your commands and does not obey every order you give him shall be put to death. Only *be strong and resolute!*" (1:18). By contrast, it is difficult to imagine anyone addressing Moses in this manner. Would Joshua be able to lead a stiff-necked people and guide them during crises?

SUN VERSUS MOON LEADERSHIP

Despite the fears that nation and reader may have experienced concerning Joshua's abilities to lead, he became one of Israel's most effective leaders. The only recorded sin of his period was that of Achan (7:1). More impressively, a nation that persistently complained throughout Moses' forty years of leadership grumbled only once in the Book of Joshua—to the *elders* (and not to Joshua) after they mistakenly struck a treaty with the Gibeonites (9:18). Most remarkably, even after their hearts "sank in total dismay" following their defeat at Ai (7:5), they did not complain to Joshua.

Paradoxically, it may be that the people had more confidence in Joshua than in Moses, precisely because Joshua himself was terrified after the loss at Ai:

"Ah, Lord God!" cried Joshua. "Why did You lead this people across the Jordan only to deliver us into the hands of the Amorites, to be destroyed by them? If only we had been content to remain on the other side of the Jordan! O Lord, what can I say after Israel has turned tail before its enemies? When the Canaanites and all the inhabitants of the land hear of this, they will turn

upon us and wipe out our very name from the earth. And what
will You do about Your great name?" (7:7–9)

Joshua sounded exactly like the majority of the spies and their
followers in the wilderness (Num. 14:1–3; Deut. 1:27). At the same
time, Joshua made an appeal similar to that of Moses, that God
should be concerned with His reputation among the nations of the
world (Num. 14:13–16).

Thus the talmudic passage cited above regarding Joshua's name
change (*Sotah* 34b) has captured Joshua's complex spirit. Joshua
first remained silent in the episode of the spies as a result of his fears;
subsequently, he courageously joined Caleb against the faithless
people. He shared in elements of both sides, thereby being uniquely
qualified to bring the teachings of Moses to an apprehensive nation.

In contrast, it may have been difficult for the people to trust the
ever-resolute Moses. Although the elders may have complained that
"Moses is like the sun, Joshua like the moon" (*Bava Batra* 75a),
there was a benefit to Joshua's being like the moon. Moses objectively was superior, but *literally* was like the sun—his people could
not even look at him, so he had to wear a veil (Exod. 34:29–35).
Moses was privileged to speak with God face to face (Num. 12:8),
but the people were unable to speak to Moses face to face!

This tension is captured by another talmudic passage:

R. Hanina further said: Everything is in the hand of heaven except the fear of heaven, as it says, "And now, O Israel, what does
the Lord your God demand of you? Only this: to revere" (Deut.
12:10). Is the fear of heaven such a little thing....Yes; for Moses
it was a small thing; as R. Hanina said: To illustrate by a parable,
if a man is asked for a big article and he has it, it seems like a
small article to him; if he is asked for a small article and he does
not possess it, it seems like a big article to him. (*Berakhot* 33b)

Moses' unparalleled awe of God was so great that he could not
fathom why his people did not trust God also. Ironically, then,

Moses' incomparable faith may have been precisely at the root of his struggles in leading the Israelites. In contrast, the people never rebelled against Joshua, because they detected his fears and therefore viewed him as one of them. Thus Joshua was able to bridge the world of Moses with their world.

In his *Sefat Emet*, Rabbi Yehudah Aryeh Leib Alter of Ger offers a further contrast between Moses and Joshua. Unlike the sun, which dominates the sky, the moon allows stars to shine.[3] From the very opening of the Book of Joshua, Joshua immediately shared his leadership, turning to the officials of the people (Josh. 1:10). When crossing the Jordan, Joshua gave the orders, but the tribal delegates, priests, Ark, and officials dominate the narrative. The same is true with the encircling of Jericho and the ceremony at Mount Gerizim-Ebal: Joshua was the leader, but the people had a far more active and prominent role than they had under Moses. Moses' brightness in the Torah narratives largely eclipsed their participation. It appears that this further element of Joshua's moon-style leadership empowered many among the people, so that they actively supported and joined in Joshua's efforts.

ONE SANDAL ON, ONE SANDAL OFF

Malbim (on Exod. 3:5) contrasts the parallel scenes between Moses at the Burning Bush and Joshua with the angelic commander outside of Jericho:

And He said, "Do not come closer. Remove your sandals [na'alekha] from your feet, for the place on which you stand is holy ground." (Exod. 3:5)

The captain of the Lord's host answered Joshua, "Remove your sandals [na'alkha] from your feet, for the place where you stand is holy." And Joshua did so. (Josh. 5:15)

Standing on holy ground, both prophets were commanded to remove their sandals for their respective revelations. However,

Malbim observes that in the Hebrew, Moses was commanded "*shal na'alekha* [the plural form for "sandals"] *me'al raglekha*," whereas the commander ordered Joshua, "*shal na'alkha* [the singular form for "sandal"] *me'al raglekha*." Ibn Caspi (on Joshua 5:15) does not think that there is any difference on the level of *peshat*, and his approach has been adopted by the NJPS commentary, which translates both as "sandals."

Malbim, however, offers a midrashic-conceptual interpretation. Shoes symbolize human involvement in the world.[4] Having reached the most exalted level of revelation, Moses was completely elevated to the realm of the metaphysical in his prophecy. Therefore, he was ordered to remove both sandals. In contrast, Joshua removed only one sandal while leaving the other on. In this manner, he entered the metaphysical realm prophetically but simultaneously remained rooted in this world. Malbim's analysis of Joshua's "one sandal on, one sandal off" leadership is a perfect depiction of his relationship to Moses and to the people. He had one foot in Moses' ideal world of prophecy, but at the same time kept the other with his people.

One may extend Malbim's argument: Moses led the nation in the wilderness, where God provided for His nation directly and super-naturally. In the wilderness, the nation needed a Moses, with "both sandals off," to lead them. Indeed, Joshua's efforts at leadership in the wilderness largely were ineffective, with the notable exception of his military campaign against Amalek, where he led the natural side of the battle while Moses spiritually led the people from atop the hill. Joshua's "one sandal on, one sandal off" leadership, however, would be more appropriate in the Land—he was uniquely qualified to bridge God's continued supervision with human efforts at cultivating a real society.

Joshua's unique combination of Moses' prophetic faith and the people's fears diminished his objective greatness in relation to Moses. His prophecy did not reach the level of Moses'. These short-comings, however, enabled Joshua to succeed as a leader in a manner that even his master could not. Precisely these weaknesses may have engendered additional trust among the people. As a result, Joshua was able to bring Moses' teachings to the people,[5] guiding a stiff-necked and rebellious people to unrivaled faithfulness as they entered the Promised Land.

NOTES

1. Joshua's connection to his tribe of Ephraim in the Book of Joshua is even less pronounced than in the Torah. Other than his inheritance (Josh. 19:49–50) and burial (24:30), we would not have known his tribal origins. He is cast as the leader of the entire nation and as Moses' disciple. Cf. Yehudah Kiel, *Da'at Mikra: Joshua* [Hebrew] (Jerusalem: Mossad HaRav Kook, 1970), p. 4.

2. Other than one reference to "Hosea" at the end of the Torah (Deut. 32:44), Joshua is always referred to by the name Moses gave him.

3. *Sefat Emet*, vol. 4 (*Bemidbar*), *Parashat Pinehas* 5657.

4. Jews are required to remove their shoes at the Temple and on Yom Kippur to elevate themselves to the level of angels. At the other end of the spectrum, mourners remove their shoes as a sign of degradation. For further discussion of the symbolism of shoes, see R. Haim David Halevi, *Mekor Hayyim ha-Shalem*, vol. 1 (Tel Aviv: Organization for the Publication of the Writings of Rabbi Haim David Halevi, 1966) pp. 32–34.

5. Viewing the sun-moon relationship from a different angle, Rabbenu Bahya (on Deut. 31:14) observes that the sun can light up the moon even after it sets. So too, Moses continued to inspire Joshua after his death.

WAR AGAINST CANAAN:
DIVINE AND HUMAN PERSPECTIVES

INTRODUCTION

Though religious war is a thorny subject, we must confront the Torah's commandment of war against Canaan. This command is not applicable today, and therefore this is a purely theoretical discussion.[1] Nonetheless, it is important to reflect on what Tanakh teaches even when there is no practical application today. This essay will explore some of the critical texts and evaluate rabbinic approaches to this topic.[2]

DEUTERONOMY 20:10–18

When you approach a town to attack it, you shall offer it terms of peace. If it responds peaceably and lets you in, all the people present there shall serve you at forced labor. If it does not surrender to you, but would join battle with you, you shall lay siege to it; and when the Lord your God delivers it into your hand, you shall put all its males to the sword. You may, however, take as your booty the women, the children, the livestock, and everything in the town—all its spoil—and enjoy the use of the spoil of your enemy, which the Lord your God gives you. Thus you shall deal with all towns that lie very far from you, towns that do not belong to nations hereabout.

In the towns of the latter peoples, however, which the Lord your God is giving you as a heritage, you shall not let a soul remain alive. No, you must proscribe them—the Hittites and the Amorites, the Canaanites and the Perizzites, the Hivites and the Je-

74

busites—as the Lord your God has commanded you, lest they lead you into doing all the abhorrent things that they have done for their gods and you stand guilty before the Lord your God. (Deut. 20:10–18)

Commentators propose two fundamental ways to read this passage. It may be understood as two sets of rules, one governing war outside of the land of Israel and the other in regard to the seven Canaanite nations. When attacking nations outside the land, the Israelites first must offer peace. Regarding the Canaanites, they must annihilate them without any peaceful gesture. Rashi and Ra'avad espouse this reading.

Alternatively, the initial two verses which instruct offering peace may apply to the entire passage. The Israelites were required to offer peace even to the seven Canaanite nations. The ensuing laws distinguish only between those cities inside and outside of the land that reject offers of peace. Rambam (*Laws of Kings* 6:1–4) and Ramban prefer this reading.[3]

These interpreters generally add that the offer of peace includes a precondition that the Canaanites abandon their immoral paganism and accept the seven Noahide laws. Though it is not explicit in the text, this assumption appears to reflect the reasoning for the war, as described in verse 18. What would be the value of making peace if the Canaanites continue to influence the Israelites toward paganism? Rashi (on Deut. 20:18) also asserts that the Israelites could accept Canaanite converts since the problem of their dwelling in Israel is their potential negative religious and moral influence. While Rashi does not require the Israelites to *offer* peace, the two views may have more common ground than it had initially seemed.

Rambam and Ramban derive additional support from two verses in the Book of Joshua:

Apart from the Hivites who dwelt in Gibeon, not a single city made terms with the Israelites; all were taken in battle. For it was the Lord's doing to stiffen their hearts to give battle to Israel, in order that they might be proscribed without quarter and wiped out, as the Lord had commanded Moses. (Josh. 11:19–20)

From these verses, it appears that every nation theoretically had the chance to make peace, but God "stiffened their hearts" and therefore all the Canaanites save the Gibeonites in Joshua 9 declined this option and chose to fight instead.

However, the rest of Book of Joshua supports the Rashi-Ra'avad reading. Aside from the conspicuous absence of references to Joshua's offering peace to Canaanites, the Gibeonites' deceitful treaty appears superfluous according to the Rambam-Ramban reading. Why would they have used deceitful tactics if they had been offered letters of peace?[4] While Rambam and others offer explanations, these appear to be based on the assumption that there were in fact letters of peace. Additionally, the passage from Joshua 11:19–20 cited above could mean simply that no other cities made treaties of any kind, not that every city was given an opportunity to make one beforehand. Therefore, it appears that Rashi-Ra'avad have the smoother overall reading of the command.

ETHICAL, NOT ETHNIC

Even within the Rashi-Ra'avad reading, it is possible for moral Canaanites to become accepted as residents in Israel. This premise is rooted in the fact that the war against Canaan was not ethnic; rather, it was a battle against their immorality. God already included this premise in the covenant with Abraham:

And they shall return here in the fourth generation, for the iniquity of the Amorites is not yet complete. (Gen. 15:16)

The Torah stresses that there was no room for negotiation as long as the Canaanites retained their pagan culture.[5] Implicit in the Abrahamic covenant is that, were the Canaanites to become righteous, they would retain the right to remain in the land.

Furthermore, the Torah and later biblical passages make it clear that Israel's presence in the land is similarly conditional on their faithfulness to the covenant. If they violated the covenant, they would meet the fate of the Canaanites and be exiled from the land (e.g., Deut. 11:13–17). If an Israelite town were to behave like Canaanites, then the rest of the nation was obligated to wage war on that town (Deut. 13:13–19). During the reign of Manasseh, the people became even worse than the Canaanites and therefore deserved their decree of exile (II Kings 21:9).

To summarize, good Israelites and Canaanites may dwell in the land, whereas bad Israelites and Canaanites are subject to punishment or exile. This view is espoused both by Rashi (on Deut. 20:18) and Rambam (*Laws of Kings* 6:1).[6] Perhaps the most poignant illustration of these principles is in the Book of Joshua when the Canaanite prostitute Rahab integrated into the Israelite people after helping them (Josh. 6:25).[7] In the following chapter, the Judahite Achan was executed for violating the ban on Jericho (Josh. 7:24–26).

THEORY VERSUS REALITY

Having discussed the moral expectations of the laws of conquest, we turn to Joshua's wars in light of the command to annihilate the Canaanites. A superficial reading of the Book of Joshua leads to the conclusion that Joshua conquered the entire land (e.g., Josh. 10:40–43; 11:16–23; 21:41–43). However, the detailed accounts in chapters 13–19 make it amply clear that he did not (e.g., Josh. 15:63; 16:10; 17:14–18; 19:47). Even the victory song in chapter 12 lists only 31 cities that were captured. It stands to reason, however, that there were many more cities in Canaan.

Furthermore, it appears that Joshua generally defeated the armies of those cities but did not actually attack the people in the cities. For example, Joshua 10:33 reports that the Israelites defeated Gezer. Yet Gezer remained a Canaanite city even afterwards:

At that time King Horam of Gezer marched to the help of Lachish; but Joshua defeated him and his army, letting none of them escape. (Josh. 10:33)

However, they failed to dispossess the Canaanites who dwelt in Gezer; so the Canaanites remained in the midst of Ephraim, as is still the case. But they had to perform forced labor. (Josh. 16:10; cf. Jud. 1:29)[8]

Gezer was not fully conquered until Pharaoh did so in the time of Solomon (I Kings 9:16).

Other cities follow this pattern. For example, Jerusalem was defeated in Joshua 10 and is listed as one of the 31 captured cities in 12:10; but Joshua 15:63 and 18:28 demonstrate that much of the city remained in Canaanite hands. Only three cities in the Book of Joshua are explicitly described as having been entirely destroyed: Jericho, Ai, and Hazor. Most of the other battles likely describe battles of armies against armies, rather than Israelite invasions of Canaanite towns.[9] The campaign described in Joshua 1–12, then, simply broke the back of the Canaanite military coalitions.

DIVINE VERSUS HUMAN STANDARDS OF JUSTICE

Did Joshua understand the command in Deuteronomy to extend only to armies rather than cities? The Torah appears explicitly to refer to all (unconverted) Canaanites. Perhaps the disparity between the Torah's command of annihilation and Joshua's military record can be traced to a surprising disjunction between God's command of war against Sihon the Amorite and Moses' offering him peace. God explicitly commanded Moses to attack, yet Moses responded to this direct command with an offer of peace:

Up! Set out across the wadi Arnon! See, I give into your power Sihon the Amorite, king of Heshbon, and his land. Begin the occupation: engage him in battle. This day I begin to put the dread and fear of you upon the peoples everywhere under heaven, so that they shall tremble and quake because of you whenever they hear you mentioned.

Then I sent messengers from the wilderness of Kedemoth to King Sihon of Heshbon with an offer of peace, as follows, "Let me pass through your country. I will keep strictly to the highway, turning off neither to the right nor to the left....But King Sihon of Heshbon refused to let us pass through, because the Lord had stiffened his will and hardened his heart in order to deliver him into your power—as is now the case. (Deut. 2:24–30)

This response appears to be a flagrant violation of God's command by Moses.

One could interpret Moses' offer of peace as strategic rather than disobedient. Perhaps he craftily attempted to lure Sihon and his troops out of the safety of their walled cities so that the Israelites could battle them in the open. However, the narrative does not indicate anything strategic about Moses' offer.

Taking into account the fact that God did not reprimand Moses for disobedience, some midrashim and later commentators maintain that inherent in God's command of warfare is an assumption that Moses (and later Joshua) would offer peace before attacking any city. As we saw earlier, Rambam and Ramban adopt this position and apply it to their reading of Deuteronomy 20.

A more revolutionary interpretation appears in other midrashic sources. According to these midrashim, Moses deliberately disobeyed, and God subsequently altered the law to reflect Moses' wishes:

R. Joshua of Siknin said in the name of R. Levi: God agreed to whatever Moses decided. How?...God commanded him to make war on Sihon, as it is said, And contend with him in battle (Deut. 2:24), but he did not do so, but [as Scripture has it], And I sent messengers, etc. (2:26). God said to him: "I have commanded you to make war with him, but instead you began with peace;

by your life, I will confirm your decision; every war upon which
Israel enters, they shall begin with [a declaration of] peace," as it
is said, WHEN YOU DRAW NEAR UNTO A CITY TO FIGHT
AGAINST IT, THEN PROCLAIM PEACE UNTO IT. (*Deut.
Rabbah* 5:13; cf. *Num. Rabbah* 19:33)[10]

According to this reading, Moses and Joshua deviated *intentionally*
from God's command of complete annihilation of the Canaanites.[11]

This interpretation would become another expression of the tension between God and people regarding justice.[12] God's method in
the time of Noah and Sodom was to annihilate all evil. He considered the same method during the sins of the Golden Calf and Spies;
yet Moses successfully interceded on behalf of the people.

With Sihon, Moses attempted peace but God hardened Sihon's
heart. Once Sihon attacked, the Israelites had no choice but to defend themselves. The same may be the case with Joshua. He did not
conquer a majority of the land, yet he was considered completely
faithful. Joshua 11:19–20, cited earlier, supports this reading as well:

Apart from the Hivites who dwelt in Gibeon, not a single city
made terms with the Israelites; all were taken in battle. For it
was the Lord's doing to stiffen their hearts to give battle to Israel, in order that they might be proscribed without quarter and
wiped out, as the Lord had commanded Moses. (Josh. 11:19–20)

Joshua succeeded in gaining control over the land, so that the Israelites had the wherewithal to eliminate Canaanism. However, subsequent generations allowed them to remain as pagan Canaanites,
and this is where the prophetic condemnation begins. Joshua can be
praised for his faithfulness even as he left vast parts of the land un-
conquered. When later generations tolerated paganism, this position
led to the downfall of Israel.

CONCLUSION

Rashi-Ra'avad seem to have the smoother reading of the command in Deuteronomy 20, which calls for the annihilation of all Canaanites without offering peace beforehand. At the same time, the Torah makes clear a moral equivalence between Canaanites and Israelites—both are expected to live religious-moral lives. If they do, they may remain in the Land. If they do not, they will not remain in the Land. The battle against Canaanites was ethical not ethnic.

Joshua generally battled against armies rather than destroying entire cities in a war of annihilation. This policy harks back to Moses' offers of peace to Sihon, which appears to have contradicted God's outright command of attack. These episodes reflect another tension between the divine imperative to eradicate all evil and the human inclination to attempt methods of resolution.

Regardless of method, the ultimate goal of God and of Moses-Joshua was to avoid pagan Canaanite influence and immorality. Later generations' allowing pagan immorality to remain in Israel's heartland ultimately led to the erosion of Israel's morality and religious spirit.

To truly support the human perspective, we need to be strong religiously and influence society for the better. That is why Moses, Joshua, and Abraham at Sodom ultimately were willing to argue with God. Their fight is now ours.

NOTES

1. For a halakhic-conceptual analysis, see Dr. Norman Lamm, "Amalek and the Seven Nations: A Case of Law vs. Morality," in *War and Peace in the Jewish Tradition*, Lawrence Schiffman and Joel B. Wolowelsky (eds.) (New York: Yeshiva University Press, 2007), pp. 201–238.

2. For this study I am particularly indebted to the collection of Hebrew articles in *Musar Milhamah ve-Kibush* (Tevunot: Yeshivat Har Etzion, 1994); and Rabbi Shalom Carmy, "The Origin of Nations and the Shadow of Violence: Theological Perspectives on Canaan and Amalek," in *War and Peace in the Jewish Tradition*, pp. 163–199.

3. Cf. Radak on Josh. 9:7; Ralbag and Abarbanel on Josh. 11:19–20. *J.T. Shevi'it* 6:1.

4. Adopting a middle position, Rashbam (on Deut. 20:16) suggests that Israel did not make peaceful gestures prior to battles with Canaanites, but were permitted to accept proactive offers of peace such as that of the Gibeonites.

5. Rabbi Shalom Carmy quotes a letter from Rabbi Abraham Isaac Kook to his student Rabbi Moshe Seidel (*Iggerot ha-Reiyah* I [Jerusalem, 1943], #99, p. 100): "Regarding war: It would have been impossible, at a time when all the neighbors were literal wolves of the night, that only Israel refrain from war. For then they would have gathered and eradicated them, God forbid. Moreover, it was necessary for them to cast their fear on the barbarians through harsh conduct, albeit with the hope of bringing humanity to the state that it ought to reach, but without prematurely anticipating it" ("The Origin of Nations and the Shadow of Violence: Theological Perspectives on Canaan and Amalek," pp. 169–170).

6. This view appears in midrashic sources as well. See, e.g., *Sifrei* 202. S. D. Luzzatto (on Deut. 23:4) does not believe that the Canaanites were given the option to convert.

7. A midrashic tradition (e.g., *Megillah* 14b) extends this premise to a remarkable extreme by positing that Rahab went on to marry Joshua.

8. Gezer also is named as a city of refuge in Josh. 21:21.

9. See, e.g., Rabbi Yaakov Medan, "The Question of the Conquest of the Land in Light of Ethical Principles—A Study in the Book of Joshua" (Hebrew), in *Musar Milhamah ve-Kibush*, pp. 24–25; Rabbi Yoel Bin-Nun, "The Book of Joshua—the Plain Sense of the Text and the Words of Our Sages" (Hebrew), in *Musar Milhamah ve-Kibush*, pp. 36–38; Rabbi Yoel Bin-Nun, "The Bible from an Historical Perspective and the Israelite settlement in the land of Canaan" (Hebrew), in *Ha-Polemos al ha-Emet ha-Historit ba-Mikra*, Yisrael L. Levin and Amihai Mazar (eds.) (Yad Yitzhak Ben Zvi, Merkaz Dinur: 2002), pp. 3–16.

10. Rabbi Shalom Carmy observes that in the narrative order of the Torah, Moses battled Sihon (Num. 21:21–31; Deut. 2:24–36) prior to the formulation of the commandment for war against the Canaanites in Deuteronomy 20 ("The Origin of Nations and the Shadow of Violence: Theological Perspectives on Canaan and Amalek," p. 199 n. 66).

11. Rabbi Abraham Isaac Kook espouses a similar view: "Even in sin its eye was not evil towards the entire human race for they did not annihilate the nations," thus exhibiting "an inner tendency to seek the welfare of all human beings, which was excessive" (*En Ayah* 2:300, 115, quoted in Rabbi Shalom Carmy, "The Origin of Nations and the Shadow of Violence: Theological Perspectives on Canaan and Amalek," pp. 176–177).

12. Rabbi Yoel Bin-Nun opens his article with this premise. God needed to command this war with absolute severity because it was against Israel's nature to fulfill this command ("The Book of Joshua—the Plain Sense of the Text and the Words of Our Sages," p. 31). It is noteworthy that even the most wicked of the Northern Israelite kings—Ahab—still was famed for being a magnanimous king (I Kings 20:31) and spared his enemies. In that instance, prophecy responded that the spared Arameans would regroup and ultimately kill Ahab (I Kings 20:42).

"I AM THE SEER":
OBJECTIVE AND SUBJECTIVE ELEMENTS OF
SAMUEL'S RELATIONSHIP TO SAUL AND THE
MONARCHY IN I SAMUEL 8–16[*]

INTRODUCTION

The first seven chapters of the Book of Samuel cast the prophet Samuel as a perfect individual and leader, completely in sync
with God's will. His prophecy is impeccable (3:19–20)[1]; he trav-
els throughout the country to judge the people, thereby inspiring a
national repentance (7:3–4, 16–17); and he attains military victory
against the Philistines by praying on Israel's behalf (7:7–11). Had
Samuel been immortal, he would have been Israel's consummate
leader for all eternity. Alas, he grew old, forcing Israel to think about
succession.

Prophets often are viewed as passive receptacles and communica-
tors of God's will. However, the Sages maintain that all prophets
aside from Moses have prophetic experiences that combine the objective encounter of God with subjective elements of their person-
alities:

All the prophets looked through a dim glass, but Moses looked
through a clear glass. (*Yevamot* 49b)[2]

This dichotomy between objective and subjective components in
prophecy plays a significant role in chapters 8–16, where Samuel
must create a monarchy despite his strong opposition to that

* This article appeared in *Milin Havivin: Beloved Words* 4 (2008–2010),
pp. 6–18. Reprinted here with minor modifications, with permission from
Milin Havivin.

institution; and later when he must anoint a successor for the rejected Saul despite the prophet's love for the king.

This essay will explore the intricate relationship between God's will and Samuel's will—where they intersect and where they might differ in these pivotal narratives in the history of Israel's leadership.

CHAPTER 8

> When Samuel grew old, he appointed his sons judges over Israel.... But his sons did not follow in his ways; they were bent on gain, they accepted bribes, and they subverted justice. All the elders of Israel assembled and came to Samuel at Ramah, and they said to him, "You have grown old, and your sons have not followed your ways. Therefore appoint a king for us, to govern us like all other nations." (8:1–5)

Samuel is growing older and expects his justice-subverting sons to succeed him.[3] That Samuel would support his unworthy sons is surprising, since he would resemble his predecessor Eli, who was rejected precisely for allowing his sinful sons to remain in office (2:27–36; 3:11–14). As late as Saul's second coronation, Samuel still insists that his sons would be preferable to a king:

> Then Samuel said to all Israel, "I have yielded to you in all you have asked of me and have set a king over you. Henceforth the king will be your leader. As for me, I have grown old and gray— but my sons are still with you—and I have been your leader from my youth to this day." (12:1–2)

Noting that God never criticizes Samuel for failure to rebuke his sons (as He did with Eli), Ibn Caspi and Abarbanel maintain that Samuel must have been unaware of their corruption. Nevertheless, the elders' statement to Samuel, "You have grown old, and your sons have not followed your ways" (8:5) indicates that the prophet likely was better informed.

Samuel was displeased that they said "Give us a king to govern us." Samuel prayed to the Lord, and the Lord replied to Samuel, "Heed the demand of the people in everything they say to you. For it is not you that they have rejected; it is Me they have rejected as their king. Like everything else they have done ever since I brought them out of Egypt to this day—forsaking Me and worshiping other gods—so they are doing to you. Heed their demand; but warn them solemnly, and tell them about the practices of any king who will rule over them." (8:6–9)

Based on the narrator's excerpting from the elders' statement, Samuel is disturbed by the request of "a king to govern us" (*melekh le-shoftenu*). Since Samuel is the *shofet* and has appointed his sons as *shofetim*, it appears that he is reacting in part from personal motivations. Perhaps he viewed the request as a rejection of his leadership and that of his sons. God confirms this reading by telling Samuel not to take the elders' request as a personal rejection, indicating that Samuel perceived it as such.[4]

Though God likens the request of monarchy to idolatry, God still accedes to the people's request. There appears to be a divergence between God's and Samuel's perspectives on the monarchy. God espouses a complex view that kingship is dangerous yet necessary.[5] Much of Samuel's response parallels God's concern that God's kingdom will be threatened by a human monarch. However, the element of personal rejection may have pressed him to unequivocal opposition to the monarchy. Thus God's response incorporates both diametrically opposed sides of the human debate. Samuel fully opposes monarchy, whereas the people fully endorse monarchy.

When Samuel heard all that the people said, he reported it to the Lord. And the Lord said to Samuel, "Heed their demands and appoint a king for them." Samuel then said to the men of Israel, "All of you go home." (8:21–22)

After God instructs Samuel to heed their demands, the prophet does not inform the elders that God has approved. Instead, he sends everyone home! This response may reflect tension between what Samuel wants and God's command.[6] Mitigating this disparity, Malbim and Kiel interpret Samuel's response to mean "go home until God gives me further instructions." However, the ensuing narrative is a textbook example of divine providence as Saul "coincidentally" arrives in Ramah searching for his father's missing donkeys. It appears that absent such providence, nothing more would have occurred.

CHAPTER 9

Now the day before Saul came, the Lord had revealed the following to Samuel: "At this time tomorrow, I will send a man to you from the territory of Benjamin, and you shall anoint him ruler of My people Israel. He will deliver My people from the hands of the Philistines; for I have taken note of My people, their outcry has come to Me." (9:15–16)

As Saul approaches Samuel, God informs the prophet that a king will alleviate the people's suffering. God presents kingship as an act of mercy rather than a concession to an illegitimate request. As is noted above, God both supports and is threatened by monarchy. These verses reflect the positive aspect—and precisely what the elders want—of the monarchy.

CHAPTER 10

Samuel summoned the people to the Lord at Mizpah and said to them, "Thus said the Lord, the God of Israel: 'I brought Israel out of Egypt, and I delivered you from the hands of the Egyptians and of all the kingdoms that oppressed you.' But today you have rejected your God who delivered you from all your troubles and calamities. For you said, 'No, set up a king over us!' Now station yourselves before the Lord, by your tribes and clans." (10:17–19)

At Saul's first coronation, Samuel publicly condemns the people's request for a king as sinful. This declaration doubtlessly had a devastating effect on Saul's monarchy. Was this denunciation a verbatim transcript of God's message, or did Samuel add words of his own? Samuel quotes God as saying that God delivered Israel in the past (v. 18), but then he refers to God in the third person when he says that the monarchy is sinful (v. 19).[7] The NJPS translation cited above follows this lead by closing God's quotation after verse 18. If Samuel is blurring the boundary between God's words and his own, the speech that likely undermined some of the monarchy's initial authority emanated more from the prophet than from God.

CHAPTER 12

Then Samuel said to all Israel, "I have yielded to you in all you have asked of me and have set a king over you. Henceforth the king will be your leader. As for me, I have grown old and gray— but my sons are still with you—and I have been your leader from my youth to this day. Here I am! Testify against me, in the presence of the Lord and in the presence of His anointed one: Whose ox have I taken, or whose ass have I taken? Whom have I defrauded or whom have I robbed? From whom have I taken a bribe to look the other way? I will return it to you." (12:1–3)

After Saul's decisive victory against Ammon in chapter 11, the people hold a second coronation. At this ceremony—Samuel's final recorded public address to the nation—Samuel casts the monarchy as a rejection of himself and his sons. The parallel of "I have been your leader" (*va-ani hithalakhti lifnekhem*) as opposed to "henceforth the king will be your leader" (*ve-atah hinneh ha-melekh mithalekh lifnekhem*) further demonstrates that Samuel feels personally rejected.[8]

Samuel surveys Israel's history to teach that God always saved Israel, so why do they rebelliously demand a king? He concludes his censure by successfully praying for a storm:

"Now stand by and see the marvelous thing that the Lord will do before your eyes. It is the season of the wheat harvest. I will pray to the Lord and He will send thunder and rain; then you will take thought and realize what a wicked thing you did in the sight of the Lord when you asked for a king." Samuel prayed to the Lord, and the Lord sent thunder and rain that day, and the people stood in awe of the Lord and of Samuel. The people all said to Samuel, "Intercede for your servants with the Lord your God that we may not die, for we have added to all our sins the wickedness of asking for a king." (12:16–19)

At his second coronation, Saul hears the nation admit that kingship is sinful, and the storm indicates divine support for Samuel and his staunch opposition to the monarchy.[9]

Thus the most unequivocally negative statements against monarchy (10:19; 12:17) emanate from Samuel in his direct speech. In contrast, God upholds a complex view of monarchy by both endorsing the people's request for a king and answering Samuel's prayer for the storm. Internalizing God's composite position, the people now concede that while they still want a king, monarchy poses a serious spiritual hazard. Prophecy, on the other hand, would acknowledge the positive aspect of monarchy only after Samuel. Yehudah Kiel observes that later prophets tend to condemn the sinful behavior of kings but do not oppose the institution of monarchy itself.[10]

CHAPTERS 13–14

"After that, you are to go down to Gilgal ahead of me, and I will come down to you to present burnt offerings and offer sacrifices of well-being. Wait seven days until I come to you and instruct you what you are to do next." (10:8)

He waited seven days, the time that Samuel [had set]. But when Samuel failed to come to Gilgal, and the people began to scatter, Saul said, "Bring me the burnt offering and the sacrifice of well-being"; and he presented the burnt offering. He had just finished presenting the burnt offering when Samuel arrived; and Saul went out to meet him and welcome him. But Samuel said, "What have you done....You acted foolishly in not keeping the commandments that the Lord your God laid upon you! Otherwise the Lord would have established your dynasty over Israel forever. But now your dynasty will not endure. The Lord will seek out a man after His own heart, and the Lord will appoint him ruler over His people, because you did not abide by what the Lord had commanded you." (13:8–14)

Saul failed to wait for Samuel because he feared danger and also his religious sentiment that he should not enter battle before an offering was brought. Nevertheless, this error cost Saul the throne. The initial impression from this passage is that Saul lost his monarchy as a result of this sin.

However, there is a redundancy between Saul's rejection in this narrative and in chapter 15, when he sins in the battle against Amalek. Radak (on 15:28) suggests two resolutions: (1) in chapter 13 Saul lost his dynasty; in chapter 15 Saul himself was rejected. (2) Saul still had an opportunity to repent after chapter 13, but the decree was sealed irrevocably after chapter 15.

However, if there were no chapter 15, chapter 13 would have been understood as a permanent rejection of Saul and his dynasty. Perhaps the following can serve as a more likely resolution. Since God never speaks in chapter 13, and the objective narrator supports Saul, it is unclear if Samuel is conveying a received prophecy or if he is speaking on his own.[11] This ambiguity may be contrasted with chapter 15, where God explicitly tells Samuel that Saul has forfeited the kingship (15:10–11). It is possible that Saul *really* loses the monarchy only after God's rejection in chapter 15 but believes that he has lost it already with Samuel's rejection in chapter 13.

Samuel's postmortem rebuke of Saul supports this reading:
The Lord has done for Himself as He foretold through me: The Lord has torn the kingship out of your hands and has given it to your fellow, to David, because you did not obey the Lord and did not execute His wrath upon the Amalekites. That is why the Lord has done this to you today. (I Sam. 28:17–18)

Significantly, the prophet does not mention Saul's failure to wait at Gilgal.[12] Perhaps Samuel in chapter 13 truly believes that Saul should be rejected at this point, even if God did not convey any such message to the prophet.[13]

Yairah Amit articulates the operative literary principles when there is a conflict between God or the narrator and other characters:
My first argument is that the narrator's reliability and that of God's image in biblical narrative are axiomatic. My second argument is that every other character, including God's human representatives, the prophets, can prove to be unreliable. My third argument is that the reliable images of the narrator and God can serve as a judgmental criterion for the reliability of the other characters. A character whose statements are consistent with those of the narrator or of God becomes reliable, while in the reverse situation he becomes unreliable.[14]

In chapter 13 the narrator stresses that Saul in fact waited seven days and Samuel arrived late (13:9–10). In the meantime, Saul's troops were deserting. Only 600 men, or 20 percent of Saul's original army, remained (13:15). Finally, Saul and Jonathan were the only soldiers with real weapons (13:19–22). When Saul justifies himself to Samuel, his claims are corroborated by the objective prophetic narrator.

CHAPTER 15

The word of the Lord then came to Samuel: "I regret (*nihamti*)
that I made Saul king, for he has turned away from Me and has
not carried out My commands." Samuel was distressed and he
entreated the Lord all night long. (15:10–12)

Although Samuel opposes monarchy, he has loved Saul from the
beginning of their association, even kissing him after anointing him
(10:1). Saul is the type of person Samuel would want as king, if
there had to be a king.[15] Once Saul is rejected by God, Samuel sinks
into mourning. Initially committed to his own sons despite their unworthiness, Samuel now stands by his beloved disciple Saul despite
explicit divine rejection.

This dichotomy between God's will and Samuel's also may be
manifest regarding whether God can change His mind:

And Samuel said to him, "The Lord has this day torn the kingship over Israel away from you and has given it to another who
is worthier than you. Moreover, the Glory of Israel does not deceive or change His mind (*ve-lo yinahem*), for He is not human
that He should change His mind." (15:28–29)

Samuel never saw Saul again to the day of his death. But Samuel
grieved over Saul, because the Lord regretted (*niham*) that He
had made Saul king over Israel. (15:35)

When speaking to Saul, Samuel insists that God does not change
His mind (15:29). How does this declaration jibe with the words
of God (15:11) and the narrator (15:35), where God *does* regret
having appointed Saul (the Hebrew root *n-h-m* is used in all three
instances)?[16] Following Targum's lead, Rashi suggests that God
regretted choosing Saul but would not strip the kingship from David
now that it had been promised to him. Alternately, this contradiction
again may blur the boundaries between what God says and Samuel's
personal views.[17]

CHAPTER 16

And the Lord said to Samuel, "How long will you grieve over Saul, since I have rejected him as king over Israel? Fill your horn with oil and set out; I am sending you to Jesse the Bethlehemite, for I have decided on one of his sons to be king." Samuel replied, "How can I go? If Saul hears of it, he will kill me." The Lord answered, "Take a heifer with you, and say, 'I have come to sacrifice to the Lord.'" (16:1–2)

Samuel's mourning over Saul continues to the point where God must order Samuel to anoint a successor. Many commentators assume that Samuel's anointing the next king would be perceived as an act of rebellion and therefore Samuel's fears are warranted.[18] Alternatively, Abarbanel maintains that Samuel is merely stalling, since he does not want Saul to be replaced.

"Invite Jesse to the sacrificial feast, and then I will make known to you what you shall do; you shall anoint for Me the one I point out to you."…When they arrived and he saw Eliab, he thought: "Surely the Lord's anointed stands before Him." But the Lord said to Samuel, "Pay no attention to his appearance or his stature, for I have rejected him. For not as man sees [does the Lord see]; man sees only what is visible, but the Lord sees into the heart." (16:3, 6–7)

Given that God ordered Samuel to wait for God's instructions before selecting a king, why does Samuel act prior to receiving prophecy? Radak and Kiel assert that the tall Eliab reminded Samuel of Saul, whom he loved. Samuel desperately hoped that this surrogate Saul would be the successor to the throne.

Now approaching the end of his public prophetic career, Samuel the seer cannot see, and his subjective personality is exposed. One midrash suggests that Samuel's vision was somewhat colored from the outset of his relationship with Saul and the institution of monarchy (chapter 9) until Samuel's error when anointing Saul's successor (chapter 16):

> And even Samuel—who was likened to Moses and Aaron—because he said "I am the seer" (9:19). God said to him: "You said 'I am the seer'; by your life tomorrow I will show you if you are indeed a seer. As it is written, 'Fill your horn with oil and set out; I am sending you to Jesse the Bethlehemite, for I have decided on one of his sons to be king.'" (16:1). When he arrived it is written, "When they arrived and he saw Eliab," he thought: "Surely the Lord's anointed stands before Him" (16:6). God replied, "You are the one who said 'I am the seer'! 'Pay no attention to his appearance'"(16:7). (*Tanhuma Buber Mikketz* 6)

By proclaiming "I am the seer," that is, by injecting his own personality into his prophetic leadership, Samuel blurred the boundaries between God's word and his own on several occasions.

R. Yeshayah of Trani and Yehudah Kiel *ad loc.* maintain that this midrash has validity in *peshat*.[19] God deliberately delayed revealing His selection of David so that Samuel would err and recognize that his will is not identical to the will of God.

Thus Samuel's love of his sons—and later of Saul—color his vision so that his objective prophecy and subjective personality blur throughout his relationships with God, the nation, Saul, and the institution of monarchy. The multifaceted presentation of the prophetic narrative encourages readers to discern various facets of Samuel's religious character—a singular privilege given Samuel's exalted status as one of Israel's greatest prophets and leaders ever.

NOTES

1. Cf. Rambam, *Hil. Yesodei HaTorah* 10:2. For analysis of the parallels between Moses and Samuel, see Amnon Bazak, *Makbilot Nifgashot: Makbilot Sifrutiyot be-Sefer Shemuel* (Hebrew), (Alon Shevut: Hegyonot, 2006), pp. 24–37.

2. For discussion of this talmudic passage and its implications, see Hayyim Angel, *Through an Opaque Lens* (New York: Sephardic Publication Foundation, 2006), pp. 15–20; Amos Hakham, "The Superiority of Moses' Vision as Opposed to the More Limited Vision: A Study of Numbers 12:6–8" (Hebrew), in *Sefer H.M.Y. Gevaryahu: Studies in the Bible and Jewish Thought*, vol. 1, ed. B. Z. Luria (Jerusalem: The Society for Biblical Study in Israel, 1989), pp. 60–67.

3. A passage in *Shabbat* 56a maintains that Samuel's sons did not accept bribes but were guilty only of not traveling around the country to judge as did their father. However, several commentators, including Radak, Abarbanel, Malbim, and Kiel, accept the plain sense of the text and assert that Samuel's sons indeed perverted justice. See discussion of rabbinic responses to this talmudic passage in Yaakov Medan, *David and Bathsheba* (Hebrew) (Alon Shevut: Hegyonot, 2002), pp. 7–24.

4. Cf. Rambam (*Hil. Melakhim* 1:2): "Why was God upset when the people asked Samuel for a king? Because they asked inappropriately; they did not ask because they wanted to fulfill the commandment but because they were rejecting Samuel's leadership." See also Malbim on 8:6; Yehudah Kiel, "Notes on the Chapters about Saul and David" (Hebrew), *Sinai* 49 (1961), pp. 289–292.

5. Coupled with the additional complexity in the Torah's formulation of the laws of monarchy (Deut. 17:14–15), it is not surprising that the nature of the Israelite monarchy has been debated throughout the ages. See Nehama Leibowitz, *Studies in Devarim*, trans. and adapted from the Hebrew by Aryeh Newman (Jerusalem: World Zionist Organization, Dept. for Torah Education and Culture in the Diaspora, 1980), pp. 175-180; Elhanan Samet, *Iyyunim be-Parashot ha-Shavua*, first series (Hebrew) (Ma'alei Adumim: Ma'aliyot, 2002), vol. 2, pp. 348–363.

6. Cf. Robert Alter, *The David Story* (New York: W.W. Norton, 1999), p. 45; Shimon Bar-Efrat, *Mikra LeYisrael: I Samuel* (Hebrew) (Tel-Aviv: Am Oved Publishers Ltd., 1996), p. 130.

7. Cf. Bar-Efrat, *Mikra LeYisrael*, p. 148.

8. Cf. Bar-Efrat, *Mikra LeYisrael*, p. 162; Moshe Garsiel, *The First Book of Samuel: A Literary Study of Comparative Structures, Analogies and Parallels* (Ramat-Gan: Revivim Publishing House, 1985), p. 69.

9. Although the plain sense of the text supports Radak and Ralbag, it

is noteworthy that Rashi (12:16–17) maintains that Samuel's primary motivation for producing the storm was to demonstrate the efficacy of his own prayers rather than God's displeasure with the monarchy.

10. Yehudah Kiel, *Da'at Mikra: I Samuel* (Hebrew) (Jerusalem: Mossad HaRav Kook, 1981), p. 111. For a survey of prophetic passages, see Moshe Elat, *Samuel and the Establishment of Monarchy in Israel* (Hebrew) (Jerusalem: Magnes Press, 1998), pp. 60–65.

11. Cf. Alter, *The David Story*, p. 73; Yairah Amit, "'The Glory of Israel Does Not Deceive or Change His Mind': On the Reliability of Narrator and Speakers in Biblical Narrative," *Prooftexts* 12 (1992), p. 209.

12. Cf. *Yoma* 22b, which also ignores Saul's failure to wait at Gilgal: "R. Huna said...Saul sinned once and it brought [calamity] upon him, David sinned twice and it did not bring evil upon him. What was the one sin of Saul? The affair with Agag. But there was also the matter with Nob, the city of the priests? [Still] it was because of what happened with Agag that Scripture says: I repent that I have set up Saul to be king."

13. See further in Moshe Greenberg, "Jewish Conceptions of the Human Factor in Biblical Prophecy," in *Justice and the Holy: Essays in Honor of Walter Harrelson*, ed. Douglas A. Knight and Peter J. Paris (Atlanta: Scholars Press, 1989), pp. 145–162.

14. Yairah Amit, "'The Glory of Israel Does Not Deceive or Change His Mind,'" p. 205.

15. Cf. Bar-Efrat, *Mikra LeYisrael*, p. 148; Shemuel Avramsky and Moshe Garsiel, *Olam HaTanakh: I Samuel* (Hebrew) (Tel-Aviv: Dodzon-Iti, 1996), p. 87; Yehudah Kiel, "Notes on the Chapters about Saul and David," pp. 289–292.

16. For an excursus on God's repentance, see Francis I. Andersen and David Noel Freedman, *Anchor Bible, Amos* (Garden City, NY: Doubleday, 1989), pp. 638–679.

17. Cf. Alter, *The David Story*, p. 92; Yairah Amit, "'The Glory of Israel Does Not Deceive or Change His Mind,'" p. 209.

18. Cf. *Pesahim* 8b; *Yevamot* 65a; *Kiddushin* 39b. Rambam (*Shemoneh Perakim*, 7) also takes Samuel's statement literally but considers Samuel's reservations as a flaw in the prophet's faith.

19. See also Meir Sternberg, *The Poetics of Biblical Narrative: Ideological Literature and the Drama of Reading* (Bloomington: Indiana University Press, 1985), pp. 94–98.

READING THE BIBLE
FORWARD AND BACKWARD:
THE SINS OF DAVID AND SOLOMON

INTRODUCTION

One of the most remarkable aspects of Tanakh is its honesty regarding even the greatest heroes.[1] Two striking examples are the David-Uriah-Bathsheba episode (II Samuel 11) and Solomon's lapse into idolatry (I Kings 11). These narratives send the unmistakable message that righteous behavior can stabilize a kingdom whereas sinful behavior can unravel it. They also teach that nobody is perfect, not even our greatest heroes. However, a question looms: how did the two founders of the Davidic dynasty fall prey to the three cardinal sins so suddenly?

Reading the David and Solomon narratives from beginning to end does not necessarily lead to expectation of their downfalls. However, once we read them, we may look backward and find evidence of buildups to their sins. This essay will consider how the Abigail-Nabal narrative in I Samuel 25 prefigures the Bathsheba-Uriah affair, and how the Solomon narratives may be simultaneously viewed as an idealized depiction of the king and his era as well as a foreshadowing of his sin.

DAVID

From David's anointing in chapter 16, the narrator establishes a stark contrast between David and Saul.[2] David finally has the chance to kill Saul in chapter 24 but heroically refrains from doing so.[3]

Amidst this extended contrast between David and Saul, we encounter the Abigail-Nabal narrative in chapter 25.

> Samuel died, and all Israel gathered and made lament for him; and they buried him in Ramah, his home. David went down to the wilderness of Paran. (I Sam. 25:1)

Even if Samuel died at this chronological point, several midrashim and later commentators derive additional meaning from its textual position. One midrash explains that the prophetic justification for David's kingship was threatened:

> Nabal answered David's servants, "Who is David? Who is the son of Jesse?" (I Sam. 25:10). [David] relied on nothing but two drops [of oil] with which Samuel anointed him. Where is Samuel and where are those drops? (*Midrash Samuel* 23:10)

In this reading, Nabal's obnoxious rebuffing of David stemmed from his belief that David no longer had any means of legitimating his royal claim.

Connecting Samuel's death to the preceding narrative, Radak suggests that Saul had just publicly admitted that David would be king (I Sam. 24:20). Thus Samuel's anointing David gained at least some acknowledgement within the prophet's lifetime. Looking ahead to the Abigail-Nabal narrative, Kara suggests that had Samuel still been alive, David never would have considered massacring Nabal and his family. The moral standing of the nation—that of David included—was jeopardized in Samuel's absence. Abarbanel favors the reading of *Midrash Samuel* 23:8, which suggests that the juxtaposition is intended as further criticism of Nabal. While the nation mourned the death of a beloved prophet, Nabal feasted!

> There was a man in Maon whose possessions were in Carmel. The man was very wealthy....At the time, he was shearing his sheep in Carmel. The man's name was Nabal, and his wife's name was Abigail. The woman was intelligent and beautiful, but the man, a Calebite, was a hard man and an evildoer. (I Sam. 25:2–3)

"Nabal" means "boor" in Hebrew, and his wife Abigail exploits this meaning: "Please, my lord, pay no attention to that wretched fellow Nabal. For he is just what his name says: His name means 'boor' and he is a boor" (I Sam. 25:25).[4] While Nabal's "Calebite" epithet refers primarily to his deriving from Caleb's family—a clan in Judah—it also may carry a negative wordplay meaning "dog-like" (Radak, Ralbag, Abarbanel). Coupled with his introduction as a "hard man and an evildoer," it is evident that the narrator intended for readers to despise Nabal from the outset.[5]

Despite the anti-Nabal bias, however, David and Abigail both acted dubiously. Though David and his men protected Nabal's sheep, Nabal did not formally owe them protection fees.[6] Indeed, David thanked Abigail for thwarting his murderous plan:

David said to Abigail, "Praised be the Lord, the God of Israel, who sent you this day to meet me! And blessed be your prudence, and blessed be you yourself for restraining me from seeking redress in blood by my own hands." (25:32–33)

When David heard that Nabal was dead, he said, "Praised be the Lord who championed my cause against the insults of Nabal and held back His servant from wrongdoing; the Lord has brought Nabal's wrongdoing down on his own head." (25:39)

One midrash scathingly criticizes David's intended plan of exterminating Nabal and his family:

Rabbi Shemuel said: Abigail was better for David than all the sacrifices in the world. Had [David] carried out his intended plan toward Nabal, all the sacrifices in the world would not have atoned for him. (*Midrash Psalms* 53:1)

A plausible explanation for David's extreme response is that he viewed Nabal as a rebel against his royal authority (e.g., Radak on 25:13). Though Saul was still king, David had been anointed by Samuel. He was the king's son-in-law, Saul had recently acknowl-

edged his impending kingship (I Sam. 24:20), and Jonathan recognized that David would be king (I Sam. 23:17). Even the Philistines
referred to him as "king of the land" (I Sam. 21:12). Abigail similarly acknowledged David's future reign:

> And when the Lord has accomplished for my lord all the good
> He has promised you, and has appointed you ruler of Israel, do
> not let this be a cause of stumbling and of faltering courage to
> my lord that you have shed blood needlessly and that my lord
> sought redress with his own hands. And when the Lord has pros-
> pered my lord, remember your maid." (I Sam. 25:30–31)

The Talmud suggests that David intended to kill Nabal because he
mistakenly believed that he already had royal authority:

> [David] said to [Abigail]: [Nabal] is a rebel against the king
> and no trial is necessary for him. She replied; Saul is still alive,
> and your fame is not yet spread abroad in the world. (*Megillah*
> 14a–b)

Moshe Garsiel derives meaning from the position of the Abigail-
Nabal narrative between the two episodes when David refrained
from killing Saul.[7] Literarily, Nabal is analogous to Saul. Both Saul
(I Sam. 24:18) and Nabal (25:21) repaid David's kindness with cruelty. The family members of both Saul and Nabal were more loyal
to David than to Saul or Nabal. David told Abishai that God would
smite Saul (26:10), and God did smite Nabal (25:38). Nabal's feast
was "fit for a king" (25:36). Nabal's retort to David that "there are
many slaves nowadays who run away from their masters" (25:10)
is something Saul could have said just as readily. It appears that
David's readiness to lash out at Nabal was a reflection of how he
wanted to kill Saul.[8]

The Abigail-Nabal narrative teaches that one's moral qualities are
not fixed. Although the Book of Samuel generally contrasts David
and Saul, the flow of chapters 24–26 softens the barriers. At the end
of chapter 24, Saul publicly admitted that he was wrong and pleaded

for forgiveness. On the other side, David almost failed with Nabal when his own ostensible authority was challenged. Like Saul, David inappropriately judged someone a rebel against his throne.

In addition to David's overreaction to a falsely considered rebel against his authority, he had a sexually charged encounter with the still married Abigail and married her immediately following Nabal's untimely demise. "And when the Lord has prospered my lord, remember your maid" (I Sam. 25:31). It can be argued that Abigail was insinuating marriage to David (see, e.g., *Megillah* 14b, Kara, Ralbag).[9]

Even after Abigail married David, she still is referred to as "Abigail wife of Nabal the Carmelite" (e.g., I Sam. 27:3; 30:5; II Sam. 2:2; 3:3). Ibn Caspi (on I Sam. 27:3) interprets these references as critical of their inappropriate interchange which contained traces of the behaviors manifest later during the Bathsheba affair. The aforementioned talmudic passage similarly views the Abigail-Nabal episode both as sexually charged and as foreshadowing the Bathsheba affair:

> [Abigail] bared her thigh and [David] went three parasangs by the light of it. He said, Listen to me. She replied, Let not this be a stumbling-block to you (I Sam. 25:31). The word "this" implies that something else would be. And what was that? The incident of Bathsheba; and so it was eventually. (*Megillah* 14b)

Both episodes involve impropriety with married women, attempts at unwarranted murder of their husbands, and immediate marriage to the widows. In the case of Abigail-Nabal, disaster was averted thanks to Abigail's intervention. David displayed greatness by stopping despite swearing to God that he would carry out his intentions. However, David did consummate the affair with Bathsheba and also may have deemed Uriah as a rebel against the throne (see, e.g., *Shabbat* 56a). Bathsheba also is referred to as "Uriah's wife" after Uriah's death (II Sam. 11:26–27), parallel to Abigail's epithet as "wife of Nabal the Carmelite".

Thus the Abigail-Nabal narrative prefigures David's downfall with Bathsheba-Uriah. As with Saul's treatment of David, David now was guilty of repaying kindness with cruelty toward his faithful soldier Uriah. To David's credit, and in contrast with Saul, David accepted Nathan's criticism as he had accepted that of Abigail in the Nabal narrative.

SOLOMON

One may view Solomon's reign as entirely good with a sudden collapse at the end, or one may detect buildups to those troubles throughout the narrative.

Solomon's reign divides into three sections. Chapters 1–2 describe Solomon's elimination of his political opposition and his subsequent attainment of stability. Chapters 3–10 reflect a utopian age: a prophetic and wise king; a religious nation; regional peace and prosperity; the people's building the Temple and God's Presence occupying it; surrounding nations coming to see Solomon and hearing his words of wisdom, thereby sanctifying God's Name. All then unraveled in chapter 11 as Solomon lapsed into idolatry, which ultimately led to the division of the monarchy.

However, once we know of Solomon's sin and the remainder of the Book of Kings, we may look back through the narratives and ascertain factors earlier in his reign that may have foreshadowed his downfall and ultimately the destruction of the Temple.

A. Pharaoh's Daughter and the Shrines

Solomon allied himself by marriage with Pharaoh king of Egypt. He married Pharaoh's daughter and brought her to the City of David [to live there] until he had finished building his palace, and the House of the Lord, and the walls around Jerusalem. The people, however, continued to offer sacrifices at the open shrines, because up to that time no house had been built for the name of the Lord. And Solomon, though he loved the Lord and followed the practices of his father David, also sacrificed and offered at the shrines. (I Kings 3:1–3)

Radak and Abarbanel puzzle over the fact that this passage does not condemn Solomon for marrying Pharaoh's daughter, reserving its criticism for when his wives led his heart astray at the end of his life (I Kings 11).

Additionally, shrines were permissible prior to the construction of the Temple. Yet the narrative introduces worship at these shrines with the critical stereotypical formula characteristic of later generations' sinfully worshipping at shrines after the Temple was built.[10]

Radak adopts a rejected minority opinion from *Yevamot* 76b and suggests that the neutral tone regarding Solomon's marriage to Pharaoh's daughter indicates that converted Egyptian women were permitted to marry Israelites. Alternatively, Abarbanel concludes that Solomon erred in his understanding of Torah law. He was young and it was good diplomacy to marry the Egyptian princess, so God did not punish or even criticize him for the actual marriage.[11]

Regarding the unexpectedly critical comment about the shrines, Radak and Abarbanel suggest that though permitted, the proliferation of shrines resembles idolatry since they established many places from which one could worship God. However, this reasoning appears difficult, since if shrines were permitted then the text should not criticize them.

A different approach emerges when one reads the narratives both forward and backward.[12] When one reads the narrative from beginning to end, it appears that Solomon failed spiritually only toward the end of his life. Once we know the tragic end of the narrative, however, it is possible to trace the roots of Solomon's failure from the beginning of his reign.

On one level, Solomon's marriage to Pharaoh's daughter was politically favorable. Yehudah Kiel notes that this is the only biblical instance of an Israelite king marrying a princess from a superpower;

there also are no extant Egyptian records of any foreigner marrying one of their princesses.[13] By the end of the narrative, however, Pharaoh's daughter led Solomon astray. Knowing that both aspects of this marriage were true, the author of Kings could place the favorable component of the marriage in the section that highlights Solomon's power and stability and defer the sinful aspect for later.

Further evidence of the framing of chapters 3–11 can be seen with a comparison between chapter 3 and chapter 11:

King Solomon loved many foreign women in addition to Pharaoh's daughter—Moabite, Ammonite, Edomite, Phoenician, and Hittite women, from the nations of which the Lord had said to the Israelites, "None of you shall join them and none of them shall join you, lest they turn your heart away to follow their gods." Such Solomon clung to and loved. He had seven hundred royal wives and three hundred concubines; and his wives turned his heart away. In his old age, his wives turned away Solomon's heart after other gods, and he was not as wholeheartedly devoted to the Lord his God as his father David had been. (I Kings 11:1–4)

Chapter 3 begins with Solomon's marriage to Pharaoh's daughter and the nation's offering sacrifices on shrines; chapter 11 has Pharaoh's daughter leading Solomon astray and Solomon sacrificing on idolatrous shrines. Chapter 3 mentions that Solomon loved God; chapter 11 notes that he loved his pagan wives. Chapter 3 reports that Solomon brought 1,000 offerings; chapter 11 has him marrying 1,000 women. In chapter 3, God gives Solomon a prophecy offering him one wish; in chapter 11, God gives Solomon a prophecy announcing the decree of doom. These parallels demonstrate a purposeful narrative that enables Solomon's reign to shine while one is reading forward, but that simultaneously suggests that the cracks of his downfall were latent from the outset of his reign.

The reverse may be said of the critical reference to shrines in chapter 3. Although shrines were permitted in the pre-Temple period, Solomon wrongfully allowed them to remain after he built the Temple. This toleration led to spiritual harm for the nation through the time of Hezekiah. Therefore, the narrator cast these shrines negatively to foreshadow the long-term damage of Solomon's reign.[14] Thus Solomon is cast as the builder of the Temple but also as the one who began to sow the seeds of its destruction.

The Talmud expresses this foreshadowing regarding the destruction of both Temples:

One verse says, For the Lord has chosen Zion (Ps. 132:13), but another verse says, For this city has been to me a provocation of My anger and of My fury from the day that they built it even unto this day (Jer. 32:31)? The former applied to the time before Solomon married the daughter of Pharaoh whereas the latter applied to the time after Solomon married the daughter of Pharaoh. (*Niddah* 70b)

Rab Judah said in Samuel's name: When Solomon married Pharaoh's daughter, Gabriel descended and planted a reed in the sea, and it gathered a bank around it, on which the great city of Rome was built. (*Shabbat* 56b)[15]

B. Horses and Wealth

After Solomon requested wisdom in his dream, God promised him riches and glory in addition to unsurpassed wisdom (I Kings 3:11–13). The lavish descriptions of Solomon's wisdom, wealth, and power in chapters 5, 9, and 10 reflect the fulfillment of these divine promises[16]:

Solomon had 40,000 stalls of horses for his chariotry and 12,000 horsemen. (I Kings 5:6)

King Solomon excelled all the kings on earth in wealth and in wisdom. All the world came to pay homage to Solomon and to listen to the wisdom with which God had endowed him....Solomon assembled chariots and horses. He had 1,400 chariots and

12,000 horses, which he stationed in the chariot towns and with
the king in Jerusalem. The king made silver as plentiful in Jerusalem as stones, and cedars as plentiful as sycamores in the
Shephelah. (I Kings 10:23–27)

Notwithstanding, the Sages and later commentators puzzle over
the prohibitions that the Torah legislates regarding kings:

Moreover, he shall not keep many horses...he shall not have
many wives, lest his heart go astray; nor shall he amass silver
and gold to excess. (Deut. 17:16–17)

Commenting on the exorbitant number of Solomon's horses,
Abarbanel explains that he retained them for the glory of his
kingdom and as a military deterrent. Given the utopian tone and
the fulfillment of divine blessings, it is difficult to sense criticism of
Solomon in this passage.

Several midrashic traditions, on the other hand, criticize Solomon's accumulation of horses and wealth:

R. Isaac also said: Why were the reasons of [some] Biblical laws
not revealed? Because in two verses reasons were revealed, and
they caused the greatest in the world [Solomon] to stumble.
Thus it is written: He shall not multiply wives to himself (Deut.
17:17), but Solomon said, I will multiply wives yet not let my
heart be perverted. Yet we read, When Solomon was old, his
wives turned away his heart (I Kings 11:4). Again it is written:
He shall not multiply to himself horses (Deut. 17:16), concerning which Solomon said, I will multiply them, but will not cause
[Israel] to return [to Egypt]. Yet we read: And a chariot came
up and went out of Egypt for six [hundred shekels of silver] (I
Kings 10:29). (*Sanhedrin* 21b)

It is written, Neither shall he multiply wives to himself (Deut.
17:17), yet he had seven hundred wives, princesses, and three
hundred concubines (I Kings 11:3). It is written, He shall not

multiply horses to himself (Deut. 17:16), yet Solomon had 40,000 stalls of horses (I Kings 5:6). It is written, Neither shall he greatly multiply to himself silver and gold (Deut. 17:17), yet the king made silver to be in Jerusalem as stones (I Kings 10:27). (*Kohelet Rabbah* 2:4)

These midrashim are attentive to Solomon's ultimate downfall. Chapters 10–11 contain references to Solomon's abundance of horses, wealth, and wives. Reading forward, chapter 10 is a positive depiction of Solomon's reign. Once Solomon's wives led his heart astray, however, the abundance of horses and wealth also appear retrospectively to have contributed to his downfall, and suddenly it seems that Solomon violated the three prohibitions in Deuteronomy 17.[17]

CONCLUSION

The multifaceted portrayals of the sins of David and Solomon help elucidate the prophetic authors' intent in teaching about them. Each king contained the ingredients of sin long before his downfall. By reading the narratives forward and then backward, we can ascertain those different layers of meaning and see how the details work together in creating a complex understanding of their sins.

NOTES

1. For general discussions of the religious ramifications of biblical heroes' sinning, see Amos Frisch, "The Sins of the Patriarchs as Viewed by Traditional Jewish Exegesis," *Jewish Studies Quarterly* 10 (2003), pp. 258–273; Mosheh Lichtenstein, *Tzir va-Tzon* (Hebrew) (Alon Shevut: Yeshivat Har Etzion, 2002), pp. 235–257; Yaakov Medan, "*David u-Bat Sheva: ha-Het, ha-Onesh, ve-ha-Tikkun*" (Hebrew) (Alon Shevut: Tevunot, 2002), pp. 7–24; and Joel B. Wolowelsky, "'*Kibbud Av*' and '*Kibbud Avot*': Moral Education and Patriarchal Critiques," *Tradition* 33:4 (Summer 1999), pp. 35–44.

2. See, e.g., Moshe Garsiel, *The First Book of Samuel: A Literary Study of Comparative Structures, Analogies and Parallels* (Ramat-Gan: Revivim, 1985), pp. 107–122.

3. See further discussion in Hayyim Angel, "Why Didn't He Do It? An Analysis of Why David Did Not Kill Saul," in *From Strength to Strength*, ed. Marc D. Angel (Brooklyn: Sefer Hermon Press, 1998), pp. 163–183; reprinted in Angel, *Through an Opaque Lens* (New York: Sephardic Publication Foundation, 2006), pp. 169–185.

4. Moshe Garsiel entertains the possibility that Nabal was his true name and the text then plays off of its meaning as "boor"; as well as the possibility that Nabal is a literary name shaped by this narrative (*The First Book of Samuel*, p. 127). See also Robert Alter, *The David Story: A Translation and Commentary of 1 and 2 Samuel* (New York: W. W. Norton & Co., 1999), p. 152; Yehudah Kiel, *Da'at Mikra: I Samuel* (Hebrew), (Jerusalem: Mossad HaRav Kook, 1981), p. 251.

5. Yehudah Kiel observes that Isa. 32:5–8 criticizes a *nabal* for not feeding the hungry. In our narrative, Nabal eats like a king (I Sam. 25:36) while not feeding David and his starving men (*Da'at Mikra: I Samuel*, p. 257). See also Jon Levenson, "1 Samuel 25 as Literature and as History," *CBQ* 40 (1978), pp. 11-28.

6. See further discussion in Yaakov Medan, "The *Nabal* Says in His Heart: 'There is no God'" (Hebrew), *Megadim* 4 (1988), pp. 23–55.

7. Moshe Garsiel, *The First Book of Samuel: A Literary Study of Comparative Structures, Analogies and Parallels*, pp. 122–133.

8. David's harsh reaction to Nabal's not feeding him resembles Saul's massacre of the priests at Nob for feeding David (I Sam. 21–22). Cf. *Kohelet Rabbah* 7:16, which offers a similar insight regarding Saul: "R. Simeon b. Lakish said: Whoever shows himself merciful in circumstances where he should be pitiless, in the end becomes pitiless when he should be merciful. Whence have we that Saul was pitiless when he should have been merciful? As it is said, And Nob, the city of the priests, smote he with the edge of the sword, both men and women, children and sucklings, and oxen, and asses, and sheep (I Sam. 22:19), and Nob should not have been treated like the seed of Amalek" (cf. I Sam. 15:3).

9. Robert Alter suggests that Abigail may have even offered to ensure Nabal's death in exchange for David's marrying her (*The David Story*, p. 159).

10. See, e.g., I Kings 15:14; 22:44; II Kings 12:3–4; 14:3–4; 15:3–4, 34–35.

11. See further discussion in Hayyim Angel, "Where the Rules of *Peshat* and *Pesak* Collide: Deuteronomy and Prophetic Narratives," printed in this volume.

12. Cf. Yoav Barzilai, "The Introduction to Solomon's Kingdom" (Hebrew), *Megadim* 11 (1990), pp. 73–97.

13. Yehudah Kiel, *Da'at Mikra: I Kings* (Hebrew) (Jerusalem: Mossad HaRav Kook, 1989), p. 50.

14. See further discussion in Yehezkel Kaufmann, "The Introduction of the Solomon Narratives" (Hebrew), in *Sefer Segal*, Yehoshua M. Grintz and Jacob Liver (eds.) (Jerusalem: Kiryat Sefer, 1965), pp. 87–93.

15. For analysis of these and other midrashic readings that generally understand Solomon's downfall to trace back to his marriage to Pharaoh's daughter, see Gilad Sasson, "'When Solomon Married Pharaoh's Daughter': Moving the Crisis Point from the End of Solomon's Reign to Its Beginning" (Hebrew), *Beit Mikra* 53 (2008), pp. 145–164.

16. Shaul Zilvesky argues that Solomon's dream is central to the ensuing narratives which demonstrate fulfillment of every aspect of the divine promises made in the dream ("God's Revelation to Solomon at Gibeon" [Hebrew], *Tarbiz* 42 [1973], pp. 247–258).

17. Marc Brettler ("The Structure of 1 Kings 1–11," *JSOT* 49 [1991], pp. 87–97) observes that 9:24–25 mentions Pharaoh's daughter and the practice of sacrificing only in the Temple. These verses close the circle with 3:1–3, which also mentions Pharaoh's daughter and sacrificing on the shrines. If so, this unit may comprise the positive aspect of Solomon's reign, and the descriptions of Solomon's wealth and horses from 9:26 onward represent Solomon's violation of the prohibitions in Deuteronomy 17. However, Chronicles' inclusion of the wealth and horses in its idealized portrayal of Solomon indicates that the author of Kings intended the narrative to be read in both directions—positive reading forward and negative reading backward.

THERE NEVER AGAIN ROSE
A PROPHET LIKE MOSES:
EXCEPT PERHAPS EZEKIEL?*

INTRODUCTION

Ezekiel prophesied in a time when religious guidance was singularly necessary. The people of Israel believed that the destruction of the Temple and national exile meant that God's relationship with Israel had been permanently severed (e.g., Ezek. 33:10; 37:11). Along with his contemporary Jeremiah, Ezekiel envisioned a brighter future for his despairing nation.

While continuing in the spirit of his predecessors, Ezekiel distinguished himself in several respects. It may be argued that Ezekiel cast himself as a second Moses who was to reveal the Torah to a generation finally worthy of receiving it. This essay will consider several major aspects of this portrayal.

THE THIRTIETH YEAR

In the thirtieth year, on the fifth day of the fourth month, when I was in the community of exiles by the Chebar Canal, the heavens opened and I saw visions of God. On the fifth day of the month—it was the fifth year of the exile of King Jehoiachin—the word of the Lord came to the priest Ezekiel son of Buzi, by the Chebar Canal, in the land of the Chaldeans. And the hand of the Lord came upon him there. (1:1-3)

* This article appeared originally in *Rav Chesed: Essays in Honor of Rabbi Dr. Haskel Lookstein*, vol. 1, ed. Rafael Medoff (Jersey City, NJ: KTAV, 2009), pp. 1-16. Reprinted here with minor modifications, with permission from the editors.

Ezekiel began to prophesy in the fifth year of the exile of Jehoiachin, or 592 B.C.E. To what, however, did Ezekiel refer in 1:1 when he mentioned the thirtieth year? This enigma generated several lines of interpretation.

Thirty years prior to Ezekiel's initiation was 622 B.C.E., the year of Josiah's reformation. While that was indeed an important episode, biblical events generally are dated from the years in a king's reign. Notwithstanding, several commentators adopt this identification. For example, Radak considers this oblique reference to be ominous. After finding the Torah scroll, Josiah tore his garments and Huldah affirmed the sealed decree against Jerusalem (II Kings 22:11-20). Ezekiel therefore dated his book from that event, which marked the first stage of the disaster to follow. Though this reading is not compelling, it is conceptually significant. We will revisit this discussion toward the conclusion of this essay.

EZEKIEL'S INITIATION
A. The Celestial Chariot[1]

Ezekiel's visions of the celestial chariot are remarkably detailed and revealing. A verse in Psalms links the revelation at Sinai to the chariot:

God's chariots are myriads upon myriads, thousands upon thousands; the Lord is among them as in Sinai in holiness. (Ps. 68:18)

Following this lead, the Sages selected Ezekiel 1 as a Haftarah for Shavuot, which commemorates the revelation at Sinai (*Megillah* 31a). The Sages interpreted Ezekiel's vision in light of Sinai, and Sinai in light of Ezekiel's vision. For example, one midrash (*Exod. Rabbah* 42:5) suggests that the Israelites saw the chariot at Sinai, which included the image of an ox (Ezek. 1:10). This vision explains why they fashioned a Golden Calf later on.[2]

Additionally, Ezekiel uses an uncommon verb tense to describe his prophetic revelation:

> As He spoke to me, a spirit entered into me and set me upon my
> feet; and I heard what was being spoken to me (Heb. *middabber*
> *elai*). (2:2)

The form *middabber* is reflexive, possibly intimating that God was
talking to Himself and Ezekiel was privileged to listen in (Rashi,
Kara). This expression occurs only two other times in Tanakh
regarding prophecy: Moses' revelation when the Tabernacle was
completed (Num. 7:89); and again regarding Ezekiel during his
Temple vision (Ezek. 43:6).

Thus, both the exalted visionary experiences and mode of prophecy of Moses and Ezekiel seem uniquely comparable.

B. Ezekiel's Hesitancy and Muteness

Following the vision of the celestial chariot, God repeatedly instructs Ezekiel to speak to the people of Israel (2:4, 7; 3:1, 4). However, the prophet passively refuses. God responds to Ezekiel's silence by exhorting Ezekiel that he is a "watchman" for Israel and
bears responsibility if he fails to warn the nation of their impending
doom (3:16-21). However, the prophet *still* does not respond! This
continued refusal sets the stage for God's informing Ezekiel that he
will be muted:

> And a spirit entered into me and set me upon my feet. And
> He spoke to me, and said to me: "Go, shut yourself up in your
> house. As for you, O mortal, cords have been placed upon you,
> and you have been bound with them, and you shall not go out
> among them. And I will make your tongue cleave to your pal-
> ate, and you shall be dumb; you shall not be a reprover to them,
> for they are a rebellious breed. But when I speak with you, I
> will open your mouth, and you shall say to them, 'Thus says the
> Lord God!' He who listens will listen, and he who does not will
> not—for they are a rebellious breed." (3:24-27)

Rashi explains that Ezekiel's staying home and his silence demonstrate that the people did not merit prophetic reproof since they were hopelessly wicked. Therefore this prophecy should be understood as a non-verbal rebuke of Israel. However, the Jews did not yet have a chance to sink further in their rebellion by rejecting Ezekiel's message, since the prophet had yet to address them. Why would God command a more severe rebuke of the people?[3]

Consequently, R. Eliezer of Beaugency maintains that muteness was God's response to Ezekiel's unwillingness to rebuke the people. Initially rebellious, Ezekiel's passivity now became a defining feature of his prophecy. No longer would he be allowed to speak spontaneously; rather, he would have to wait for God's command and in this manner would fulfill his prophetic mission.[4]

Rashi and R. Eliezer agree that there is an additional dimension to the muteness prophecy:

In the twelfth year of our exile, on the fifth day of the tenth month, a fugitive came to me from Jerusalem and reported, "The city has fallen." Now the hand of the Lord had come upon me the evening before the fugitive arrived, and He opened my mouth before he came to me in the morning; thus my mouth was opened and I was no longer speechless. (33:21-22; cf. 24:26-27)

Once the destruction came, Ezekiel was vindicated. Thus Ezekiel's muteness also symbolizes his lack of credibility prior to the destruction (cf. 16:63; 29:21 for similar expressions of prophetic vindication).

Regardless of the precise meaning of Ezekiel's "muteness," his prolonged reluctance to prophesy approximates that of Moses. Additionally, Moses stalled by referring to himself as being "of uncircumcised lips" (e.g., Exod. 4:10; 6:12, 30)—a feature which appears to be reflected in Ezekiel's "muteness." Finally, Moses employed that argument specifically in regard to his credibility:

But Moses appealed to the Lord, saying, "The Israelites would not listen to me; how then should Pharaoh heed me, a man of impeded speech!" (Exod. 6:12)

EXODUS-REDEMPTION (CHAPTER 20)

A. Laws That Were Not Good

In one of his scathing historical surveys, Ezekiel relates that God chose Israel in Egypt and told them to renounce idolatry (20:5–7). That generation failed. God wanted to destroy them while they were yet in Egypt but refrained from doing so in order to avoid desecrating His Name. After God redeemed them, they failed again in the desert. God again spared them in order to avoid the desecration of His Name, but He also prevented them from entering the Land of Israel (20:10–17).

When the second generation also failed, God gave them "laws that were not good":

> Moreover, I gave them laws that were not good and rules by which they could not live: When they set aside every first issue of the womb, I defiled them by their very gifts—that I might render them desolate, that they might know that I am the Lord. (20:25-26)

Interpreters have suggested a number of explanations for this enigmatic prophecy, which seems to intimate that God had commanded child-sacrifice:

1. God allowed the people to succumb to their evil inclinations and sacrifice their children but of course never commanded them to perform this horrible act (Targum, Rashi).
2. By exiling the Jews, God forced them to endure the pagan practices imposed on them by their host nations (Radak; R. Menahem b. Shimon; Ibn Caspi).
3. The verse is elliptical: "Moreover, I gave them laws that were not good [in their own eyes], and rules by which they [did not want to] live" (R. Yeshayah of Trani, Malbim).
4. The Torah's commandments are bad for you if you are wicked (Abarbanel #1).
5. These verses refer not to the laws of the Torah, but rather to the curses for the non-fulfillment of the Torah (Abarbanel #2).

Abarbanel's first explanation—that the Torah's commandments are bad for those who are wicked—seems closest to the mark.[5] In Ezekiel's perception, the Torah was a failed project because the Israelites never were faithful to it. In the future, God would ensure that Israel would fulfill the Torah's covenant:

> I will give them one heart and put a new spirit in them; I will re-move the heart of stone from their bodies and give them a heart of flesh, that they may follow My laws and faithfully observe My rules. Then they shall be My people and I will be their God. (11:19-20; cf. 36:25-27)

The new heart will relate to the same Torah, but this time it will contain "good laws" for them, that is, they will be faithful to that covenant.

B. The Wilderness of the Peoples

> With a strong hand and an outstretched arm and overflowing fury I will bring you out from the peoples and gather you from the lands where you are scattered, and I will bring you into the wilderness of the peoples; and there I will enter into judgment with you face to face.... I will remove from you those who rebel and transgress against Me; I will take them out of the countries where they sojourn, but they shall not enter the land of Israel. Then you shall know that I am the Lord. (20:34-38)

Strikingly, this prophecy of deliverance casts redemption as a punishment. It fits Ezekiel's contention that Israel never deserved redemption; God will save them because He wants to avoid the desecration of His Name (cf. 11:19; 14:21-23; 16:59-63; 36:16-36).

Ezekiel does not refer to a Babylonian downfall in this proph-ecy. In his introduction to Ezekiel, Abarbanel submits that since the prophet lived in Babylonia, it would be dangerous to prophesy the downfall of his host nation. Therefore God did not reveal to Ezekiel prophecies about Babylonia's downfall.[6]

Beyond this utilitarian reason, there also appears to be a more fundamental purpose for Ezekiel's omission of Babylonia. Babylonia is not the new Pharaoh in the exile-redemption model. Israel has replaced Pharaoh, and God therefore must rescue Israel from herself and her own hardened heart of stone (Ezek. 11:19; 36:26). Consequently, Israel will be plagued and some even killed in the "wilderness of the peoples." Some then will be redeemed "with a strong hand and an outstretched arm and overflowing fury." Just as the Torah repeats the expression "and the Egyptians shall know that I am the Lord" (e.g., Exod. 7:5; 10:2; 14:4, 18), a refrain of the Book of Ezekiel is "and they shall know that I am the Lord" (some sixty times).

In this regard, Ezekiel resembles Moses at the head of the nation, as God will redeem Israel completely unassisted. This time the redemption would work. It was to be contrasted with the original exodus, where the Israelites failed.

THE TEMPLE VISION (CHAPTERS 40-48)

The strongest parallels between Ezekiel and Moses occur in Ezekiel's final major prophecy, the Temple vision in chapters 40-48.[7]

In the twenty-fifth year of our exile, the fourteenth year after the city had fallen, at the beginning of the year, the tenth day of the month—on that very day—the hand of the Lord came upon me, and He brought me there. He brought me, in visions of God, to the Land of Israel, and He set me down on a very high mountain on which there seemed to be the outline of a city on the south. (40:1-2)

God communicates the vision to Ezekiel on Temple Mount, parallel to Moses on Sinai. God reveals His Presence and there is a thundering sound at the revelation (43:2). Ezekiel receives a visual outline of the Temple, is given the rules that will govern the priests, and is assigned the task of leading the Temple dedication (43:19). These elements parallel God's commands to Moses regarding the Tabernacle and its dedication ceremony in Exodus 25-31. Most strikingly, Ezekiel's vision is the *only* time in Tanakh that God reveals legislation to a prophet after Moses.

Not only does Ezekiel legislate prophetically; several laws in this section differ from those in the Torah. Some are additions, and others are even contradictory. Many commentators observe that these new laws do not eliminate any laws of the Torah; rather, they prescribe higher standards. On other occasions, they are temporary rulings for that Temple dedication, rather than ongoing legislation that would become permanently binding.[8]

To summarize, Ezekiel began reluctant to prophesy and "mute" as was Moses. He perceived the celestial chariot and prophecy in a manner resembling the case with Moses. Ezekiel received laws on a mountain, occasionally with even higher standards than in the Torah. He was designated to preside over the rededication of the new Temple as Moses did over the dedication of the Tabernacle. Ezekiel was to be the Moses of a new world order, with the redemption (= the new exodus) to occur within his lifetime. God would rescue Israel from her own hardened heart, and Israel finally would be purified and follow the Torah's "good laws" with her new "heart of flesh."[9]

Returning to the "thirtieth year" in 1:1, discussed at the outset of this essay, R. Eliezer of Beaugency suggests that since Ezekiel acted as a new Torah-giver, he dated his prophetic career back to the finding of the Torah scroll in Josiah's time:

[Ezekiel] did not explain from what date he was counting thirty years. Even though the Targum is straight, and points to the time when Hilkiah the priest found the Torah scroll, this is not a common way for verses to speak. Admittedly there is no alternative, even though we do not understand why he would count in this manner. However, it appears in light of the entire book that we can offer a reason: you will not find a prophet exhorting his generation about Torah and the commandments except for [Ezekiel]. Most of his words echo the style of the Torah, and he repeated nearly the entire Torah to them...as though he were giving the Torah to them anew.... Therefore he counted the date from the time [the scroll of the Torah] was found, since the essence of his book was dependent on it. (R. Eliezer of Beaugency, introduction to Ezekiel)

THE SAGES

The Sages were concerned with the unusually close association between Moses and Ezekiel. Specifically, the levels of Moses' and Ezekiel's prophecy in the celestial chariot vision; and Ezekiel's functioning as a lawgiver raised alarm. Consequently, the Book of Ezekiel was the only prophetic book that risked censorship by the Sages.[10] Instead of removing the Book of Ezekiel from Tanakh, the Sages instead took pains to establish that Moses and Ezekiel were fundamentally different in these two areas.

A. The Celestial Chariot

The Rabbis taught: There was once a child who was reading at his teacher's house the Book of Ezekiel, and he apprehended what Hashmal was, whereupon a fire went forth from Hashmal and consumed him. So they sought to suppress the Book of Ezekiel. (*Haggigah* 13a)

Because of the revelation described by Ezekiel, the Sages cautioned against studying the true essence of that passage and teaching it to the uninitiated. They also emphasized that Ezekiel's vision was inferior to that of Moses:

R. Judah said: Through nine lenses did the prophets behold [prophetic visions]. This is indicated by what is said, And the appearance of the vision which I saw was like the vision that I saw when I came to destroy the city; and the visions were like the vision that I saw by the River Chebar; and I fell upon my face (Ezek. 43:3); but Moses beheld [prophetic visions] through one lens, as it is said, With him do I speak... in a vision, and not in dark speeches (Num. 12:8). The Rabbis said: All the other prophets beheld [prophetic visions] through a blurred lens, as it is said, And I have multiplied visions; and by the ministry of the angels have I used similitudes (Hos. 12:11). But Moses beheld [prophetic visions] through a polished lens, as it is said, The similitude of the Lord does he behold (Num. 12:8). (*Lev. Rabbah* 1:14; cf. *Yevamot* 49b)

B. Ezekiel's Prophetic Legislation

Rab Judah said in the name of Rab, That man is to be remembered for good, and Hanina b. Hezekiah is his name; for were it not for him the Book of Ezekiel would have been suppressed, since its sayings contradicted the words of the Torah. What did he do? He took up with him three hundred barrels of oil and remained there in the upper chamber until he had explained away everything. (*Shabbat* 13b; *Haggigah* 13a; *Menahot* 45a)

While several Sages in *Menahot* 45a believed that some contradictions between the Torah and the Book of Ezekiel defied reconciliation and would require Elijah the prophet to elucidate them, Hanina b. Hezekiah somehow found a means of harmonizing the conflicts. Unfortunately, as Rashi (on 45:22) and Radak (on 45:20; 40:13) lament, we have lost these resolutions.[11] As was noted above, several commentators maintain that Ezekiel is not eliminating any laws of the Torah but rather is prescribing higher standards. On other occasions, Ezekiel presents temporary rulings for that Temple dedication rather than ongoing legislation that will be permanently binding.

In addition to the discrepancies between Ezekiel's prophetic legislation and the Torah, the Sages were troubled by the fact that Ezekiel legislated altogether:

"These are the commandments" (Lev. 27:34), which implies that no prophet is at liberty to introduce anything new henceforward. (*Sifra Behukkotai* 8:13; cf. *Shabbat* 104a; *Yoma* 80a; *Megillah* 2b–3a; *Temurah* 16a)

Rather than looking to Ezekiel as a second Moses, then, some Sages turned to Ezra—a nonprophetic Sage—to fill that role:

R. Yosei said: Had Moses not preceded him, Ezra would have been worthy of receiving the Torah for Israel. (*Sanhedrin* 21b)[12]

NOTES

1. As Ezekiel's vision is called in rabbinic literature. See, e.g., Mishnah *Haggigah* 2:1; *Haggigah* 13a.

2. See further in Lieve Teugels, "Did Moses See the Chariot? The Link between Exod 19-20 and Ezek 1 in Early Jewish Interpretation," in *Studies in the Book of Exodus: Redaction-Reception-Interpretation*, ed. Marc Vervenne (Leuven: University Press, 1996), pp. 595-602.

3. Conscious of this problem, R. Yosef Hayyun assumes that Ezekiel must have exhorted the people and they ignored him. That he needed to add this detail points to its conspicuous absence in the text.

4. See further discussion in Moshe Greenberg, "On Ezekiel's Dumbness," *JBL* 77 (1958), pp. 101-105. Rimon Kascher ("Ezekiel's Muteness [Ezek. 3:22-27]" [Hebrew], *Beit Mikra* 43 [1998], pp. 227-244) adds that the muteness prophecy serves as a transition from Ezekiel's initiation to the symbolic actions in chapters 4-5. It redefined Ezekiel's mission, since he still refused to speak to the people. It also is the first of Ezekiel's symbolic actions that continue in the following chapters.

5. See further elaboration on Abarbanel's position in Lippman Bodoff, "Ezekiel 20:25-26—Did God Ever Command the Sacrifice of Israel's Firstborn Sons?" *Bekhol Derakheka Daehu* 10 (2000), pp. 23-36.

6. Cf. Yehiel Moskowitz, *Da'at Mikra: Ezekiel* (Hebrew) (Jerusalem: Mossad HaRav Kook, 1985), pp. 105–106.

7. See also Henry McKeating, "Ezekiel the 'Prophet Like Moses'?" *JSOT* 61 (1994), pp. 97-109.

8. See, e.g. Moskowitz, *Da'at Mikra: Ezekiel*, pp. 353, 360.

9. Although the primary prophecies of redemption leave the purification process to God, Ezekiel elsewhere states that some aspects of redemption may have remained contingent on Israel's behavior: "[Now] you, O mortal, describe the Temple to the House of Israel, and let them measure

its design. But let them be ashamed of their iniquities: When they are ashamed (*ve-im nikhlemu*) of all they have done, make known to them the plan of the Temple and its layout, its exits and entrances—its entire plan, and all the laws and instructions pertaining to its entire plan. Write it down before their eyes, that they may faithfully follow its entire plan and all its laws" (43:10-11).

Rashi and several later commentators observe that *ve-im nikhlemu* might mean "if" they are ashamed, rather than "when" they are ashamed (as translated by the NJPS). If so, the redemption ultimately would be conditional on Israel's being ashamed and repenting. Cf. 18:31-32: "Cast away all the transgressions by which you have offended, and get yourselves a new heart and a new spirit, that you may not die, O House of Israel. For it is not My desire that anyone shall die—declares the Lord God. Repent, therefore, and live!"

For an analysis of the tension between the deterministic and anti-deterministic tendencies in the Book of Ezekiel, see Yair Hoffmann, "Free Choice and Decree in the Book of Ezekiel" (Hebrew), in *Hagut ba-Mikra* vol. 2, ed. Meir Hovav (Tel-Aviv: Am Oved, 1973), pp. 79-89.

10. See Asher Weiser, "'Were it not for Him the Book of Ezekiel Would Have Been Suppressed'" (Hebrew), *Sinai* 51 (1962), pp. 37-45. Weiser also lists other potential discrepancies between the Torah and the Book of Ezekiel. For analysis of the rabbinic sources on the potential withdrawal of biblical books, see Sid Z. Leiman, *The Canonization of Hebrew Scripture: The Talmudic and Midrashic Evidence* (New Haven, CT: The Connecticut Academy of Arts and Sciences, 2nd ed., 1991), pp. 72–86.

11. Tosafot *Menahot* 45a quotes a *Sifrei* that may preserve the only extant resolution of R. Hanina.

12. See further discussion in Hayyim Angel, "The First Modern-Day Rabbi: A Midrashic Reading of Ezra," in Angel, *Revealed Texts, Hidden Meanings: Finding the Religious Significance in Tanakh* (Jersey City, NJ: KTAV-Sephardic Publication Foundation, 2009), pp. 217–226.

EZEKIEL: PRIEST-PROPHET*

INTRODUCTION

The Book of Ezekiel distinguishes itself from other prophetic books in several significant ways. Ezekiel's prophetic tenure is entirely in the exile. There is a high level of visionary revelation of God and the angelic host. Ezekiel's name hardly appears in the book; instead, God consistently refers to him as *ben adam* (Son of Man). Ezekiel is surprisingly silent, often acting out symbolic actions. For the most part, redemption is not contingent on Israel's behavior; rather, God redeems Israel for His Name's sake. Even after Israel returns to her Land, the war of Gog will occur.

It appears that Ezekiel's combination of prophecy and priesthood can explain many of the distinctive aspects of his book. Ezekiel's prophetic calling parallels the priestly career he would have had in Jerusalem in better times. By serving as a priest-prophet in exile, Ezekiel was able to encourage the Jews at the time of the destruction that God remains with them even in exile. Additionally, the passive nature of Ezekiel's prophecy allows God's personality to occupy center stage.

PRIESTHOOD IN THE TORAH

In his analysis of the priesthood in the Torah, Rabbi Eitan Mayer explains the wide range of priestly functions.[1] Among their many tasks, priests offer sacrifices, conduct the Temple service, and bless

* This article appeared originally in the *Jewish Bible Quarterly* 39:1 (2011), pp. 35-45. Reprinted here with minor modifications, with permission from the *Jewish Bible Quarterly*, POB 29002, Jerusalem, Israel; www.jewishbible.org.

the people. The High Priest represents Israel before God, with his accoutrements bearing the names of the twelve tribes (Exod. 28:11, 21, 29–30). The priesthood is responsible for teaching (Lev. 10:8–11), judging (Deut. 17:8–11), and mediating through the *Urim ve-Tummim* (Num. 27:21).

Sorting these functions into two broad categories, the priesthood serves as a bridge from God to the people through teaching, judging, mediating, and conferring the priestly blessing. It also serves as a bridge from the people to God through participation in the Temple service and wearing accoutrements inscribed with the names of the twelve tribes.

Priests were anointed like the utensils during the Tabernacle dedication ceremony (Exod. 29:7, 21; 30:25-33, 40:9-16). The special clothing worn by the priests are mandatory during service (Exod. 28:35; 29:9).

Perhaps the most extreme manifestation of the passive nature of the priesthood in the Torah is the injunction prohibiting Aaron from mourning the death of his sons Nadab and Abihu during the dedication of the Tabernacle:

> And Moses said to Aaron and to his sons Eleazar and Ithamar, "Do not bare your heads and do not rend your clothes, lest you die and anger strike the whole community. But your kinsmen, all the house of Israel, shall bewail the burning that the Lord has wrought. And so do not go outside the entrance of the Tent of Meeting, lest you die, for the Lord's anointing oil is upon you." And they did as Moses had bidden. (Lev. 10:6-7)

While performing the Temple service, the priest's personal identity is eclipsed by his position. A bridge between God and the people must stand still in order to function properly.

EZEKIEL CHAPTERS 1-3

Ezekiel was exiled from Jerusalem in 597 B.C.E. along with King Jehoiachin and some 10,000 of Jerusalem's elite citizens (II Kings

24:11-14). Though he could not serve in the soon-to-be-destroyed Temple, Ezekiel's priesthood plays a central role in his prophetic mission.

A. "THE THIRTIETH YEAR"

In the thirtieth year, on the fifth day of the fourth month, when I was in the community of exiles by the Chebar Canal, the heavens opened and I saw visions of God. On the fifth day of the month—it was the fifth year of the exile of King Jehoiachin— the word of the Lord came to the priest Ezekiel son of Buzi, by the Chebar Canal, in the land of the Chaldeans. And the hand of the Lord came upon him there. (Ezek. 1:1-3)

Ezekiel began his prophetic tenure in the fifth year of Jehoiachin's exile, or 592 B.C.E. To what, however, does "the thirtieth year" refer (1:1)? This enigma generated several lines of interpretation.

Thirty years prior to Ezekiel's initiation was Josiah's reformation, in 622 B.C.E. While that event was important, however, biblical events generally are dated from the years of a king's reign. The issue of dating notwithstanding, several commentators adopt this interpretation.

In some midrashim, Ezekiel's initiation occurred in the thirtieth year since the previous Jubilee year, which coincided with Josiah's reformation (*Arakhin* 12a). Rashi, R. Yosef Kara, and Radak cite this view as well.

R. Menahem ben Shimon (thirteenth-century Provence) cites a third view, that Ezekiel was thirty years old when he received his initiation prophecy. Had he not been exiled, Ezekiel would have begun his priestly service at age thirty, assuming that priests began their service at the same age as regular Levites (see Num. 4:3, 23, 30).[2] Instead of beginning his service in the Temple, Ezekiel's turning thirty was marked by his prophesying from exile about the impending destruction of that Temple. Within this line of interpretation, Ezekiel received the Temple vision (chapters 40–48) twenty years after his initiation (see 40:1, the twenty-fifth year of the exile = 572 B.C.E.), or at age fifty, when a priest normally would retire from service.[3] Though it is difficult to prove this reading over any other, it is possible that Ezekiel's prophetic career fundamentally spanned the years he otherwise would have served as a priest in the Temple.[4]

B. "SON OF MAN"

And He said to me, "O mortal, stand up on your feet that I may speak to you." (Ezek. 2:1)

After Ezekiel's initial vision, God speaks, curiously addressing the prophet as *ben adam* (Son of Man). Throughout Tanakh, God calls prophets *ben adam* 94 times. Of those 94 instances, 93 are in regard to Ezekiel, the other lone reference being to Daniel (Dan. 8:17).

Rashi and several later commentators suggest that God wanted to remind Ezekiel of his humanness specifically during these exalted visions in the presence of the angelic host. However, Isaiah experienced a similar vision (Isa. 6), and God had no need to humble Isaiah. Additionally, God consistently refers to Ezekiel as *ben adam*, even when communicating regular prophecies. Clearly, *ben adam* is characteristic of the Book of Ezekiel.

In fact, Ezekiel's name appears only twice in the entire book (1:2; 24:24), and the first reference belongs to the superscription. By way of contrast, Jeremiah's name occurs 129 times in his book, which is replete with personal and biographical information about Jeremiah. Though Jeremiah also was a priest (Jer. 1:1), that aspect of his pedigree plays virtually no role in his prophetic career. Ezekiel resembles a priest who does not exert his personality during service.

C. EZEKIEL'S MUTENESS

God repeatedly orders Ezekiel to speak to the people (2:4, 7; 3:1, 4). However, the prophet silently refuses when he returns to them (3:15). God responds to this silence by exhorting Ezekiel that he is a "watchman" for Israel and bears responsibility if he fails to warn the nation of their impending doom (3:16-21). However, the prophet *still* does not respond! This continued refusal sets the stage for God's informing Ezekiel that he will be muted:

> And a spirit entered into me and set me upon my feet. And He spoke to me, and said to me: "Go, shut yourself up in your house. As for you, O mortal, cords have been placed upon you, and you have been bound with them, and you shall not go out among them. And I will make your tongue cleave to your palate, and you shall be dumb; you shall not be a reprover to them, for they are a rebellious breed. But when I speak with you, I will open your mouth, and you shall say to them, 'Thus says the Lord God!' He who listens will listen, and he who does not will not—for they are a rebellious breed." (Ezek. 3:24-27)

Rashi suggests that Ezekiel's staying home while mute demonstrates that the people did not merit prophetic reproof since they were hopelessly wicked. According to the sequence of the text, however, the Jews did not yet have a chance to sink further in their rebellion since the prophet had thus far refused to address them. Why would God rebuke the people further?

R. Eliezer of Beaugency maintains that God was responding to Ezekiel's unwillingness to rebuke the people. Initially an act of rebellion, Ezekiel's silent passivity now was transformed into a defining feature of his prophecy.[5]

EZEKIEL'S PRIEST-PROPHET ROLE IN CHAPTER 4
A. 4:1-3, PLAYING GOD'S ROLE

And you, O mortal, take a brick and put it in front of you, and incise on it a city, Jerusalem. Set up a siege against it, and build towers against it, and cast a mound against it; pitch camps against it, and bring up battering rams roundabout it. Then take an iron plate and place it as an iron wall between yourself and the city, and set your face against it. Thus it shall be under siege, you shall besiege it. This shall be an omen for the House of Israel. (Ezek. 4:1-3)

In the first symbolic action of chapter 4, Ezekiel makes a brick representing Jerusalem and then holds a metal pan between the brick and himself. Following the talmudic interpretation in *Berakhot* 32b, Abarbanel, Malbim, and Yehiel Moskowitz[6] explain that in this instance Ezekiel is acting in God's stead. God shields His face from Jerusalem so that the city may be destroyed.

B. 4:4-8, PLAYING GOD'S AND ISRAEL'S ROLES

Then lie on your left side, and let it bear the punishment of the House of Israel; for as many days as you lie on it you shall bear their punishment (*tissa et avonam*).... Then, with bared arm, set your face toward besieged Jerusalem and prophesy against it. Now I put cords upon you, so that you cannot turn from side to side until you complete your days of siege. (Ezek. 4:4-8)

In the second symbolic action of chapter 4, Ezekiel lies on his sides for a total of 430 days so that he may "*tissa et avonam*." There appear to be multiple meanings of this expression and action: (1) Ezekiel bears Israel's punishment, that is, he represents Israel, who will be besieged. (2) He bears Israel's sin, representing God, Who had patiently borne Israel's sins for many years but now is prepared to destroy them. (3) In 4:7 Ezekiel represents God by staring with hostility and baring his arm against Jerusalem. (4) In 4:8 Ezekiel's bound state represents the people of Jerusalem who will be paralyzed during the siege (similar to 3:24–27). In this symbolic action, Ezekiel represents both God and the people.

C. 4:9-17, PLAYING ISRAEL'S ROLE

"Further, take wheat, barley, beans, lentils, millet, and emmer. Put them into one vessel and bake them into bread...you shall bake it on human excrement before their eyes. So," said the

Lord, "shall the people of Israel eat their bread, unclean, among
the nations to which I will banish them." (Ezek. 4:9-13)

During the famine that would result from the siege of Jerusalem,
people would be forced to combine whatever ingredients they had
available. There also would be a shortage of wood, so they would
use human excrement as fuel to bake their bread (Rashi, Yehiel
Moskowitz[7]). In this symbolic action, Ezekiel represents the people.

To summarize the symbolic actions in chapters 3–4: In 3:24–27
Ezekiel's role as a prophet of rebuke is transformed into a mission
of muteness and passivity; he also symbolizes Israel's paralysis during the upcoming siege. In 4:1–3 Ezekiel represents God by hiding
his face from Jerusalem. In 4:4–8 Ezekiel represents God by bearing
the people's sins and by glaring at the city with wrath, and represents the people by lying paralyzed and bearing their punishment. In
4:9–17 Ezekiel represents the people by experiencing their famine.
Thus Ezekiel's unique priest-prophet mission enables him to serve
as a bridge between God and the nation.

OTHER SIGNIFICANT REFERENCES
A. AN ANGEL DRESSED AS A PRIEST
In chapter 8 God gives Ezekiel a virtual tour of Jerusalem and its
sins to justify the extreme decree of destruction. Ezekiel then experiences a vision of angels destroying Jerusalem, followed by God's
Presence abandoning the city (chapters 9–10):

Then He called loudly in my hearing, saying, "Approach, you
men in charge of the city, each bearing his weapons of destruction!" And six men entered by way of the upper gate that faces
north, each with his club in his hand; and among them was another, clothed in linen, with a writing case at his waist. They
came forward and stopped at the bronze altar. (9:1-2)

One of the angels is dressed in linen. A midrash suggests an
interpretation of his attire:

R. Berekiah and R. Jeremiah in the name of R. Hiyya said: Like the ministration on high so was the ministration below. As in the case of the ministration on high there was One man in the midst of them clothed in linen (Ezek. 9:2) so in the case of the ministration below: He shall put on the holy linen tunic (Lev. 16:4). (*Lev. Rabbah* 21:11)

According to this midrash, God created the heavenly angelic host in parallel with the Temple and priests. The angel wearing linen corresponds to the priests, who wear linen in the Temple. If this interpretation can explain the plain sense of the vision,[8] Ezekiel's priest-prophet mission might affect his perception of the metaphysical arena also.

B. THE PROHIBITION AGAINST MOURNING

O mortal, I am about to take away the delight of your eyes from you through pestilence; but you shall not lament or weep or let your tears flow. Moan softly; observe no mourning for the dead....Tell the House of Israel: Thus said the Lord God: "I am going to desecrate My Sanctuary, your pride and glory, the delight of your eyes and the desire of your heart; and the sons and daughters you have left behind shall fall by the sword. Accordingly, you shall do as I have done: you shall not cover over your upper lips or eat the bread of comforters. (Ezek. 24:16–22)

Immediately preceding the siege of Jerusalem, God commands Ezekiel to abstain from mourning the death of his wife. This shocking inaction serves as a model to the Jews who similarly may not mourn the upcoming destruction. God's commandment resembles the prohibition of Aaron from mourning when his sons Nadab and Abihu perished. Ezekiel is essentially in service throughout his tenure as a priest-prophet.[9]

THE SIGNIFICANCE OF PROPHECY-PRIESTHOOD

Similar to priesthood, prophecy also serves as a bridge between God and Israel. The prophet transmits God's word to the people and intercedes to God on behalf of the people. Prophecy also generally has a more creative component, where the prophet's personality impacts his message. Jeremiah epitomizes this component, since his book is replete with his personal prayers and biographical information. In contrast, Ezekiel merges the function of priesthood into his prophetic mission. He has little creative personality, thereby functioning as a bridge to represent both sides of the God-Israel relationship.

On one level, Ezekiel's unique prophetic mission is critical because of the historical circumstances in which he lived. The Jews in Babylonia believed that God had rejected them permanently (e.g., 33:10; 37:11). That God could appear to a prophet and serve as a "small sanctuary" (11:16) in exile was revolutionary to them. By serving as a priest-prophet in the exile, then, Ezekiel played a vital role in encouraging his community that God was indeed with them in their suffering.[10] While of course this "small sanctuary" was no replacement for the real Temple in Jerusalem, Israel's connection with God continued into the exile. As a prophet in Babylonia, Ezekiel functioned as the "priest" of this "small sanctuary," serving as a bridge between God and the Jews in exile.[11]

On a different plane, Ezekiel's passivity and namelessness keep his personality out of the way of his revelation. In this respect he becomes a bridge primarily from God to the people. Consequently, readers are exposed to an unparalleled display of God's Presence and emotions.

The metaphysical destruction of Jerusalem occurs several years prior to its physical destruction, when the angels throw coals onto Jerusalem and then God's Presence abandons the city (chapters 9-10). This detailed description occupies two full chapters.[12] In contrast, the report of the physical destruction several years later is described coldly in just two words:

In the twelfth year of our exile, on the fifth day of the tenth month, a fugitive came to me from Jerusalem and reported, "The city has fallen" (*hukketah ha-ir*). (Ezek. 33:21)

As was noted above, the people were forbidden from showing signs of mourning (24:21-22).

God goes into exile as the Temple is destroyed, and God is the primary subject of redemption as well. The restoration in the Book of Ezekiel generally does not require Israel's repentance as a prerequisite, since God needs to sanctify His Name regardless (e.g., 11:14-21; 14:21-23; 16:59-63; 20:33-44; 36:16-36).[13] This phenomenon also explains why the war of Gog would occur even after Israel's return to her land (see 38:8, 11, 14).[14] The ultimate redemption in the Book of Ezekiel is of God rather than of Israel, and therefore the need for God to eradicate all human evil and for all humanity to recognize that God is paramount.

CONCLUSION

The unique nature of Ezekiel as a priest-prophet explains several of the distinctive features of his book. It is plausible that the book is structured around the years of Ezekiel's life when he otherwise would have served as a priest in the Temple. His prophetic tenure in Babylonia functioned as his priesthood in the "small sanctuary" of exile.

Ezekiel's namelessness, his silent passivity as he performed a series of actions symbolizing both God and Israel, and his being prohibited from mourning the loss of his wife all can be explained as aspects of serving as a priestly bridge between God and Israel. The priestly nature of his prophecy also can explain why Ezekiel exhibits little creative personality and the fact that human emotions are all but absent from the book—even when the people learn of the Temple's destruction. Ezekiel perceives one of the angels dressed like a priest.

As a priest-prophet, Ezekiel teaches Israel that God's Presence, prophecy, and some diminished manifestation of priesthood can exist even in the exile. This realization no doubt enlivened a demoralized group of exiles who believed that their relationship with God had been permanently severed. Moreover, Ezekiel served as a passive bridge between God and Israel, revealing to his audience a striking and unprecedented display of God's personality.

NOTES

1. Eitan Mayer, Parsha Themes Tetzaveh, at http://www.yu.edu/faculty/emayer/parsha_shiurim/21tetzaveh.html.

2. Halakhah does not assume that priests had age limits as did Levites. See Mishnah *Hullin* 1:6 (24a): "The disability which does not disqualify priests disqualifies Levites." If this halakhah were already in effect in Ezekiel's time and Ezekiel's prophetic message is governed by this halakhah, then this age point would not be relevant to our discussion. If the halakhic ruling were later than Ezekiel; or if the literary point of Ezekiel is not governed by the strict halakhah, then this point may stand.

3. R. Yosef Hayyun accepts this reading as most likely. See also James E. Miller, "The Thirtieth Year of Ezekiel 1:1," *Revue Biblique* 99 (1992), pp. 499–503.

4. 29:17-21, an appendix to Ezekiel's prophecies against Egypt, dates to the twenty-seventh year (570 B.C.E.), or two years after the Temple vision in chapters 40-48. Nevertheless, this minor insertion does not detract from the argument that the overall framework of the book spans the twenty year period from 592-572 B.C.E.

5. See further in Moshe Greenberg, "On Ezekiel's Dumbness," *JBL* 77 (1958), pp. 101-105.

6. Yehiel Moskowitz, *Da'at Mikra: Ezekiel* (Hebrew) (Jerusalem: Mossad HaRav Kook, 1985), p. 25.

7. Yehiel Moskowitz, *Da'at Mikra: Ezekiel*, pp. 29-30.

8. See, e.g., Rimon Kascher, *Mikra LeYisrael Ezekiel 1–24* (Hebrew) (Tel-Aviv: Am Oved Publishers Ltd., 2004) p. 259; Yehiel Moskowitz, *Da'at Mikra: Ezekiel*, p. 54.

9. For several other illustrations, see Andrew Mein, "Ezekiel as a Priest in Exile," in *The Elusive Prophet: The Prophet as a Historical Person, Literary Character, and Anonymous Artist*, ed. J. C. De Moor (Leiden: Brill, 2001), pp. 199-213.

10. See Ps. 91:14-16; *Megillah* 29a; *Exod. Rabbah* 23:5.

11. On this point, cf. Andrew Mein, "Ezekiel as a Priest in Exile," p. 213.

12. The painstaking description of God's Presence abandoning Jerusalem inspired one midrash to depict God as crying and kissing the Temple as He left: "R. Aha said: The Shekhinah may be likened to a king who left his palace in anger. After going out, he came back and embraced and kissed the walls of the palace and its pillars, weeping and exclaiming, 'O the peace of my palace, O the peace of my royal residence, O the peace of my beloved house! O peace, from now onward let there be peace!' (*Lam. Rabbah, Prologue* 25). While this midrashic reading extends far beyond the biblical text, it poignantly captures the overall spirit of the book.

13. Although the primary prophecies of redemption leave the purification process to God, Ezekiel elsewhere states that some aspects of redemption are contingent on Israel's behavior (18:31-32; 43:10-11). While this remained the idealized vision of Ezekiel, the primary prophecies of redemption assume that Israel would not repent until after God redeems them. For an analysis of the tension between these deterministic and anti-deterministic tendencies, see Yair Hoffmann, "Free Choice and Decree in the Book of Ezekiel" (Hebrew), in *Hagut ba-Mikra* vol. 2, ed. Meir Hovav (Tel-Aviv: Am Oved, 1973), pp. 79-89.

14. See e.g., Rambam *Hil. Melakhim* 12:2, who takes for granted that the war of Gog is an earlier stage of the redemption. See also Yehiel Moskowitz (*Da'at Mikra: Ezekiel*, p. 302) for a list of aggadic sources that similarly place the war of Gog before the final redemption.

THE BOOK OF JOEL:
ANTICIPATING A POST-PROPHETIC AGE*

INTRODUCTION

Of the fifteen "Latter Prophets," Joel's chronological setting is the most difficult to identify. Yet the dating of the book potentially has significant implications for determining the overall purposes of Joel's prophecies.

The book's outline is simple enough. Chapters 1–2 are a description of and response to a devastating locust plague that occurred in Joel's time. Chapters 3–4 are a prophecy of consolation predicting widespread prophecy, a major battle, and then ultimate peace and prosperity.[1] This essay will consider the dating of the Book of Joel, the book's overall themes, and how Joel's message fits into his likely chronological setting.

DATING

Midrashim and later commentators often attempt to identify obscure figures by associating them with known figures or events. One midrash quoted by Rashi identifies the prophet Joel with the son of Samuel (c. 1000 B.C.E.):

> When Samuel grew old, he appointed his sons judges over Israel. The name of his firstborn son was Joel, and his second son's name was Abijah; they sat as judges in Beer-sheba. But his sons did not follow in his ways; they were bent on gain, they accepted bribes, and they subverted justice. (I Sam. 8:1–3)

---

* This article is forthcoming in *Milin Havivin: Beloved Words* 5 (2011). Printed here with minor modifications, with permission from *Milin Havivin*.

Since Samuel's son was wicked, one midrash explains that he must have repented in order to attain prophecy. Additionally, the midrash needs to explain why the prophet Joel's father Pethuel in fact refers to Samuel:

> Now the name of his firstborn was Joel; and the name of his second, Abijah (I Sam. 8:2). R. Judan explained in the name of R. Simeon that ultimately they repented.... For this reason they attained the privilege of divine inspiration; hence it is written, The word of the Lord that came to Joel the son of Pethuel (Joel 1:1) and Pethuel is Samuel. Why was he called by the name of Pethuel? Because he won over (*pittah*) the Holy One, blessed be He, by his prayer. (*Num. Rabbah* 10:5)

However, there is no textual record of Samuel's son's repentance. Additionally, it is difficult to identify Samuel with Joel's father Pethuel at the level of *peshat*. Consequently, Ibn Ezra rejects this midrashic identification, and R. Yosef Kara and Radak do not even quote it.

One passage in the Talmud (*Ta'anit* 5a) associates Joel's locust plague with the seven-year famine in the time of Jehoram, reported in II Kings 6:24–8:1 (851–842 B.C.E.). Rashi, R. Yosef Kara, and Radak cite this view. Of course, there also was a drought in Elijah's time, and it is plausible that Joel is describing a different famine otherwise unattested in Tanakh. Additionally, the Kings narrative does not mention a locust plague. So while possible, this view also has no textual support.

A third possibility is raised in *Seder Olam Rabbah* 20[2]: Joel prophesied during the reign of Manasseh (697–642 B.C.E.) along with Nahum and Habakkuk. According to this midrashic view, the Book of Kings does not name the prophets who were active during the reign of Manasseh (II Kings 21:10–15) because Manasseh was so exceptionally wicked. Once again, however, this view is possible but has no textual support.

Abarbanel rejects all three midrashic opinions since they lack textual support. Turning instead to the ordering of the Twelve Prophets, and noting that Hosea and Amos (who flank the book of Joel) both prophesied in the eighth century B.C.E., Abarbanel submits that Joel prophesied during the tenure of Hosea, who prophesied into Hezekiah's reign. Joel continued into the time of Hezekiah's son Manasseh, consistent with the *Seder Olam Rabbah* chronology.

However, most commentators maintain that the Twelve Prophets are not arranged in chronological order. Rather, there are thematic and linguistic links between Hosea-Joel-Amos.[3] Insofar as the attempts at dating Joel adduce no compelling textual support, Ibn Ezra (on 1:1) concludes, "We have no means of knowing his generation."

Although attempts at dating biblical books from internal evidence generally are speculative, there do appear to be some textual clues that may provide some guidance.[4] Joel reports that the famine in the wake of the devastating locust plague had caused the Temple services to stop:

Offering and libation have ceased from the House of the Lord;
the priests must mourn who minister to the Lord. (1:9; cf. 1:13, 16; 2:14)

This reference indicates that a Temple was standing. This means that Joel prophesied either before 586 B.C.E., when the First Temple was destroyed, or after 516 B.C.E., when the Second Temple was completed. R. Yosef Ibn Caspi (on 1:1; 3:1) already made this observation.

In chapter 4 Joel appears to describe the return of the exiles of Judah and Jerusalem:

For lo! In those days and in that time, when I restore the fortunes of Judah and Jerusalem.... (4:1)

Egypt shall be a desolation, and Edom a desolate waste, because of the outrage to the people of Judah, in whose land they shed the blood of the innocent. But Judah shall be inhabited forever, and Jerusalem throughout the ages. (4:19–20)

These references most likely point to a period following the destruction and exile in 586, after Jehoiachin's exile in 597, or at least following the decree of destruction in Manasseh's time (697–642), when the impending exile was known to the prophets (II Kings 21:10–15).[5]

Additionally, Edom was permanently devastated by Malachi's time:

I have made his hills a desolation, his territory a home for beasts of the desert. (Mal. 1:3)

Therefore, Joel—who predicts Edom's demise in 4:19—likely preceded Malachi.

In light of the evidence, it appears that the most likely times for Joel to have prophesied are:

1. After Jehoiachin's exile but before the destruction of the First Temple (597–586).

2. During or after Manasseh's time (697–642), when the decree of destruction and exile was known to the prophets.

3. At the beginning of the Second Temple period (post-516), before Edom was destroyed (pre-Malachi).

It also must be stressed that Joel did not have to prophesy all four chapters on the same day. Perhaps the locust plague struck prior to the destruction of the First Temple in 586, and Joel prophesied chapters 3–4 after the destruction and exile. We will bear these issues of dating in mind as we analyze several textual elements in the Book of Joel.

CHAPTERS 1–2

> Listen to this, O elders, give ear, all inhabitants of the land. Has the like of this happened in your days or in the days of your fathers? Tell your children about it, and let your children tell theirs, and their children the next generation! What the cutter has left, the locust has devoured; what the locust has left, the grub has devoured; and what the grub has left, the hopper has devoured. (1:2–4)

Rashi, Ibn Ezra, and Malbim argue that Joel is predicting a plague that has not yet occurred. Joel's implied message is that the people should repent before the plague strikes.

In contrast, Amos Hakham maintains that Joel is describing a plague that has already occurred.[6] Joel is using this plague as an opportunity to call for repentance and to learn from calamity (1:13–14, 19; 2:12–17). Joel indicates that people can see the damage for themselves:

> For food is cut off before our very eyes, and joy and gladness from the House of our God. (1:16)

It therefore appears more likely that Hakham's view is correct and all the people were able to see what Joel saw.

In his lectures at Yeshiva University, Rabbi Shalom Carmy has observed that the Book of Joel is unique in prophetic literature in not identifying any sin as cause for a specific disaster nor as impetus for repentance. Following the teachings of Rabbi Joseph Soloveit-chik, Rabbi Carmy explains that there are two types of repentance: response for sins, and introspection as the result of adversity. When tragedy strikes, we must examine ourselves and try to come closer to God, even if we cannot ascertain any specific sins of which we are guilty.[7]

This point can be pushed further. Joel did not need to be a prophet in order to speak to the people as he did. Everyone witnessed the plague. Joel is calling for a fast and repentance, which any religious leader can do with or without prophecy. Indeed, the Sages of the Talmud used Joel's prayer as a model for their own prayers during public fast days:

> What is the order [of service] for fast days?...The elder among them addresses them with words of admonition [to repentance]: thus, our brethren, Scripture does not say of the people of Nineveh, and God saw their sackcloth and their fasting, but, as God saw their works, that they turned from their evil way (Jon. 3:10); and in the prophets it is said, And rend your heart and not your garments... (Joel 2:13). (Mishnah *Ta'anit* 15a)

Returning to our discussion about the dating of the Book of Joel, this observation would be particularly meaningful if Joel prophesied at the end of the First Temple period or the beginning of the Second Temple period. Several midrashim and later commentaries explain that the destruction of the First Temple crippled the existence of prophecy, even if it continued briefly into the Second Temple period with Haggai, Zechariah, and Malachi.[8] Additionally, several commentators posit that the last prophets were conscious of the fact that the age of prophecy was coming to a close.[9] Perhaps they received prophecies informing them of the coming end, or perhaps they observed the scarcity of prophets in their time. If this is the case regarding Joel (though we have no means of knowing this textually), Joel might be anticipating the cessation of prophecy and teaching people how to respond to crisis when there is no prophecy.

This hypothesis is supported further by Joel's increased appeal to earlier sacred texts—a hallmark of the post-prophetic age. Of the 73 verses in the Book of Joel, 25 are strikingly similar to other verses elsewhere in Tanakh. It is more likely that Joel borrowed or anthologized from many others, rather than influencing so many different writers.[10]

CHAPTERS 3–4

> After that, I will pour out My spirit on all flesh; your sons and
> daughters shall prophesy; your old men shall dream dreams, and
> your young men shall see visions. I will even pour out My spirit
> upon male and female slaves in those days. (3:1–2)

Many commentators maintain that chapters 3–4 pertain to the
messianic redemption.[11] In light of our previous discussion of Joel's
chronological setting, the emphasis on the restoration of prophecy
in chapter 3 might take on additional meaning if Joel was prophetically anticipating the end of prophecy. Joel may also have observed
a decline in prophecy in his time.

> Beat your plowshares into swords, and your pruning hooks into
> spears. Let even the weakling say, "I am strong." (4:10)

Amos Hakham interprets this verse as a parody of the utopian visions of Isaiah and Micah (Isa. 2:4; Mic. 4:3).[12] Assuming that Joel
prophesied after those eighth-century prophets, he intimates that in
the future the world will be perfected as nations beat their swords
into plowshares. However, that ideal age will be preceded by a terri-
ble war that will require people to beat farm implements into weapons. Additionally, Joel blends agricultural imagery and wars in this
prophecy, thereby connecting the two halves of the book. Joel uses
agricultural terminology when describing the downfall of Israel's
enemies:

> Swing the sickle, for the crop is ripe; come and tread, for the
> winepress is full, the vats are overflowing! For great is their
> wickedness. (4:13)

Joel also describes the locusts using military imagery, so the two
halves of his book are joined in both directions:

> They have the appearance of horses, they gallop just like steeds.
> With a clatter as of chariots they bound on the hilltops, with
> a noise like a blazing fire consuming straw; like an enormous

horde arrayed for battle....They rush like warriors, they scale a wall like fighters. And each keeps to his own track. (2:4–7)

The conclusion of the book also promises agricultural prosperity in addition to peace from the military invaders:

And in that day, the mountains shall drip with wine, the hills shall flow with milk, and all the watercourses of Judah shall flow with water; a spring shall issue from the House of the Lord and shall water the Wadi of the Acacias. (4:18)

Amos Hakham similarly addresses the connections between the two halves of the book. In the first half, God emphasizes that after the locust plague ended, Israel no longer would be degraded by other nations (2:19, 27). Even when Israel had food, however, they still were oppressed and mocked during the destruction of the Temple and ensuing exile. Joel therefore emphasizes that the end of locust plague would be followed by a permanent salvation from enemy nations. As locusts swarmed in Israel, causing damage and desolation, nations would invade Israel and cause damage and desolation. As the locusts were completely destroyed, so will Israel's enemies be.[13]

In several regards, Joel sounds more like a precursor to the Sages than a conventional prophet. He teaches people how to respond to crisis, does not specify the sin behind the locust plague, and frequently alludes to earlier biblical texts. If Joel prophesied at the end of the First Temple period or the beginning of the Second Temple period, he was part of a new era that soon would lose prophecy. Therefore he taught people how to respond religiously to crises without having prophets in their midst. He also began his prophecy of redemption by envisioning a future time when everyone would prophesy.

THE "SON" OF SAMUEL

We may return to the midrashic identification of the prophet Joel with the son of Samuel (*Num. Rabbah* 10:5), cited at the outset of this essay. While this identification is not viable at the level of *pe-shat*, it may be understood in a conceptual-*derash* manner. Joel's role and envisioned utopian era is similar to that of Samuel, who lived some 500 years earlier. Samuel was born at a time when prophecy was scarce:

> Young Samuel was in the service of the Lord under Eli. In those days the word of the Lord was rare; prophecy was not widespread. (I Sam. 3:1)

Over the course of his lifetime, Samuel trained others to be prophets to the point where those approaching him attained some degree of inspiration:

> Saul sent messengers to seize David. They saw a band of prophets speaking in ecstasy, with Samuel standing by as their leader; and the spirit of God came upon Saul's messengers and they too began to speak in ecstasy....He was on his way there, to Naioth in Ramah, when the spirit of God came upon him too; and he walked on, speaking in ecstasy, until he reached Naioth in Ramah. Then he too stripped off his clothes and he too spoke in ecstasy before Samuel; and he lay naked all that day and all night. That is why people say, "Is Saul too among the prophets?" (I Sam. 19:20–24; cf. I Sam. 10:5, 10–12)

In a midrashic sense, then, Joel is conceptually the "son" of Samuel, teaching people how to live without prophecy but envisioning the future return and widespread prevalence of revelation.

Tying further to this midrash, there is a connection to Samuel as Pethuel, "because he won over (*pittah*) the Holy One, blessed be He, by his prayer." Joel teaches his audience and subsequent generations how to pray and react to crisis. Samuel is similarly famed for his effective prayers. He prays for the defeat of the Philistines and is immediately answered (I Sam. 7:5–11); and God similarly responds when Samuel prays for a storm to prove that Israel's request of kingship was sinful (I Sam. 12:16–19). Later biblical writers hail Samuel as one of the most effective pray-ers ever:

The Lord said to me, "Even if Moses and Samuel were to intercede with Me, I would not be won over to that people. Dismiss them from My presence, and let them go forth! (Jer. 15:1)

Moses and Aaron among His priests, Samuel, among those who call on His name—when they called to the Lord, He answered them. (Ps. 99:6)

Rabbi Joseph B. Soloveitchik similarly viewed prayer as the natural heir to prophecy. When prophecy ceased, the Men of the Great Assembly refused to allow dialogue between God and Man to cease:

If God had stopped calling man, they urged, let man call God. So the covenantal colloquy was shifted from the level of prophecy to that of prayer.[14]

Living around the time of the destruction of the First Temple or the beginning of the Second Temple period, Joel began to build a bridge between the age of prophecy and post-prophecy. He used a contemporaneous locust plague to teach people how to respond religiously to crisis with prayer and repentance. He frequently alluded to earlier sacred texts. Simultaneously, his message of consolation features the prevalence of prophecy during the ultimate redemption. In this manner, Joel paved the way for a continued dialogue between God and Israel even after prophecy ceased.

NOTES

1. R. Eliezer of Beaugency and Abarbanel insist that chapters 1–2 are a parable that describes enemy invaders, and chapters 3–4 are the true meaning of that parable. This essay will follow the majority opinion that Joel is describing a real locust plague. For evaluation of the textual

evidence in support of an actual locust plague, see Amos Hakham, *Da'at Mikra: Joel*, in *Twelve Prophets* vol. 1 (Hebrew) (Jerusalem: Mossad HaRav Kook, 1990), introduction p. 4.

2. In Radak and Abarbanel's version of that midrash. Rashi cites this view in the name of Behag rather than *Seder Olam Rabbah*.

3. Amos Hakham (*Da'at Mikra: Joel*, introduction p. 3) notes the thematic connections to Amos: see Joel 4:16–18 – Amos 1:2, 9:13. The blessing described at the end of Joel is similar to that in Hosea 14:8.

4. See James L. Crenshaw, *Anchor Bible 24C: Joel* (New York: Doubleday, 1995), pp. 22–29; Mordechai Cogan, *Mikra LeYisrael: Joel* (Hebrew) (Tel-Aviv: Am Oved, 1994), introduction, pp. 5–6.

5. Zephaniah similarly assumes that there will be an exile though he prophesied before it, during Josiah's reign (640–609 B.C.E.; see Zeph. 2:7).

6. Amos Hakham, *Da'at Mikra: Joel*, p. 6.

7. From one of his student's notes from his lectures at Yeshiva College (1996), and this phrasing is confirmed by R. Carmy. See also R. Aharon Lichtenstein's formulation of R. Joseph Soloveitchik's position: "I presume we are inclined to acknowledge the justice enunciated by the Rav, zt"l [i.e., R. Soloveitchik], that Judaism has not confronted suffering primarily as a speculative matter. Rather, it has related to it as an existential and experiential reality, to be dealt with pragmatically and normatively. Response, not explanation, is focal. Its message, in sum, is: 'Don't waste your passional experiences; utilize them; exploit them; let every passional experience become a point of departure for a higher and nobler life.'" From "The Duties of the Heart and Response to Suffering," in *Jewish Perspectives on the Experience of Suffering*, ed. Shalom Carmy (Northvale, NJ: Jason Aronson Inc., 1999), pp. 22–23.

For further discussion, see Hayyim Angel, "The Uncertainty Principle of Repentance in the Books of Jonah and Joel," in Angel, *Revealed Texts, Hidden Meanings: Finding the Religious Significance in Tanakh* (Jersey City, NJ: KTAV, 2009), pp. 148–161.

8. For more on the destruction of the First Temple playing a role in the cessation of prophecy, see, e.g., Lam. 2:9; *Yoma* 21b; *Pesikta D'Rav Kahana* 13; Radak on Ezek. 9:3. For further discussion, see Hayyim Angel, "The End of Prophecy: Malachi's Position in the Spiritual Development

of Israel," *Conversations* 9 (Winter 2011), pp. 112-118, reprinted in this volume.

9. See, e.g., Abarbanel and Malbim on Zech. 1:5–6; Ibn Ezra and Abarbanel on Mal. 1:1; R. Yosef Kara and Malbim on Mal. 3:22.

10. Cf. James L. Crenshaw, *Anchor Bible 24C: Joel*, pp. 27–28, 36.

11. For example, Rashi, R. Yosef Kara, Radak, Abarbanel, and Malbim. Ibn Ezra quotes R. Moshe Ibn Gikatilah, who maintains that Joel's prophecy in chapters 3–4 was fulfilled during the reign of Jehoshaphat (876–852 B.C.E.).

12. Amos Hakham, *Da'at Mikra: Joel*, p. 23.

13. Amos Hakham, *Da'at Mikra: Joel*, introduction, pp. 4–5; cf. Mordechai Cogan, *Mikra LeYisrael: Joel*, introduction, pp. 5–6.

14. Rabbi Joseph B. Soloveitchik, *The Lonely Man of Faith* (New York: Doubleday, 1992), p. 58.

THE END OF PROPHECY:
MALACHI'S POSITION IN THE SPIRITUAL DEVELOPMENT OF ISRAEL[*]

INTRODUCTION

God communicated through prophecy for nearly the entire biblical period, from Adam until Malachi. According to a prevalent Jewish tradition, prophecy ceased with Malachi, not to be renewed until the messianic age.

This essay will consider a few traditional explanations of why prophecy ceased and note some spiritual implications for Judaism over the ensuing 2,500 years and counting.

OVERVIEW OF MALACHI

Unlike Haggai and Zechariah, whose prophecies pulsated with messianic potential, Malachi lived a generation or two later, when that messianic potential appears to have been lost. The people's political and economic suffering contributed to their feelings of rejection by God (1:2–5), corruption of the priesthood (1:6–2:9), rampant intermarriage (2:10–16), and laxity in tithing (3:8–12).

God-fearing people were losing heart as well. Why remain righteous? Their sinful compatriots were successful while God-fearing people suffered (2:17; 3:13–21). All Malachi could answer was that for now the mere fact of Israel's continued existence proved that God still loved them (1:2–5). Only in some unspecified future would God bring complete justice (3:13–24).

---

* This article appeared originally in *Conversations* 9 (Institute for Jewish Ideas and Ideals, Winter 2011), pp. 112-118. Reprinted here with minor modifications, with permission from the editor.

According to several classical rabbinic sources, Malachi was the last prophet (see, for example, Tosefta *Sotah* 13:3; *Yoma* 9b; *Sanhedrin* 11a). That his book is positioned last in the Twelve Prophets does not prove he was the last prophet, though, since the book is not arranged in chronological order. However, it seems from textual evidence that he likely was the last of the Twelve. Radak and Abarbanel observe that unlike Haggai and Zechariah, Malachi does not mention the Temple construction; it was in use already. Malachi also condemns intermarriage (Mal. 2:10–16), a shared concern of Ezra and Nehemiah (458–432 B.C.E., see Ezra 9–10; Neh. 13:23–28). The widespread laxity in tithing (Mal. 3:8–12) also likely dates to Nehemiah's time (Neh. 10:35–40; 12:44; 13:5, 10–12).

Even if Malachi were the last of the biblical prophets, there is no statement at the end of his book or anywhere else in Tanakh stating categorically that prophecy had ceased. For example, Nehemiah battled false prophets (Neh. 6:5–7, 11–13) but did not negate the existence of prophecy in principle.

Nevertheless, the tradition that Malachi was the last prophet opened the interpretive possibility that Malachi was *conscious* of the impending end of prophecy.

A pronouncement (*massa*): The word of the Lord to Israel through Malachi. (Mal. 1:1)

Most commentators understand the book's opening word *massa* as another generic term for "prophecy." However, Abarbanel notes that the term could also mean "burden." One midrash similarly understands *massa* in this vein:

[Prophecy] is expressed by ten designations.... And which is the severest form? ... The Rabbis said: Burden (*massa*), as it says, As a heavy burden (Ps. 138:5). (*Gen. Rabbah* 44:6)

Within this interpretation, it is possible that Malachi viewed his mission with additional weight, conscious of his being the last of the prophets.

Similarly, several interpreters understand the book's closing verses as a self-conscious expression that prophecy was about to end:

> Be mindful of the Teaching of My servant Moses, whom I charged
> at Horeb with laws and rules for all Israel. Lo, I will send the
> prophet Elijah to you before the coming of the awesome, fear-
> ful day of the Lord. He shall reconcile parents with children and
> children with their parents, so that, when I come, I do not strike
> the whole land with utter destruction. (Mal. 3:22–24)

Kara (on 3:22), Ibn Ezra (on 1:1), Abarbanel (on 1:1), and Malbim
(on 3:22) explain that Malachi was aware that prophecy would stop
with him. The word of God would henceforth be available only
through the written word of Tanakh. Malbim links the exhortation
to observe the Torah to the prediction of Elijah's coming. With the
end of prophecy, the Torah would sustain the people of Israel until
the messianic era, at which point prophecy would resume.

WHY PROPHECY STOPPED

We now turn to three leading trends in traditional Jewish thought
as to why prophecy ceased: sin, the destruction of the Temple, or a
metaphysical spiritual transition.

Sin

Some sources suggest that the loss of prophecy was punishment
for sin. Over 200 years before Malachi, Amos predicted the cessation of prophecy:

> A time is coming—declares my Lord God—when I will send a
> famine upon the land: not a hunger for bread or a thirst for water,
> but for hearing the words of the Lord. Men shall wander from
> sea to sea and from north to east to seek the word of the Lord,
> but they shall not find it. (Amos 8:11–12)

Avot D'Rabbi Nathan B:47 explains that prophecy ceased as a
consequence of people's mocking the prophets.

Radak (on Hag. 2:5) suggests more generally that lack of fidelity to the Torah resulted in the loss of prophecy. A midrash (*Pesikta Rabbati* 35) states that many Jews failed to return to Israel after Cyrus gave them permission, and therefore prophecy ceased. Commenting on *Yoma* 9b, which blames the lack of redemption in the Second Temple period on the fact that many Jews did not return to Israel, Maharsha similarly states that prophecy ceased as a consequence of the lackluster return from exile.

Destruction of the Temple

Ezekiel chapters 8–10 describe a vision wherein God shows the prophet the rampant idolatry in Jerusalem. God's Presence abandons the Temple and goes into exile. Radak (on Ezek. 9:3) explains that the absence of God's Presence ultimately contributed to the disappearance of prophecy.

Although Haggai, Zechariah, and Malachi prophesied after the destruction of the First Temple, a number of sources consider the destruction to have dealt a fatal blow to prophecy.

In five things the first Sanctuary differed from the second: in the ark, the ark-cover, the Cherubim, the fire, the Shekhinah, the Holy Spirit [of Prophecy], and the *Urim ve-Thummim* [the Oracle Plate]. (*Yoma* 21b)

As Benjamin is the last tribe, so Jeremiah is the last prophet. But did not Haggai, Zechariah, and Malachi prophesy after him? R. Lazar says: they had limited prophecy. R. Samuel b. Nahman says: [Jeremiah's] prophecy already was given to Haggai, Zechariah, and Malachi. (*Pesikta D'Rav Kahana* 13)

The last prophets were diminished or, alternatively, were mere transmitters of Jeremiah's message. Malbim (on Zech. 1:5–6) presents a different form of this approach:

I will not send new prophets, since there is no longer any need for prophets as you have seen all the prophecies of doom fulfilled against you...there is no longer any need for prophecy since you already understand God's hand in history.

According to Malbim, there no longer was any need for prophecy since the message had already been given through earlier prophets.

Metaphysical Transition

Seder Olam Rabbah 30 states that prophecy ceased in the time of Alexander the Great. Based on the rabbinic chronology, the Greek Empire began immediately following the end of the biblical period, so this time frame would synchronize with Malachi. Following this chronological assumption, R. Zadok HaKohen of Lublin observed that a metaphysical transition to an age of reason occurred in Israel and in Greece at the same time:

> The proliferation of idolatry and sorcery in the gentile world paralleled divine revelation and prophecy in Israel. When prophecy ceased and the era of the Oral Law commenced, there appeared Greek Philosophy, which is to say, mortal wisdom. (*Resisei Laylah*, 81b, Bezalel Naor translation)

This idea meshes with a talmudic statement that at the beginning of the Second Temple period the temptation for idolatry ceased being the force it had been during the First Temple period (*Yoma* 69b). R. Yehudah HeHasid argued that once the urge for idolatry vanished, there no longer existed the need for prophecy to counterbalance magic (*Sefer Hasidim*, Wistenetzky ed., p. 544; cf. R. Elijah of Vilna, commentary on *Seder Olam Rabbah* 30; R. Zadok, *Divrei Soferim*, 21b).

Similarly, a certain spiritual intensity was lost. Once the urge to idolatry had declined, prophetic revelation would have too much power if left unchecked. To preserve free will, prophecy had to cease as well (R. Eliyahu Dessler, *Mikhtav me-Eliyahu* III, pp. 277–278).

RELIGIOUS IMPLICATIONS

According to the sin approach, the deprivation of the supreme gift of prophecy was a devastating punishment that has diminished the connection between God and humanity for the past 2,500 years since Malachi. Within the destruction of the Temple approach, the disappearance of prophecy was a necessary corollary of that cataclysmic event.

Although the loss of prophecy was a spiritual catastrophe, there still are some spiritual benefits to its suspension, particularly within the approach that there was a metaphysical shift from prophecy-idolatry to human reason. In 1985 Professor Yaakov Elman published two articles analyzing the position of R. Zadok HaKohen of Lublin in reference to the transition from the age of prophecy to the age of Oral Law. According to R. Zadok, the end of prophecy facilitated a flourishing of the development of the Oral Law, a step impossible as long as people could turn to the prophets for absolute religious guidance and knowledge of God's Will. Sages needed to interpret texts and traditions to arrive at rulings, enabling them to develop axioms that could keep the eternal Torah relevant as society changed.

Although the decline of revelation distanced people from ascertaining God's Will, it simultaneously enabled mature human participation in the mutual covenant between God and humanity. This religious struggle is captured poignantly by the following talmudic passage:

> And they stood under the mount: R. Abdimi b. Hama b. Hasa said: This teaches that the Holy One, blessed be He, overturned the mountain upon them like an [inverted] cask, and said to them, "If you accept the Torah, it is well; if not, there shall be your burial." R. Aha b. Jacob observed: This furnishes a strong protest against the Torah. Said Rava, Yet even so, they re-accepted it in the days of Ahasuerus, for it is written, [the Jews] confirmed, and took upon them [etc.]: [i.e.,] they confirmed what they had accepted long before. (*Shabbat* 88a)

Rather than explaining away R. Aha's question, Rava understood that revelation in fact crippled an aspect of free will. He proposed Purim as the antidote, since that represents the age when revelation ceased.

Although prophecy was the ideal state—and we long for its return—its absence enables the flourishing of human reason, as we no longer have access to absolute divine knowledge. We must take initiative in our relationship with God or else the relationship suffers. R. Zadok applied this human endeavor to the realm of Torah study. Rabbi Joseph Soloveitchik understood prayer as replacing prophecy, precisely with the imperative of our responsibility to keep the lines of communication between God and humanity open:

> In short, prayer and prophecy are two synonymous designations of the covenantal God-man colloquy. Indeed, the prayer community was born the very instant the prophetic community expired and, when it did come into the spiritual world of the Jew of old, it did not supersede the prophetic community but rather perpetuated it…. If God had stopped calling man, they urged, let man call God. (*The Lonely Man of Faith* [New York: Doubleday, 1992], pp. 57–58)

Institutionalized prayer rescued intimacy with God by creating a new framework for this sacred dialogue.

Although prophecy disappeared some 2,500 years ago, the underlying spiritual struggle continues to be manifest in contemporary society. Many people long for absolute knowledge of God's Will. Consequently, there exists a compelling pull toward holy men (*rebbes*, kabbalists) or the over-extension of a *da'at Torah* concept that accords near-infallibility to Torah scholars. Though that appeal may be understandable, it must be remembered that (a) these individuals are not prophets and therefore do not have the certain divine knowledge that many accord to them; and (b) in an age lacking prophecy we have a far greater responsibility to learn Torah and pray, and to take that spiritual energy to infuse every aspect of our lives with sanctity. Doing this requires a healthy dose of human reason and effort, coupled with an ongoing consultation with spiritual guides who can help us grow.

For further study, see:
- Hayyim Angel, "The First Modern-Day Rabbi: A Midrashic Reading of Ezra," in Angel, *Revealed Texts, Hidden Meanings: Finding the Religious Significance in Tanakh* (Jersey City, NJ: KTAV-Sephardic Publication Foundation, 2009), pp. 217–226.
- Hayyim Angel, "The Theological Significance of the *Urim VeThummim*," in Angel, *Through an Opaque Lens* (New York: Sephardic Publication Foundation, 2006), pp. 195–214.
- Gerald Blidstein, "In the Shadow of the Mountain: Consent and Coercion at Sinai," *Jewish Political Studies Review* 4:1 (1992), pp. 41–53.
- Yaakov Elman, "R. Zadok HaKohen on the History of Halakha," *Tradition* 21:4 (Fall 1985), pp. 1–26.
- Yaakov Elman, "Reb Zadok HaKohen of Lublin on Prophecy in the Halakhic Process," in *Jewish Law Association Studies I: Touro Conference Volume*, ed. B. S. Jackson (Chico, CA: Scholars Press, 1985), pp. 1–16.
- Lawrence Kaplan, "*Daas Torah*: A Modern Conception of Rabbinic Authority," in *Rabbinic Authority and Personal Autonomy*, ed. Moshe Sokol (Northvale, NJ: Jason Aronson Inc., 1992), pp. 1–60.
- Bezalel Naor, *Lights of Prophecy* (New York: Union of Orthodox Congregations, 1990).

GOD INSISTS ON TRUTH:
RABBINIC EVALUATIONS OF
TWO AUDACIOUS BIBLICAL PRAYERS*

This essay will consider the diversity of response to two sharply formulated prayers in Tanakh. Habakkuk appears to accuse God of poor judgment by allowing the wicked Babylonians to conquer Judah, and then boldly demands a response. Psalm 89 lashes out at God for abrogating the permanent covenant He had struck with the Davidic dynasty.

Traditional interpreters assume that everything in Tanakh is divinely inspired and is applicable to all later generations (see, e.g., *Megillah* 14a). At the same time, several midrashim and later exegetes are uncomfortable with the bluntness of these prayers and therefore attempt to restrict their applicability. These commentators adopt variations of at least five options:

1. The prophet/psalmist acted religiously appropriately, and therefore we should emulate his prayer.

2. The prophet/psalmist acted religiously appropriately, but most people have not attained a sufficiently high spiritual level to emulate that kind of prayer. Therefore they should speak more diffidently before God.

3. The prophet/psalmist was objectively wrong himself.

* This article appeared originally in the *Jewish Bible Quarterly* 38:1 (2010), pp. 3–9. Reprinted here with minor modifications, with permission from the *Jewish Bible Quarterly*, POB 29002, Jerusalem, Israel; www.jewishbible.org.

4. The prophet/psalmist was quoting someone else rather than speaking for himself.

5. The text needs to be supplemented or reinterpreted in order to remove the sting of the more literal reading.

HABAKKUK

How long, O Lord, shall I cry out and You not listen, shall I shout to You, "Violence!" And You not save? Why do You make me see iniquity [why] do You look upon wrong? – Raiding and violence are before me, strife continues and contention goes on. That is why decision fails and justice never emerges; for the villain hedges in the just man – therefore judgment emerges deformed. (Hab. 1:2–4)

I will stand on my watch, take up my station at the post, and wait to see what He will say to me, what He will reply to my complaint. (2:1)

Habakkuk had difficulty with the favor God was to show the Babylonians at the time of the destruction of the Temple. Although Israel may have deserved punishment for her sins, it should not have come at the hands of a nation far more wicked (Abarbanel on 1:13). Habakkuk believed that the success of the wicked Babylonians would reduce faithfulness, since people would conclude that there is no justice in the world (Ibn Ezra, Radak on 1:4). Additionally, Habakkuk expresses frustration that God had not yet responded to his prayers, suggesting a long history of protest prior to the opening of the biblical book.

One midrash is uncomfortable with Habakkuk's tone and sharply criticizes him:

"Keep your mouth from being rash" (Eccl. 5:1) .... When Habakkuk said "I will stand on my watch, Take up my station at the post" (Hab. 2:1) .... This teaches that he drew a form, and stood in its midst. He said "I will not move from here until You answer me."...God replied, "You are not an ignoramus, but rather a Torah scholar!"...When Habakkuk heard this, he fell on his face and supplicated. He said, "Master of the Universe! Do not judge me as a willful transgressor, but rather as an inadvertent sinner [*shogeg*]." This is what is written, "A prayer of the prophet Habakkuk. In the mode of *Shigionoth*" (Hab. 3:1). (*Midrash Psalms* 7:17)

This midrash deems Habakkuk guilty of speaking rashly before God, emulating an ignoramus rather than a prophet. It proceeds to explain Habakkuk 3 – prefaced with *al shigionoth* (midrashically explained as deriving from *s-g-g* [error]) – as a psalm of repentance by the prophet.[1]

A different approach is espoused in the Talmud (*Ta'anit* 23a), where Habakkuk's story is likened to that of Honi the Circle Drawer: "[Honi] thereupon drew a circle and stood within it in the same way as the prophet Habakkuk had done." Both brazenly and successfully demanded responses from God. Habakkuk received his theological answer, and Honi got the rain he requested. In the Talmud, both figures are praised for their saintliness and for God's positive responses. Despite Honi's success, however, Shimon ben Shetah was deeply concerned with his conduct:

If you were not Honi I would have excommunicated you.... But what can I do to you who acts petulantly before the Omnipresent and He grants your desire, as a son who acts petulantly before his father and he grants his desires.... Of you Scripture says, "Your father and mother will rejoice; She who bore you will exult" (Prov. 23:25). (*Ta'anit* 23a)

Shimon ben Shetah believed that it was religiously inappropriate to make such demands of God. Nevertheless, he recognized that Honi enjoyed a unique relationship with God.[2] This talmudic passage appears to espouse the view that Habakkuk and Honi were objectively correct in their prayers. Shimon ben Shetah, concerned that others might emulate them, restricted the applicability of these prayers to an exclusive elite.[3]

Ibn Ezra (on Hab. 1:1, 12) adopts yet another response to Habakkuk's prayers. Rather than admit that a prophet spoke those words himself, Ibn Ezra asserts that Habakkuk was quoting others of his generation. Thus Ibn Ezra avoids the need to ask whether this prophetic prayer may be used as a model or not; Habakkuk was not the originator of those words.

Then again, perhaps Habakkuk spoke for himself, concerned about the religious ramifications the destruction likely would cause. Most commentators do not ascribe these words to other speakers, nor do they think Habakkuk was repenting in chapter 3. Additionally, God responded directly to Habakkuk without any tone of criticism. Therefore Habakkuk's prayer may have been fully appropriate, and God's positive response supports this view.[4]

PSALM 89

Yet You have rejected, spurned, and become enraged at Your anointed. You have repudiated the covenant with Your servant; You have dragged his dignity in the dust. You have breached all his defenses, shattered his strongholds. (Ps. 89:39–41)

Psalm 89 is one of the most jarring of the psalms. For 38 verses, the psalmist speaks elatedly of God's eternal covenant with the Davidic monarchy. God swore that it would endure forever, like the sun, moon, and heavens. But then the psalm turns abruptly in verses 39–52, as the psalmist explodes at the abrogation of the covenant when the monarchy ended. It appears that the psalmist is directly accusing God of violating His oath.

Rashi, Meiri, and Metzudat David attempt to mitigate the protest by inserting an admission of sin: "You have been meticulous with [David's] descendants to weigh their sins until You rejected and spurned them in the time of Zedekiah." From this point of view, the psalmist is shifting blame onto Israel, rather than accusing God. However, the flow of the psalm appears to militate against this reading. While the psalmist admits that sin would elicit punishment, the monarchy itself was supposed to endure:

> I will establish his line forever, his throne, as long as the heavens last. If his sons forsake My Teaching and do not live by My rules; if they violate My laws, and do not observe My commands, I will punish their transgression with the rod, their iniquity with plagues. But I will not take away My steadfast love from him; I will not betray My faithfulness. (Ps. 89:30–34)

Nevertheless, one can appreciate why these commentators reinterpreted the verses. The plain sense of the text is sharp indeed.

Those who accept the simplest reading must confront this challenge directly. Ibn Ezra (on 89:2) mentions a Spanish sage who considered this psalm blasphemous and therefore censored it: "In Spain, there was a great and pious sage, and this psalm was difficult for him. He would not read it, nor was he able to listen to it since the psalmist speaks sharply against God...." Ibn Ezra agrees that those verses are blasphemous, but he is unwilling to entertain the possibility that an inspired biblical psalmist would speak inappropriately. Therefore he asserts that the psalmist is quoting the words of the enemies of God who blaspheme.

Radak, in turn, censures the anonymous sage and Ibn Ezra:
> Many have expressed astonishment over how this psalmist could speak these words against God [he then quotes the anonymous sage and Ibn Ezra]....I am astonished by their astonishment, for the psalms were written through divine inspiration, and it is unthinkable that something in them is untrue! (Radak on 89:39)

Isaiah of Trani and Amos Hakham likewise consider these words to be of the psalmist. The words are religiously acceptable by definition, since they appear in the mouth of a divinely inspired writer. Providing a framework for these harsh words, Hakham quotes talmudic passages stating that the righteous do not flatter God. Rather, they stand honestly before their Creator, pouring out all their emotions.[5] Does this mean that everyone may emulate this style of prayer? That might be a matter of debate, as was discussed in the case of Habakkuk (and Honi). In practice, Jewish liturgy did not include this psalm.

GOD INSISTS ON TRUTH

Ever sensitive to minor nuances, the Talmud compares the formulations of four verses scattered throughout Tanakh:

For the Lord your God is God supreme and Lord supreme, the *great*, the *mighty*, and the *awesome* God. (Deut. 10:17)

O *great* and *mighty* God whose name is Lord of Hosts. (Jer. 32:18)

O Lord, *great* and *awesome* God, who stays faithful to His covenant with those who love Him and keep His commandments! (Dan. 9:4)

And now, our God, *great, mighty*, and *awesome* God, who stays faithful to His covenant. (Neh. 9:32)

Focusing on the fact that Moses had said "the great, the mighty, and the awesome God," the Sages recognized that Jeremiah and Daniel used only parts of that formulation and that the leaders of the prayer in Nehemiah 9 returned to Moses' complete formula. Midrashically, they posited the following reasoning behind this development:

Why were they called Men of the Great Assembly? Because they restored the crown of Divine attributes to its ancient completeness. Moses had said, "the great, the mighty, and the awesome God." Then Jeremiah came and said, Aliens are destroying His Temple! Where are His awesome deeds? Therefore he omitted "awesome." Daniel came and said, Aliens are enslaving

His sons. Where are His mighty deeds? Therefore he omitted "mighty." But they came and said, On the contrary! He performs mighty deeds by suppressing His wrath.... He performs awesome deeds, since were it not for the fear of Him, how could one nation persist among the nations! But how could [Jeremiah and Daniel] abolish something established by Moses? R. Eleazar said: Since they know that the Holy One, blessed be He, insists on truth, they would not ascribe false [things] to Him. (*Yoma* 69b)

This talmudic passage sensitively balances the tension of truthfulness and deferential respect before God. On the one hand, the Men of the Great Assembly are praised for their optimism and for restoring Moses' account of God's attributes to its original full form. Indeed, the Talmud gives them the final word, and the first benediction of the Amidah contains this complete formulation.[6] At the same time, however, the Talmud applauds the profound religious integrity of Jeremiah and Daniel.

Throughout biblical tradition, the lions of faith have challenged God – already beginning with Abraham and Moses:

Far be it from You to do such a thing, to bring death upon the innocent as well as the guilty, so that innocent and guilty fare alike. Far be it from You! Shall not the Judge of all the earth deal justly? (Gen. 18:25)

Now, if You will forgive their sin [well and good]; but if not, erase me from the record which You have written! (Exod. 32:32)

One talmudic passage captures the daring spirit of Moses' prayer:

R. Abbahu said: Were it not explicitly written, it would be impossible to say such a thing: this teaches that Moses took hold of the Holy One, blessed be He, like a man who seizes his fellow by his garment and said before Him: Sovereign of the Universe,

I will not let You go until You forgive and pardon them. (*Berakhot* 32a)

Whether to pray for the manifestation of God's justice, or to intervene on Israel's behalf, prophets and other biblical writers often spoke brazenly before God. Precisely our spiritual heroes—who generally must be emulated—are those who enjoyed the most intimate relationships with God, affording them a certain comfort level that may be too great for most people. The diversity of rabbinic responses to these and related prayers attests to the power of this paradox that likely never will be resolved.

NOTES

1. Rashi, Kara, and Metzudat David (on 3:1) adopt this midrashic reading. Abarbanel (on 2:4) also criticizes Habakkuk for speaking too sharply. For a survey of the dimmer views of Habakkuk's prayer, see Aron Pinker, "Was Habakkuk Presumptuous?" *Jewish Bible Quarterly* 32 (2004), pp. 27–34. As we will see below, there are indeed those who criticize Habakkuk for his prayer, but there are other means of responding as well.
2. Two pages later in the Talmud, there is further criticism of speaking brazenly before God: "Levi ordained a fast but no rain fell. He thereupon exclaimed: Master of the Universe, You went up and took Your seat on high and have no mercy upon Your children. Rain fell but he became lame. R. Eleazar said: Let a man never address himself in a reproachful manner towards God, seeing that one great man did so and he became lame, namely, Levi" (*Ta'anit* 25a).
3. Cf. Moshe Greenberg's assessment: "These heroes of faith have achieved a standing with God that ordinary mortals do not enjoy.... The situation of the ordinary mortal is quite different. With neither a vocation to God's service nor the heroism of these figures of legend, self-assertiveness and autonomy in relation to God would be considered presumptuous ... the storming of heaven by prophets hardly served as a model for the ordinary (or even the extraordinary) pious Israelite" ("On the Refinement of the

Conception of Prayer in Hebrew Scriptures," *Association for Jewish Studies Review* 1 [1976], p. 58).

4. Francis I. Andersen (*Anchor Bible: Habakkuk* [New York: Doubleday, 2001], p. 133) observes that there are no instances in Tanakh where God rebuked someone for questioning God's justice. In the Book of Job, God criticized Job's shortsightedness but vindicated his justness as well. It is worth noting that one psalmist does rebuke those who question God's ways (Ps. 94:8–10), and that type of rebuke is unique in Psalms.

5. Amos Hakham, *Da'at Mikra: Psalms* vol. 2 (Hebrew), (Jerusalem: Mossad HaRav Kook, 1979) pp. 156–157. See, for example, J.T. *Berakhot* 7:4 (11c); B.T. *Yoma* 69b.

6. Rabbi Binyamin Lau (*Hakhamim* vol. 1 [Hebrew] [Jerusalem: Eliner-Bet Morasha, 2006], pp. 36–37) explains that the Men of the Great Assembly taught that we are different from prophets. Prophets know God's ways so they can speak the truth as they perceive it. After prophecy ceased, the Men of the Great Assembly explained that absent prophecy, we cannot see or know how God works in this world. Our religious obligation is to use the Torah and tradition to pray to build a connection with God. The Torah uses the formulation "the *great,* the *mighty*, and the *awesome* God." This prayer will bind all generations.

THE DIFFERENCES BETWEEN
THE WISE AND THE FOOLISH IN PSALMS:
THEODICY, UNDERSTANDING PROVIDENCE,
AND RELIGIOUS RESPONSES*

INTRODUCTION

Happy is the man who has not followed the counsel of the wicked, or taken the path of sinners, or joined the company of the insolent; rather, the teaching of the Lord is his delight, and he studies that teaching day and night. He is like a tree planted beside streams of water, which yields its fruit in season, whose foliage never fades, and whatever it produces thrives. Not so the wicked; rather, they are like chaff that wind blows away. Therefore the wicked will not survive judgment, nor will sinners, in the assembly of the righteous. For the Lord cherishes the way of the righteous, but the way of the wicked is doomed. (Psalm 1)

Ultimately, one of the 150 psalms had to be chosen as the very first of the Book of Psalms. Aside from Psalm 1, several other psalms also are addressed to other people rather than to God (e.g., Psalms 4, 37, 49, 62). Nevertheless, it is interesting that the passage selected as Psalm 1 is not a prayer to God; it is wisdom from the psalmist to his audience. Most psalms express words of prayer to God.

Radak (on 1:1) maintains that the Book of Psalms begins with this proclamation of faith because of the centrality of the themes of

* This article appeared originally in the *Jewish Bible Quarterly* 38:3 (2010), pp. 157–165. Reprinted here with minor modifications, with permission from the *Jewish Bible Quarterly*, POB 29002, Jerusalem, Israel; www.jewishbible.org.

reward-punishment and divine providence: "In this psalm, David included the laws of man and what should happen to him in this world, i.e., the reward for the righteous and punishment for the wicked. This psalm is very exalted, and therefore he began his book with it." Belief in providence and justice is critical for prayer in general.

Amos Hakham suggests another reason for the primary position of Psalm 1: it is an exhortation—those approaching God must be righteous.[1] Nahum Sarna adds that Psalm 1 stresses Torah study, treating it as an act of profound worship in addition to prayer.[2] Thus Psalm 1 makes for an excellent opening to the Book of Psalms. It creates the religious foundation upon which many of the psalms are based.[3]

MANIFESTATIONS OF THIS EXPECTATION IN PSALMS

Many psalms are based on the assumption that the persecuted is righteous and therefore worthy of salvation. To cite two examples:

He brought me out to freedom; He rescued me because He was pleased with me. The Lord rewarded me according to my merit; He requited the cleanness of my hands; for I have kept to the ways of the Lord, and have not been guilty before my God; for I am mindful of all His rules; I have not disregarded His laws. I have been blameless toward Him, and have guarded myself against sinning; and the Lord has requited me according to my merit, the cleanness of my hands in His sight. (18:20–25)

Preserve my life, for I am steadfast; O You, my God, deliver Your servant who trusts in You. Have mercy on me, O Lord, for I call to You all day long. (86:2–3)

Amos Hakham suggests that the psalmists are not bragging about their righteousness so much as teaching that even a divinely chosen king is obligated to remain faithful to God.[4] However, the psalmists are not boasting about themselves; they are praying or thanking God for manifesting justice in the world.

Psalm 37 is concerned with people becoming demoralized by the success of the wicked and the suffering of the righteous: "Do not be vexed by evil men; do not be incensed by wrongdoers; for they soon wither like grass, like verdure fade away" (37:1). Like Psalm 1, Psalm 37 argues that the wealth and success of the wicked is illusory. The tone of these two psalms is notably different, though. Psalm 1 is a confident proclamation of faith, whereas Psalm 37 expresses concern with what many people think and the need to defend the traditional belief system.

Strikingly, Psalm 37 appeals to personal observation to verify its thesis: "I have been young and am now old, but I have never seen a righteous man abandoned, or his children seeking bread" (37:25). Could it be that the psalmist never saw the righteous suffer? Many commentators cannot accept this statement at face value. Ibn Ezra, Radak, and Meiri modify the verse by maintaining that the righteous are never *totally* abandoned. These commentators argue for some poetic flexibility as they attempt to bridge the literal reading of the verse with actual human experience.

Similarly, some commentators struggle with some of the sweeping formulations in Psalm 107:

Some lived in deepest darkness, bound in cruel irons, because they defied the word of God, spurned the counsel of the Most High. He humbled their hearts through suffering; they stumbled with no one to help. (107:10–12)

There were fools who suffered for their sinful way, and for their iniquities. All food was loathsome to them; they reached the gates of death. (107:17–18)

According to the literal reading of these verses, all prison terms and illnesses are attributed to sinful behavior. Rashi and Ibn Ezra therefore explain that anyone who is ill is called a fool (v. 17), since by definition he or she must have sinned. However, Ibn Ezra (on 107:11, 42) modifies this principle with regard to prison sentences:

most people who are in prison must have sinned, but it is possible that some have not and are being unjustly punished.

On 107:17, Radak explains the verse differently: "Had they been wise, they would think: why has God sent this illness upon us? ...But fools are insensitive to this matter, and do not repent until their illness becomes very great." According to Radak, the difference between wise people and fools is not that wise people never get ill whereas fools do. Rather, wise people who get ill utilize their illness as a religious opportunity for introspection and repentance, whereas fools do not. Thus Radak frames the contrast between the wise and fools primarily as one of religious response, not as a guarantee of a higher quality of life for the righteous.

Perhaps the most unusual response to the suffering of the righteous is found in Psalm 94: "Happy is the man whom You discipline, O Lord, the man You instruct in Your teaching" (94:12). Rather than calling upon his audience to wait patiently for ultimate justice, or insisting that the righteous never suffer, this psalmist views suffering as a sign of divine favor.[5]

Moreover, the psalmist in 94 is unique in his rebuke of those who do not fully trust in God's supervision and fairness: "Take heed, you most brutish people; fools, when will you get wisdom? Shall He who implants the ear not hear, He who forms the eye not see? Shall He who disciplines nations not punish, He who instructs men in knowledge?" (94:8–10). In contrast, other psalmists do not fault those who question God's justice; they simply attempt to answer their doubts.

To summarize the main approaches to conflicts with the beliefs set out in Psalm 1 and the commentators' responses:

1. There are no conflicts, and wise people can perceive justice all the time (37:25, 107:11).

2. In the end, all will be righted, so be patient (Psalm 1, 37). Psalm 37 explains this principle to a doubting audience; Psalm 94 rebukes those who doubt God's justice.

3. The principles of justice always work, and therefore one may pray to God to apply them, or thank God after they are applied (18:20–25; 86:2–3).

4. Suffering may be a sign of God's love rather than punishment (94:12).

And two modifications of the commentators:

5. The principles of justice apply *most* of the time (Ibn Ezra, Radak, Meiri on 37:25; Ibn Ezra on 107:11).

6. The wise use their suffering as a religious opportunity to reach out to God and to introspect, whereas fools abandon faith (Radak on 107:11).

THE CONCERNS OF PSALMISTS

Although the principles underlying Psalm 1 are affirmed by many of the psalmists, some are confronted with spiritual struggle. For example, Psalm 39 opens with a raging internal battle as the psalmist attempts to restrain himself:

I resolved I would watch my step lest I offend by my speech; I would keep my mouth muzzled while the wicked man was in my presence. I was dumb, silent; I was very still while my pain was intense. My mind was in a rage, my thoughts were all aflame; I spoke out. (Ps. 39:2–4)

Amos Hakham explains that although the psalmist started by trying to control himself, he eventually spoke out and did not conclude with any theological resolution. However, he remains steadfastly devoted to God through his suffering, praying that God eliminate his torments.[6]

Perhaps the most remarkable prayer in this regard is Psalm 73, which presents the psalmist's struggle:

As for me, my feet had almost strayed, my steps were nearly led off course, for I envied the wanton; I saw the wicked at ease.... It was for nothing that I kept my heart pure and washed my hands in innocence, seeing that I have been constantly afflicted, that each morning brings new punishments. Had I decided to say these things, I should have been false to the circle of Your disciples. So I applied myself to understand this, but it seemed a hopeless task till I entered God's sanctuary and reflected on their fate. (73:2–17)

This psalmist portrays himself as one who almost lost his faith as a result of his witnessing the success of the wicked and enduring his own suffering.[7] Not until he entered God's sanctuary were his difficulties resolved (v. 17).[8] He proceeds with the same response as in Psalms 1, 37, and others: the wicked ultimately will meet their sudden doom (73:18–20).

Unlike those psalms that use patience as a resolution, however, Psalm 73 continues: "My mind was stripped of its reason, my feelings were numbed. I was a dolt, without knowledge; I was brutish toward You" (73:21–22). Though he had reached a response in verses 17–20, the psalmist breaks chronological boundaries with this flashback, indicating an ongoing religious struggle. It also is noteworthy that this conclusion was not obvious to this psalmist as it is to those of Psalms 1 and 37. He needed to enter God's sanctuary after reaching a state of near-despair.

The conclusion of Psalm 73 suggests a different contrast between the wise and foolish:

Yet I was always with You, You held my right hand; You guided me by Your counsel and led me toward honor. Whom else have I in heaven? And having You, I want no one on earth. My body and mind fail; but God is the stay of my mind, my portion forever. Those who keep far from You perish; You annihilate all who are untrue to You. As for me, nearness to God is good; I have made the Lord God my refuge, that I may recount all Your works. (73:23–28)

The psalmist concludes that he is close to God (v. 23) whereas the wicked are far away from Him (v. 27). The success of the wicked may be short-lived, but that is not the main resolution of Psalm 73. Instead, the psalmist ultimately uses his suffering and theological torment as an opportunity to draw closer to God.[9]

Rather than viewing this psalm as exceptional, one midrash contends that Psalm 73 contains the true essence of the Book of Psalms: "I was a dolt, without knowledge, etc. (73:22): This should have been the beginning of the Book, but there is no chronological order in the Torah" (*Ecc. Rabbah* 1:12). Instead of the confident declaration of faith in Psalm 1, the Sages of this midrash appear to have considered the struggle of Psalm 73 to be central to the religious nature of Psalms. The response of the wise contrasts with that of the fool, even if both might live the same successful—or tormented—lifestyles. However, the wise do not necessarily perceive justice any more than fools do.[10]

This tension between the potential primacy of Psalm 1 or Psalm 73 is captured poignantly by Radak's comments on Psalm 92:

How great are Your works, O Lord, how very subtle Your designs! A brutish man cannot know, a fool cannot understand this: though the wicked sprout like grass, though all evildoers blossom, it is only that they may be destroyed forever. But You are exalted, O Lord, for all time. (92:6–9)

Typically, these verses are understood as contrasting the wise and fools. Wise people have patience, confident that the success of the wicked is illusory. In contrast, fools do not understand this truth (Rashi, Amos Hakham). Radak, however, struggles with the flow of these verses and their underlying religious implications:

Subtle Your designs: the reasons for difficult matters in this world were not revealed to the wise... *A brutish man*: this verse may be connected to [the verse] above or [the verse] below. If above, then its interpretation is thus....Every man is a fool (*ish—ba'ar lo yeda*), who cannot know this, i.e., to understand Your designs. If below, it will be explained thus: *A brutish man cannot know—though the wicked sprout like grass*, i.e., why they succeed in this world. However, the wise understand that *they may be destroyed forever*....One also may interpret the verse as even relating to what is below, yet its meaning is the same as the first interpretation: Every man is a fool and does not understand the success of the wicked in this world nor the suffering of the righteous in this world; for even though he said that *they may be destroyed forever*...there remain difficult questions on this matter. Our Sages (*Berakhot* 7a) have said that even Moses our Teacher did not understand. (Radak on 92:6–9)

Thus Radak is unsure if 92:7 should be translated as "A brutish man cannot know"—whereas the wise man does know; or whether "man is a brute and cannot know," that is, *no* man—not even Moses our Teacher—can fathom the success of the wicked. This ambiguity resembles the tension between Psalm 1 and Psalm 73 as theoretical competitors for the primary position in the Book of Psalms. Specifically when reading verses that appear to contrast the knowledge of the fools with that of the wise, Radak suggests that all people are fools when it comes to understanding God's ways.

CONCLUSION

There are two poles depicted within the Book of Psalms. Sometimes the wise person clearly understands God's ways whereas the fool does not. At other times, nobody—not even the psalmist—understands. Sometimes it is assumed that the righteous person necessarily will live a happier life than the wicked, at least in the long run; at other times nobody can perceive this justice.

Yet there consistently remain two differences between the wise and the fool in Psalms. One is how they respond to conflicts between religious principle and perceived reality. Because of unfairness in this world, the wicked abandon God: "The benighted man thinks, 'God does not care'" (14:1). In contrast, the righteous develop their relationship with God, sometimes by remaining steadfast in their belief that everything must ultimately be fair, and sometimes by protesting or pleading. Whatever their response, they create a dynamic connection to God. "Yet I was always with You" (73:23), proclaims the troubled psalmist. The second is that the wise continually move back to the beliefs set out in Psalm 1, whereas fools despair of God's ultimate justice.

Psalms offer various ways of approaching God in all situations, good and bad. These matters, of course, reach far beyond the simple meaning of verses in the Book of Psalms—they shape the very nature of prayer and religious experience.

NOTES

1. Amos Hakham, *Da'at Mikra: Psalms* vol. 1 (Hebrew), (Jerusalem: Mossad HaRav Kook, 1979), pp. 5–6.

2. Nahum Sarna, *On the Book of Psalms: Exploring the Prayers of Ancient Israel* (New York: Schocken Books, 1993), pp. 26–29.

3. It is worth noting that the aforementioned commentators offer their explanations based on the current canonical form of the Psalms. However, the Talmud (*Berakhot* 9b–10a) suggests that Psalms 1–2 were initially combined. Notwithstanding, the Book of Psalms' introduction with its opening verses still may be interpreted along the lines of Radak, Hakham, and Sarna.

4. Amos Hakham, *Da'at Mikra: Psalms* vol. 1, pp. 85–87, 95–96.

5. Cf. Deut. 8:5: "Bear in mind that the Lord your God disciplines you just as a man disciplines his son." Eliphaz appeals to this argument as well: "See how happy is the man whom God reproves; Do not reject the discipline of the Almighty" (Job 5:17). Cf. *Berakhot* 5b, which maintains that it is a daily occurrence that some people suffer without sin.

6. Amos Hakham, *Da'at Mikra: Psalms* vol. 1, p. 227.

7. Amos Hakham (*Da'at Mikra: Psalms* vol. 2, p. 10) suggests that the

psalmist may be speaking autobiographically, but it also is possible that he is speaking as a sage describing the experience of many.

8. Amos Hakham (*Da'at Mikra: Psalms* vol. 2, p. 6) interprets this verse to mean that by coming to the Temple precincts, the psalmist met with sages and prophets, who taught him the proper response.

9. See further discussion of this psalm and its theological implications in J. Clinton McCann, Jr., "Psalm 73: A Microcosm of Old Testament Theology," in *The Listening Heart: Essays in Wisdom and the Psalms in honor of Roland E. Murphy*, Kenneth G. Hoglund et al. (eds.) (Sheffield: JSOT Press, 1987), pp. 247–257.

10. It might also be significant that Psalm 73 begins the third collection of Psalms, and thus the second half of Psalms. If so, the very structure of the book may waver between the confidence of Psalm 1, which begins the first half; and the uncertainty of Psalm 73, which begins the second half. Cf. Walter Brueggemann & Patrick D. Miller, "Psalm 73 as a Canonical Marker," *JSOT* 72 (1996), pp. 45-56. It must be stressed, however, that it is impossible to ascertain the underlying purposes of the current canonical arrangement of the Psalms, and therefore this suggestion belongs to the realm of intriguing speculation.

A WOMAN OF VALOR HAS BEEN FOUND: RUTH AMIDST A SEA OF AMBIGUITY*

INTRODUCTION

Simple glass reflects the beam of light that shines on it only once. A precious gem, in contrast, reflects different sparks with its many facets; a single beam of light that shines on it is reflected and is returned to us greatly enhanced. (Feivel Meltzer)[1]

We may use this analogy as a guide for understanding a literary gem, Megillat Ruth. Seldom do we come across such an ideal society, characterized by *hesed* (loyalty, loving-kindness), heroes, and no villains. At worst, there are average characters such as Orpah, Boaz's foreman, and So-and-so who serve as foils to highlight the greatness of Naomi, Boaz, and Ruth.[2] R. Ze'ira's classic statement captures the essence of the Megillah:

R. Zei'ra said: This scroll [of Ruth] tells us nothing either of cleanliness or of uncleanliness, either of prohibition or permission. For what purpose then was it written? To teach how great is the reward of those who do deeds of kindness. (*Ruth Rabbah* 2:14)

---

* An abridged version of this article appeared in *The Jewish Bible Quarterly* 33:2 (2005), pp. 91–99, entitled "A Midrashic View of Ruth amidst a Sea of Ambiguity," and was reprinted in Angel, *Through an Opaque Lens* (New York: Sephardic Publication Foundation, 2006), pp. 296–306. This expanded version was published in *Shabuot Reader* (New York: Tebah Educational Services, 2009), pp. 103–117, and is reprinted here with permission of the editors.

Although it appears that *hesed* is the predominant theme of our megillah, there is considerably less clarity over how to define that *hesed*, or what other religious lessons emanate from the text of Megillat Ruth. Which characters truly epitomize R. Ze'ira's statement? What is the relationship between divine providence and human *hesed*? Additionally, what is the connection between Megillat Ruth and the period of the Judges?

In an article on the syntactic ambiguity of Ruth 2:20, Mordechai Cohen sets out two criteria for ascertaining deliberate ambiguities in a biblical text: (1) one must establish the cogency of two separate readings; (2) one must demonstrate how the ambiguity contributes to the literary context by expressing something that could not be expressed in unambiguous language.[3] Taking this argument to a different level, one might contend that much in Megillat Ruth fits these criteria.

Many elements that initially appear clear are more elusive after further scrutiny. Rather than limiting ourselves to one side or another, it is preferable to see how these viewpoints can coexist. By doing so, one stands to gain a more comprehensive understanding of the text and its messages. This essay will consider some of the major issues of the Megillah with an eye toward its overall purposes.

THE FIRST FIVE VERSES: PUNISHMENT FOR SINS?

Some midrashim and later commentators contend that Elimelech and his sons deserved their respective deaths. Elimelech left the Land of Israel[4] and a starving community behind,[5] while his sons lingered in Moab and intermarried.[6]

Perhaps the juxtaposition of Elimelech's leaving and his death and the juxtaposition of the sons' intermarriages and their deaths suggest these conclusions. However, there is a ten-year gap between the sons' marrying Moabites and their deaths. By including the lengthy time separating the two events, the Megillah appears to exclude intermarriage as a direct cause of their deaths.[7] We also are not told how long Elimelech remained in Moab before he died. Additionally,

Abraham also left during a famine in Canaan (Gen. 12), and most commentators there justify his behavior.[8] Should Elimelech and his family be held to a higher standard of faith than Abraham?[9]

These uncertainties yield at least three possible lines of interpretation:

1. *Elimelech, Mahlon, and Chilion simply died:* They legitimately left during a famine. Ibn Ezra (on 1:2, 15) insists that Ruth and Orpah converted prior to their marriages to Elimelech's sons. These verses are primarily background setting the stage for the main story of Naomi, Ruth, and Boaz, and should not be understood as punishment for sins.

2. *This story is parallel to Job:* Like Job, Naomi first complained about her God-given lot (1:20–21) but was happy at the end of the narrative. The deaths and suffering at the outset of Ruth are theologically significant, but the reader is not told how.

Unlike the Book of Job, however, where God's direct involvement is discussed in the beginning and end of the book, in Ruth it is not. Additionally, the characters in Megillat Ruth played an active role in changing their fate, whereas Job did not. It is unclear whether Megillat Ruth was intended to parallel the Book of Job or whether the two books should be contrasted, with Ruth's characters held responsible for their original suffering and credited for their eventual happiness.[10]

3. *This is a story of sin/punishment and then hesed/reward:* Unlike Abraham, Elimelech and his family left a starving community behind. The unwarranted lingering of Mahlon and Chilion in Moab led them to intermarry. Likewise, the happy ending of Megillat Ruth may be viewed as God's reward for everyone's *hesed* over the course of the story.

Does the text yield a sin/punishment conclusion? This reading is possible, but no more compelling than a non-sin/punishment reading. This uncertainty encapsulates our difficulty in pinpointing any one specific interpretation of the ephemeral characters in the opening verses of Megillat Ruth.

NAOMI

Was Naomi a passive follower of her husband, or an active participant in the abandonment of the community (assuming that there *was* anything negative about their leaving!)? Midrashim address both sides of the question:

> He was the prime mover and his wife secondary to him, and his two sons secondary to both of them. (*Ruth Rabbah* 1:5)[11]

> Why did the text mention him, his wife, and his children? To teach that all of them were stingy. (*Ruth Zuta* 1:2)

From the text, it is difficult to determine whether Naomi did anything wrong, if she was an innocent victim of her family members' sins, or if she was a victim of the unexplained deaths of her family members. The motives behind Naomi's efforts to persuade her daughters-in-law to remain in Moab also remain elusive. Although Naomi emphasized the marital prospects of Ruth and Orpah (in 1:8–15), it is possible that she was driven by other considerations as well:

> R. Shemuel b. Nahmani said in the name of R. Yehudah b. Hanina: Three times is it written here "turn back," corresponding to the three times that a would-be proselyte is repulsed; but if he persists after that, he is accepted. (*Ruth Rabbah* 2:16)

> Why did Naomi want to return them? So that she would not be embarrassed by them. We find that there were ten markets in Jerusalem, and they [i.e., the classes of people who shopped at each] never intermingled....The people were recognized by their clothing—what one class wore, another would not. (*Ruth Zuta* 1:8)

Ruth Rabbah 2:16 casts Naomi as unwilling to compromise Jewish religious standards. This view receives textual support from Naomi's observation that Orpah's return to Moab came with religious consequences as well: "So she said, 'See, your sister-in-law has returned to her people *and her gods*. Go follow your sister-in-law'" (1:15; cf. Ibn Ezra, Malbim).

In contrast, *Ruth Zuta* 1:8 depicts a less flattering aspect of Naomi. Her professed concern for the welfare of her Moabite daughters-in-law cloaked a desire to protect her own noble self-image in Judean society. The inordinate emphasis on Ruth as a "Moabite" (seven times in this tiny megillah!) could support this reading as well.

Despite the potentially complex nature of her generosity, Naomi certainly emerged successful by the end of the narrative. She had her estate redeemed by Boaz; she was the toast of the town; and Ruth's son was born into the family. How might one view this happy ending?

It appears that there are several textually valid readings of Naomi's character:

1. *Hesed*: Who could ask for a better mother-in-law than Naomi? Bereft of her husband and sons, with only Ruth and Orpah to comfort her, Naomi was more concerned with their welfare than with tending to her own loneliness. Moreover, Naomi never stopped caring for Ruth, helping her find security via matrimony. We may add the midrashic idealism in Naomi's concern with the religious conversion issues associated with taking them back with her to Israel. As a consequence of her *hesed*, God rewarded Naomi at the end of the Megillah with family, friends, and land (4:14–17).

2. *More self-centered:* Although Naomi always verbally expressed interest in her daughters-in-law, she really was more concerned for herself. She joined her family in being stingy, abandoning her community. She wanted to drive her Moabite daughters-in-law away because they would harm her social status upon return. Naomi knew she could benefit from Boaz's intervention; therefore, she orchestrated the encounter between Boaz and Ruth to help herself. Fittingly, the narrative concludes with Naomi's happiness—she took the child and had the blessings of her friends along with her land. Ruth is only a tangential figure in the Megillah's climactic frame.[12]

3. *Naomi is similar to Job:* she suffered without any explanation, complained against God, and then was restored in the end:

She said to them, Call me not Naomi; call me Mara; for the Almighty has dealt very bitterly with me (*ki hemar Shaddai li me'od*). (Ruth 1:20)

As God lives, who has taken away my judgment; and the Almighty, who has tormented my soul (*ve-Shaddai hemar nafshi*). (Job 27:2)

Although Naomi used similar language to that of Job, possibly indicating that she viewed herself as suffering unjustly, the narrator remains conspicuously noncommittal as to whether or not Naomi's story parallels that of Job.

4. *Complexity:* Naomi was concerned with herself, and also for Ruth. One might view the happy ending either as a consequence of Naomi's and the other characters' actions, or as a providential reward for her goodness. This view combines the above explanations, and each layer of motivation appears to be simultaneously sustained by the text.

BOAZ

Boaz was a hero. He protected Ruth from harassment (2:9, 15) and helped her in other ways unbeknownst to Ruth (2:15–17). He provided sustenance for Naomi (3:15), completed the redemption of Naomi's field, and married Ruth (3:18–4:10). Boaz deserves praise for overcoming the anti-Moabite biases of Judean society.

However, Boaz allowed Ruth to glean for approximately three months (cf. *Ruth Rabbah* 5:11) and needed prodding from Naomi and Ruth before he took more substantial action. Why didn't he help earlier, especially given his awareness of Ruth's character and outstanding accomplishments (2:11–12)?

Perhaps the Moabite issue figures decisively in answering that question. But was Ruth's background a legitimate cause for delay, or an excuse for inaction? Once confronted with Ruth at the threshing floor, Boaz acknowledged that everyone knew Ruth to be an *eshet hayil* (woman of valor) and that she *did* have other marital options within that society (3:10–11). More significantly, the Moabite excuse could explain Boaz's possible reluctance to marry Ruth; but how do we justify his allowing her to glean in his field for so long? As Feivel Meltzer observes (on 2:8 n. 20), "it is impossible to understand adequately why Boaz did not see it fit to visit the widows and attend their needs."

Sensitive to these cues, some midrashim cast Boaz as one who acted kindly only when he knew he would receive something in return:

R. Yitzhak commented: The Torah teaches you that when a person performs a good deed he should do so with a cheerful heart....If Boaz had known that the Holy One, blessed be He, would have it written of him that he 'Gave her parched corn' (2:14), he would have given her fatted calves! (*Lev. Rabbah* 34:8)

Rabbah, son of R. Huna, said in the name of Rav: Ibzan is Boaz. What does he come to teach us [by this statement]?...Boaz made for his sons a hundred and twenty wedding feasts, for it is said, And he [Ibzan] had thirty sons, and thirty daughters he sent abroad, and thirty daughters he brought in from abroad for his sons; and he judged Israel seven years (Jud. 12:9); and in the case of every one [of these] he made two wedding feasts, one in the house of the father and one in the house of the father-in-law. To none of them did he invite Manoah, [for] he said, 'Whereby will the barren mule repay me?' All these died in his lifetime. (*Bava Batra* 91a)

Boaz spoke more than any other figure in the Megillah (21 verses for him, 17 for Naomi, 11 for Ruth). These midrashim perceived that his flowery talking did not fully match his actions.

To summarize: Boaz certainly is a paragon of *hesed*. At the same time, however, some midrashim view Boaz's *hesed* as insufficient and motivated at least partially by his own interests. Both lines of interpretation are simultaneously supported by the text.

DIVINE–HUMAN CONTINUUM IN MEGILLAT RUTH

There is an apparent ambiguity in 2:20:

Naomi said to her daughter-in-law, "Blessed is he to the Lord, who has not abandoned His kindness with the living and with the dead."

or

Naomi said to her daughter-in-law, "Blessed to the Lord is he who has not abandoned his kindness with the living and with the dead."[13]

It is unclear whether Naomi acknowledged God for orchestrating the upward turn of events, or whether she blessed Boaz for his efforts in treating Ruth well and for his potential as a redeemer. Mordechai Cohen views this verse as intentionally ambiguous, highlighting the complex relationship between human and divine action in Megillat Ruth. This ambiguity runs through all of the Megillah, as it often is unclear where human initiative stops and God's intervention begins.

While Boaz blessed Ruth by saying that God should reward her for coming under His wings (*tahat kenafav*, 2:12), Ruth eventually realized that nothing would get done unless Boaz actively spread his "wings" over Ruth (*u-parastah kenafekha al amatekha*, 3:9). Earlier, Naomi had prayed that God grant marital security (*menuhah*) to her daughters-in-law (1:9); but she ultimately had to orchestrate the threshing floor scene to provide that security (*mano'ah*) for Ruth (3:1). One might view the happy ending as a consequence of the concerted actions of the characters. It is equally possible to view the human actions as mirroring God's plan—the divine blessings people had wished on one another had been realized.

It is noteworthy that the only two times the narrator explicitly mentions God's involvement are with the end of the famine (1:6), and Ruth's getting pregnant (4:13). This omission leaves the extent of God's involvement subject to speculation. Does the Megillah teach that God "withdrew" Himself to allow greater human action, or does it reveal God's providential hand constantly assisting these paragons of *hesed*?

THE RELATIONSHIP BETWEEN RUTH AND JUDGES

The opening verse of Megillat Ruth connects the narrative to the period of the Judges. What is the connection between the Dark Age of Judges and the display of *hesed* in Megillat Ruth, where the Judeans were religiously faithful and kind to one another?

R. Yisrael Rozen suggests that the root cause of the failure during the period of Judges was that people were too self-centered. Shiloh—the home of the Tabernacle at that time— plays an insignificant role in Judges and is mentioned only twice in passing (Jud. 18:31; 21:19), symptomatic of the lack of unity during that period. R. Rozen observes that in Judges, the word *hesed* appears only twice, and both in negative contexts. In Judges 1:24 the tribe of Joseph asks a Canaanite to do them *hesed* by betraying his countrymen and revealing the entrance to Bethel. In Judges 8:35 the Israelites are said *not* to have done *hesed* to Gideon's family after his death. In the tiny Book of Ruth, in contrast, the word *hesed* appears three times and plays a central role (1:8; 2:20; 3:10).[14]

Is Megillat Ruth a contrast to the period of the Judges, or an organic component of that period? The Megillah does not offer greater precision in dating the narrative than that it occurred in the period of the Judges—a period spanning centuries. Some midrashim link Ruth to the time of the earlier judges,[15] while others identify Boaz with the later judge Ibzan (Jud. 12:8).[16] Malbim, however, suggests a literary interpretation: since the story of Ruth is not dated precisely, the story may be viewed as representative of the entire period.

How Megillat Ruth is representative of the period of the Judges, however, remains problematic. Malbim asserts that Megillat Ruth parallels the negativity of Judges. The opening verses demonstrate that people were concerned primarily for themselves, and this self-ishness was characteristic of the period. According to Malbim, Me-gillat Ruth's connection to the period of Judges is limited primarily to its opening verses. In contrast, the remainder of Megillat Ruth is characterized by *hesed.*

Alternatively, one might argue that Megillat Ruth is characteristic of the period, but in a more complex manner. Most people were good, or at least average. However, the unwillingness of tribes and individuals to help one another demonstrates a general lack of *hesed.* People helped others primarily when they could gain something themselves. The Gemara (*Bava Batra* 91a) cited earlier regarding Boaz—one of the great figures of that era—captures this theme. Boaz certainly demonstrated *hesed*; but the Gemara accuses even this hero of not inviting Samson's father Manoah to his children's wedding feasts since he would never get a reciprocal invitation. To remedy this societal problem, and to break out from the cycle of the period, they needed an outsider like Ruth to teach them what true *hesed* was. One midrash captures this message:

> God said: may Ruth, who is a convert, and who did not chal-lenge her mother-in-law—come and rebuke Israel who has re-belled against Me. (*Ruth Zuta* 1:7)

This midrash looks beneath the surface reading of Megillat Ruth, where the Judeans are not depicted as "rebels." Rather, the midrash forges an intimate connection between Megillat Ruth and Judges and determines the root problem inherent in Israel's society to be consistent with R. Rozen's characterization of that period.

CONCLUSION

There is one character in this Megillah who is less ambiguous than the others: Ruth. Ruth reflects genuine *hesed.* She sacrificed heroically to accompany Naomi and to accept God. Ruth is compared to Abraham in leaving her family to serve God:

> The Lord said to Abram, "Go forth from your native land and from your father's house to the land that I will show you. I will make of you a great nation, and I will bless you; I will make your name great, and you shall be a blessing." (Gen. 12:1–2)

> Boaz said in reply [to Ruth], "I have been told of all that you did for your mother-in-law after the death of your husband, how you left your father and mother and the land of your birth and came to a people you had not known before." (Ruth 2:11)

Through this comparison, one might argue that Ruth is portrayed even more favorably than Abraham. God had spoken directly to Abraham and promised him reward. In contrast, Ruth came voluntarily and hardly could have expected anything but a lifetime of begging and discrimination in return for her sacrifices. Ruth also declined marriage opportunities with younger Judeans in order to marry Boaz to preserve Mahlon's name.

Ruth lived in a world where ambiguity was pervasive. The extent of God's intervention in her suffering and salvation is unclear, and so are the motivations of the members of the society on whom she depended. Nevertheless, she remained steadfast in her commitment to Naomi, Mahlon, and God. Ruth has the distinction of being the *only* biblical woman explicitly called by the epithet *eshet hayil* (woman of valor, 3:11). While Ruth struggled mightily to preserve Mahlon's name, she in fact has immortalized her own name, winning the hearts of readers generation after generation.

Megillat Ruth is characterized by deliberate ambiguity. Not only are multiple readings possible; these ambiguities are precisely the vehicles through which the short narrative captures so many subtleties in so short a space. These complexities guide readers to delve more deeply into the Megillah and recognize the religious implications for their own lives.

NOTES

1. *Da'at Mikra: Ruth*, in *Five Megillot* (Hebrew) (Jerusalem: Mossad Ha-Rav Kook, 1973), introduction p. 3 n. 1.
2. See especially Meltzer, introduction to *Da'at Mikra: Ruth*, p. 8; Moshe Garsiel, "Literary Structure, Development of Plot, and the Goal of the Narrator in Megillat Ruth" (Hebrew), in *Hagut ba-Mikra*, vol. 3, ed. E. Menahem (Tel Aviv: Israel Society for Biblical Research, 1979), pp. 66–83.
3. Mordechai Cohen, "*Hesed*: Divine or Human? The Syntactic Ambiguity of Ruth 2:20," in *Hazon Nahum: Studies in Jewish Law, Thought, and History Presented to Dr. Norman Lamm*, ed. Yaakov Elman and Jeffrey S. Gurock (Hoboken, NJ: KTAV, 1997), pp. 11–38, esp. pp. 32–33.
4. See *Bava Batra* 91a; *Gen. Rabbah* 25:3; Rashi (on 1:2), Meltzer, *Da'at Mikra*.
5. See *Ruth Rabbah* 1:4; *Tanhuma Behar* 3; *Zohar Hadash Ruth* 77b; Rashi (on 1:2).
6. See *Ruth Rabbah* 2:9; Rashi (on 1:12), Malbim (on 1:4), who maintain that Ruth and Orpah did not convert prior to their marriages to Mahlon and Kilyon. Ibn Ezra (on 1:2, 15) disagrees, as does *Zohar Hadash Ruth* 79a. Rambam (*Hilkhot Melakhim* 5:9) maintains that the family members were punished because they were communal leaders and therefore held to a higher standard of conduct. Malbim adopts a middle position: the initial departure of Elimelech and family was justified, since they went only as a temporary measure (*la-gur*); once they elected to stay permanently, however (*va-yeshevu sham*), they brought punishment upon themselves.
7. Sensitive to this difficulty, *Tanhuma Buber Behar* 8 states: "For those ten years, God was warning them. When He saw that they were not repenting, He began to strike their camels and cattle—yet they still did not repent. When He saw that they did not repent, immediately (!) 'Mahlon and Chilion died also.'" See also *Ruth Zuta* 1:4: "This teaches that decrees are suspended for ten years." Of course, without these modifications, the text is far less clear in presenting their deaths as punishment.
8. According to the majority opinion, the Torah teaches that in the absence of explicit prophetic instructions, one may not depend on supernatural intervention in times of crisis. See, for example, *Pesahim* 8b; *Kiddushin*

39b; *Bava Kamma* 60b; *Hullin* 142a. For further sources, see *Encyclopedia Talmudit*, vol. 1, s.v. *"en somekhin al ha-nes,"* pp. 679–681. For elaboration on Ramban's dissenting position, see David Berger, "Miracles and the Natural Order in Nahmanides," in *Rabbi Moshe Nahmanides (Ramban): Explorations in His Religious and Literary Virtuosity*, ed. Isadore Twersky (Cambridge, MA: Harvard University, Center for Jewish Studies, 1983), pp. 107–128.

9. It should be noted, however, that the rest of the Bethlehemites remained at home and survived the famine while Elimelech left with his family. In contrast, Abraham brought his whole family to Egypt rather than leaving others behind.

10. See further discussion in R. Amnon Bazak, "The World Is Built on *Hesed*: Between Megillat Ruth and Job" (Hebrew), *Megadim* 18–19 (1993), pp. 169–175.

11. Cf. Rashi, Malbim.

12. The dialogue in chapter 4 intimates that Boaz considered Naomi's field to be the primary element in the redemption altogether; Ruth is mentioned only in passing (4:3, 9–10). Ezra Z. Melammed ("Megillat Ruth in Light of the Halakhah" [Hebrew], *Sinai* 24 [1961], p. 156) maintains that Ruth was the more important aspect of the deal, but Boaz emphasized the field out of respect for Ruth.

13. See the survey of opinions on this verse in Mordechai Cohen, *"Hesed*: Divine or Human? The Syntactic Ambiguity of Ruth 2:20," pp. 11–38. The above translations are from his article, pp. 11–12.

14. R. Yisrael Rozen, "The Days When the Judges Judged: Generations of Vanity" (Hebrew), in *El Asher Telekhi: Studies in Megillat Ruth, Memorial Volume for the Fallen Soldier, Ariel Reviv, of Blessed Memory*, ed. Elisha Buchreis (Jerusalem: Ketav va-Sefer, 2002), pp. 159–177.

15. *Ruth Rabbah* 1:1; *Seder Olam Rabbah* 12; cf. *Makkot* 23a.

16. *Bava Batra* 91a.

PESHAT AND *DERASH*
IN MEGILLAT ESTHER*

INTRODUCTION

Elisha ben Avuyah said: one who learns as a child, to what is he compared? To ink written upon a new writing sheet; and one who learns [when] old, to what is he compared? To ink written upon an erased writing sheet. (Avot 4:20)

Megillat Esther is among the most difficult biblical books to study anew, precisely because it is so familiar. Many assumptions accompany us through our study of the Megillah, occasionally clouding our perceptions of what is in the text and what is not.

Any serious study of the *peshat* messages of the Megillah must begin with a clear sense of what is explicitly in the text, what can be inferred legitimately from the text, and what belongs primarily in a thematic exposition, using the text as a springboard for important religious concepts. This essay will consider some pertinent examples from Megillat Esther.

PESHAT CONSIDERATIONS IN THE MEGILLAH
A. THE SAUL–AGAG REMATCH

On five occasions in the Megillah, Haman is called an "Agagite."[1] Several early traditions consider this appellation a reference to Ha-

* An earlier version of this article appeared as a Review Essay of *Hadassah Hi Esther* in *Tradition* 34:4 (Winter 2000), pp. 79–97 and was reprinted in Angel, *Through an Opaque Lens* (New York: Sephardic Publication Foundation, 2006), pp. 307–330. This modified version was published in *Purim Reader* (New York: Tebah Educational Services, 2009), pp. 59–76, and is reprinted here with permission from the editors.

man's descent from King Agag of Amalek, whom Saul defeated (I Sam. 15).[2]

Similarly, several midrashic traditions identify the Kish of Mordecai's pedigree (2:5) with Saul's father (I Sam. 9:1).[3] From this vantage point, Mordecai's recorded pedigree spans some five centuries in order to connect him and Esther to Saul. If indeed Haman is of royal Amalekite stock, and Mordecai and Esther descend from King Saul, then the Purim story may be viewed as a dramatic rematch of the battle between Saul and Agag.

However, neither assumption is rooted in the text of the Megillah. The etymology of "Agagite" is uncertain; while it could mean "from King Agag of Amalek," it may be a Persian or Elamite name.[4] Had the author of the Megillah wanted to associate Haman with Amalek, it could have dubbed him "the Amalekite." The same holds true for Mordecai and Esther's descent from King Saul (Ibn Ezra). It is possible that the Kish mentioned in the Megillah is Mordecai's great-grandfather rather than a distant ancestor.[5]

Regardless of the historical factuality of the aforementioned identifications, a strong argument can be made for a *thematic* rematch between the forces of good and evil which runs parallel to Saul's inadequate efforts to eradicate Amalek. In this case, the association can be inferred from the text of the Megillah itself.[6] Thus the conflict between Mordecai and Haman as symbolic of a greater battle between Israel and Amalek is well taken conceptually, but it is tenuous to contend that the biological connections are manifest in the text of the Megillah itself. However, if the midrashim had received oral traditions regarding these historical links, we accept them—*ve-im kabbalah hi, nekabbel.*

B. ASSIMILATION

On the basis of various midrashic readings, it is often argued that the turning point of the Megillah is when the Jews fast (4:1–3, 16–17; 9:31), thereby repenting from earlier assimilationist tendencies demonstrated by their sinful participation in Ahasuerus' party. However, there is no theological explanation of why the Jews "deserved" genocide in the Megillah; on the contrary, the sole textual motivation behind Haman's decree is Mordecai's refusal to show obeisance to Haman (3:2–8). By staunchly standing out, Mordecai jeopardizes his own life and the lives of his people.[7]

Moreover, there is no indication in the Megillah that the Jews ever did anything wrong. On the contrary, the references to the Jews display them mourning and fasting,[8] first spontaneously, and then at Mordecai's directive (4:1–3, 16–17; 9:31). They celebrate their victory by sending gifts to each other and giving charity to the poor (9:16–28). Moreover, the Jews were given express permission to plunder their adversaries (8:11), yet the Megillah repeatedly stresses that they refrained from doing so (9:10, 15, 16).[9]

Consider also Haman's formulation of his request to exterminate the Jews: "their laws are different from every nation" (3:8). Several midrashim find in Haman's accusation testimony that the Jews observed the commandments and stood distinctly apart from their pagan counterparts.[10]

Curiously, the only overt indications of foreign influence on the Jews in the Megillah are the names Mordecai and Esther, which likely derive from the pagan deities Marduk[11] and Ishtar.[12] However, the use of pagan names need not indicate assimilation of Mordecai and Esther, nor of the community at large.[13]

Not only is there no textual evidence of Jewish assimilation—on the contrary, the Megillah consistently portrays Jews positively—but there is no rabbinic consensus on this matter either. The oft-quoted Gemara used to prove assimilation reads:

R. Shimon b. Yohai was asked by his disciples, Why were the enemies of Israel (a euphemism for the Jews) in that generation deserving of extermination? He said to them: Answer the question. They said: Because they partook of the feast of that wicked one. [He said to them]: If so, those in Shushan should have been killed, but not those in other provinces! They then said, answer the question. He said to them: It was because they bowed down to the image. They said to him, then why did God forgive them (i.e., they really deserved to be destroyed)? He replied: They only pretended to worship, and He also only pretended to exterminate them; and so it is written, "For he afflicted not from his heart." (*Megillah* 12a)

R. Shimon b. Yohai's students suggested that the Jews deserved to be destroyed because of their willing participation in Ahasuerus' party, but they did not state what was wrong with this participation. *Shir HaShirim Rabbah* 7:8 states that the Jews sinned at the party by eating nonkosher food. Alternatively, *Esther Rabbah* 7:13 considers prostitution the primary sin at the party.[14]

A contrary midrashic opinion is found in *Midrash Panim Aherim* 2, which relates that the Jews specifically *avoided* the party. In related sources, the Jews cried and mourned over Ahasuerus' festivities.[15]

From the aforementioned rabbinic opinions, we find controversy over what was wrong with the party and the extent of the Jews' participation (if any). But this entire discussion becomes moot when we consider that R. Shimon b. Yohai *rejects* his students' hypothesis on the grounds that only Shushan's Jewry participated; the Jews in other provinces never attended either of Ahasuerus' parties.[16]

R. Shimon b. Yohai then submits his own opinion: the Jews bowed to "the image." Rashi avers that the image refers to the statue of Nebuchadnezzar (see Daniel chapter 3), while Meiri (*Sanhedrin* 74b) quotes an alternative reading of our Gemara, which indicates that the "image" was an idol that Haman wore as people bowed to him.[17]

Both possibilities present difficulties: According to Rashi, the Jews were to be punished for the transgression of their ancestors, though there is no evidence in the Megillah that they perpetuated this sinful conduct. According to Meiri's alternative reading, the question of R. Shimon b. Yohai to his students simply becomes more acute:

only the members of the king's court in Shushan bowed to Haman. Most Jews of Shushan, and all Jews from the outer provinces, never prostrated before Haman.

In any case, the Gemara concludes that the Jews bowed without conviction. God "externally" threatened the Jews in return, that is, the threat was perceived, not real. Thus the Gemara never resolves the theological question. The Jews in the Megillah are consistently portrayed in a favorable light, and the Gemara's ambivalence over the theological cause of the Purim story only supports this reading. As a result, we must relegate discussions of assimilation completely to the realm of *derekh ha-derash*, that is, assimilation is something to be criticized, but the Megillah is not engaged in this condemnation—it has other religious purposes.

C. RELIGIOUS OBSERVANCE

The Megillah makes no mention of the distinctly commandment-related behavior of the heroes, nor of the nation. Other than the term *Yehudi(m)*, there is nothing distinctly Jewish in the Megillah. Most prominent is the absence of God's Name. Also missing are any references to the Torah or specific commandments. The holiday at the end of the Megillah could be viewed as a nationalistic celebration of victory. The only sign of religious ritual is fasting; but even that conspicuously is not accompanied by prayer.[18] The omission of God's Name and prayer is even more striking when we contrast the Masoretic Text with the Septuagint additions—where the Jews pray to God and God intervenes on several occasions. In the Septuagint version of the Megillah, God's Name appears over *fifty* times.[19] It appears unmistakable that the author of the Megillah intended to stifle references to God and Jewish religious practice. The second section of this essay will address this question.

D. MORDECAI'S DISOBEDIENCE

Mordecai's rationale for not prostrating himself involves his Jewishness (3:4), but the Megillah does not explain how. Many biblical

figures bow to kings and nobles as a sign of respect, not worship;
notably Esther bows to Ahasuerus in 8:3.[20] The text suggests that
Mordecai did not want to honor the *king* and his command (see 3:2–
4), but this explanation seems puzzling. Would Mordecai endanger
his own life and the lives of all Jews[21] for this reason? *Esther Rabbah* 6:2 finds it unlikely:

> But Mordecai did not bow down nor prostrate himself before
> him (3:2). Was Mordecai then looking for quarrels or being dis-
> obedient to the king's command? The fact is that when Ahasu-
> erus ordered that all should bow down to Haman, the latter fixed
> an idolatrous image on his breast for the purpose of making all
> bow down to an idol.[22]

Other rabbinic sources contend that rather than wearing an idol,
Haman considered himself a deity.[23]

Nevertheless, the text never alludes to idolatry in regard to Haman, nor anywhere else in the Megillah.[24] It appears that technical
idolatry did not figure into Mordecai's refusal to bow to Haman.
The second section of this essay will consider alternative responses
to this question.

To conclude, we find that certain midrashic assumptions are without clear support in the biblical text, and there often is disagreement
in rabbinic sources. Both Mordecai and Esther's biological connection to Saul and Haman's descent from King Agag of Amalek are
debatable. There is no evidence of Jewish assimilation in the Megillah, nor is there testimony to overtly Jewish religiosity. Finally, it is
unclear why Mordecai refused to bow to Haman, which is surprising
given the centrality this episode has in the narrative.

Although these ambiguities make an understanding of the Megillah more complicated, they also free the interpreter to look beyond
the original boundaries of explanation and to reconsider the text and
its messages anew. We now can turn to some of the central messages
which do arise from the text of the Megillah.

THE CENTRAL MESSAGES OF THE MEGILLAH
A. AHASUERUS AS THE MAIN CHARACTER

In determining the literary framework of the Megillah, Rabbi David Henshke notes that, viewed superficially, chapter 1 contributes Vashti's removal, making way for Esther. However, the text elaborately describes the king's wealth and far-reaching power. This lengthy description highlights the fact that there is a different plot in the Megillah: the king's power is described in detail because it is central to the message of the Megillah. Moreover the Megillah does not end with the Jews' celebration. It concludes with a description of Ahasuerus' wealth and power, just as it begins. Thus the Purim story is played out on Ahasuerus' stage.[25]

The other major characters of the Megillah—Esther, Mordecai, and Haman—are completely dependent on the good will of the king. For example, the political influence of Esther and Mordecai ostensibly contributed significantly to the salvation of the Jews. However, their authority was subject to the king's moods. Esther knew that Vashti had been deposed in an instant. The king even held a second beauty contest immediately after choosing Esther as queen (2:19). When the moment to use her influence arrived, Esther was terrified to confront the king to plead on behalf of her people. The fact that she had not been summoned for thirty days reminded her of her precarious position (4:11).

Mordecai, who rose to power at the end of the Megillah, likewise recognized the king's fickleness. Just as the previous vizier was hanged, Mordecai never could feel secure in his new position.

Rabbi Henshke points out that after Haman parades Mordecai around Shushan (a tremendous moral victory for Mordecai over his archenemy), Mordecai midrashically returns to his sackcloth and ashes (see *Megillah* 16a). After Haman is hanged, which should have ended the conflict between Mordecai and Haman, only *the king* is relieved, because the threat to his own wife is eliminated (7:10). Even after Ahasuerus turns Haman's post over to Mordecai, Esther still must grovel before the king (8:1–6). The Jews remain in mortal fear because of the *king's decree*, irrespective of Haman.

B. GOD AND AHASUERUS

The main characters of the Megillah have counterparts: Mordecai opposes Haman; Esther is contrasted to Vashti (and later Zeresh). On the surface of the Megillah, only Ahasuerus does not have a match—but behind the scenes, he does: it is God.[26] While God's Name never appears in the Megillah, "the king" appears approximately 200 times. It would appear that Ahasuerus' absolute power is meant to occupy the role normally assigned to God elsewhere in Tanakh. [27]

Everyone must prostrate himself to the king's vizier—how much more respect is therefore required for the one who appointed him! And one who enters the throne room without the king's permission risks his or her life—reminiscent of the Jewish law of the gravity of entering the Holy of Holies, God's "throne room." Even the lavish parties at the beginning of the Megillah fit this theme. Instead of all the nations of the world coming to the Temple in Jerusalem to serve God (Isa. 2:2–4), all the nations of the world come to the palace in Shushan to see Ahasuerus' wealth and to get drunk.

C. THE MEGILLAH AS SATIRE[28]

Although the king's authority and power are demonstrated amply throughout the Megillah, so are his caprice and foolishness. Ahasuerus rules the world, but his own wife does not listen to him. He makes decisions while drunk and accepts everyone's advice. Rabbi Henshke convincingly argues that the primary point of the Megillah is to display the ostensible power of a human king while satiring his weaknesses.

The patterns established in chapter 1 continue throughout the Megillah. Haman is promoted simply because the king wants to promote him. This promotion occurs right after Mordecai saves the king's life and is not rewarded at all. Despite the constant emphasis on the king's laws, Ahasuerus readily sells an innocent nation for destruction and drinks to that decision (3:11–15). Later he still has the audacity to exclaim, "*mi hu zeh ve-ezeh hu!*" (who is he and where is he, 7:5). Despite the king's indignant proclamation, the reader discerns the answer to Ahasuerus' question: it is the king himself![29]

The striking parallel between Haman's decree (3:11–15) and Mordecai's (8:7–14) further illustrates the king's inconstancy: both edicts follow the identical legal procedure and employ virtually the same language, yet one allows the Jews to be exterminated while the other permits the Jews to defend themselves. Ahasuerus is subservient to his own decrees to the point where he cannot even retract them himself (1:19; 8:2, cf. Dan. 6:9, 13, 16). Finally, the Bigtan and Teresh incident (2:21–23) serves as a reminder that the king's power was precarious and that his downfall could arise suddenly from within his Empire.[30]

D. MORDECAI'S DISOBEDIENCE

What does Haman's parading of Mordecai add to the plot of the Megillah? Rabbi Henshke responds that once it is demonstrated that Ahasuerus is the primary character of the Megillah, the parade becomes vital to the plot. True, Mordecai had rescued the king; but he also had flouted the king's laws by not bowing to Haman. Moreover, Mordecai was still subject to the impending decree against the Jews! Thus Mordecai's victory over Haman failed to end the story, so long as he and his people still were subject to the menacing decree of the king. Haman's parading Mordecai illustrates the absence of values in Ahasuerus' world.

One should add that the Megillah ascribes importance to this parade: Zeresh and Haman's advisors all recognized that somehow, this parade was the harbinger of Mordecai's triumph over Haman (6:13)—and they were proven correct.

To summarize: In the surface plot, which reflects the conflict between Mordecai and Haman, the parade marked the beginning of the victory of Mordecai over Haman. On a deeper level, the parade is a banner example of the perverse and capricious world of the king.

In a similar vein, we may identify two layers of motivation for Mordecai's not bowing to Haman: Rabbi Yaakov Medan asserts that Mordecai does not bow because he needs to send a strong message to Israel: passivity in the face of evil can cause even more harm in the future.[31]

In light of Rabbi Henshke's analysis, another answer emerges: Mordecai wishes to oppose the king's command (3:2, 4). Once the king promotes Haman (especially right after Mordecai had saved the king's life yet received no reward), Mordecai recognizes the repulsive character of the king. Even further, Mordecai perceives that Ahasuerus had "replaced" God as the major visible power in Shushan. Thus Mordecai finds himself battling on two spiritual fronts. On the surface, he opposes Haman, but he also engages in a spiritual battle against Ahasuerus. Therefore the text stresses that Mordecai was violating the king's decree by refusing to prostrate before Haman.

The Gemara lends conceptual support for this dual battle of Mordecai: After Mordecai learns of the decree of annihilation, he begins to mourn:

> "And Mordecai knew all that had been done" (4:1)—what did he say? Rav says: Haman has triumphed over Ahasuerus. Shemuel says: the higher king has triumphed over the lower king (Rashi: a euphemism for "Ahasuerus has triumphed over God"). (*Megillah* 15a)

According to Rav, Haman was the primary threat to Mordecai and the Jews. Mordecai bewails Haman's manipulation of the weaker Ahasuerus. According to Shemuel, Mordecai perceives that Ahasuerus was too powerful. That Ahasuerus allowed such a wicked individual to rise to power weakened the very manifestation of God in this world. Rav's response addresses the surface plot, the conflict between Haman and Mordecai. Shemuel reaches to the struggle behind the scenes—God's battle with Ahasuerus.

E. AN ALTERNATIVE TO THE WORLD OF AHASUERUS

Instead of stopping at its satire of the king, the Megillah offers an alternative lifestyle to the world of Ahasuerus. As was mentioned earlier, the Megillah consistently portrays the Jews' character in a positive light. In 3:8, Haman contrasts the laws of the Jews with the laws of the king. Thus the Megillah stresses that the Jewish laws and practices are an admirable alternative to the decrepit values represented by Ahasuerus' personality and society.

Ahasuerus is a *melekh hafakhpakh*, a whimsical ruler. His counterpart in the Megillah, God, works behind the scenes to influence the Purim story through the process of *ve-nahafokh hu* (9:1), a primary theme in the Megillah.[32] In the world of the *hafakhpakh* everything is arbitrary, self-serving, and immoral. There is no justice: a Haman can be promoted, as can a Mordecai. In contrast, God's world of *ve-nahafokh hu* is purposeful and just.[33] Although the reader is left wondering why the Jews were threatened in the first place, God had justice prevail in the end.

However, one must note that even in their victory, the Jews remain entirely under the power of Ahasuerus. As a result, Purim is crippled as opposed to most other holidays:

> [Why do we not say Hallel on Purim?]...Rava said: There is a good reason in that case [of the exodus] because it says [in the Hallel], Praise ye O servants of the Lord, who are no longer servants of Pharaoh — But can we say in this case, Praise ye, servants of the Lord and not servants of Ahasuerus? We are still servants of Ahasuerus! (*Megillah* 14a)

CONCLUSION

The showdown between Haman and Mordecai is central to the surface plot of the Megillah, whereas the more cosmic battle that pits God and Mordecai against the world of Ahasuerus permeates the very frame of the Megillah from beginning to end.

The reader is left helpless in the face of the question of why the Jews deserved this decree. The Jews appear completely righteous, and it specifically is the religious and national heroism of Mordecai which endangers them in the first place. Yet the reader of the Megillah, like Job, is led to confront God honestly, confident by the end that there is justice in the world, even when it is not always apparent to the human eye. This piercingly honest religiosity has been a source of spiritual inspiration throughout the Jewish world since the writing of the Megillah. The Megillah challenges us and brings us ever closer to God—who is concealed right beneath the surface of the Megillah, battling the insidious and arbitrary world of Ahasuerus.

NOTES

1. See 3:1, 10; 8:3, 5; 9:24.
2. Mishnah *Megillah* 3:4 requires that *Parashat Zakhor* (Deut. 25:17–19) be read the Shabbat preceding Purim. Mishnah 3:6 mandates that the narrative of Amalek's attack on the Israelites in the wilderness (Exod. 17:9–17) be read as the Torah portion of Purim. Josephus (*Antiquities* XI:209) asserts that Haman was an Amalekite.
3. See, for example, *Megillah* 13b.
4. Yaakov Klein, Mikhael Heltzer, and Yitzhak Avishur et al., *Olam HaTanakh: Megillot* (Tel-Aviv: Dodson-Iti, 1996, p. 217) write that the names Haman, Hamedata, and Agag all have Elamite and Persian roots.
5. Cf. Amos Hakham, *Da'at Mikra: Esther* (Hebrew) (Jerusalem: Mossad HaRav Kook, 1973), in his comments to 2:5.
6. Hakham suggests that "Agagite" may be a typological name, intended to associate Haman conceptually with "Amalek," i.e., he acts as one from Amalek (the same way many contemporary Jews refer to anti-Semites as "Amalek" regardless of their genetic origins). Jon D. Levenson (*Old Testament Library: Esther* [Louisville, KY: Westminster John Knox Press, 1997], pp. 56–57) adds that Saul lost his kingdom to David as a result of not killing Agag; now Mordecai will reclaim some of Saul's glory by defeating Haman the Agagite—although the Davidic kingdom stopped ten years after Jeconiah was exiled (2:6).
7. See discussion in R. Haim David Halevi, *Mekor Hayyim ha-Shalem* (Hebrew), vol. 4, pp. 347–351.

8. Although the Jews' mourning and fasting may indicate that they were repenting from sins, the text avoids any reference to what these sins might have been. These religious acts just as easily could indicate a petition to God in times of distress.

9. This emphasis demonstrates that the Jews were fighting for their very survival (Hakham). On a more conceptual level, the Megillah may be contrasting the Jews' behavior with that of Saul and his soldiers, who plundered Amalek (Gavriel H. Cohn, *Da'at Mikra: Esther*, introduction p. 14).

10. See *Esther Rabbah* 7:12; cf. *Megillah* 13b; *Abba Gorion* 26; *2 Panim Aherim* 68; *Aggadat Esther* 30–31; *Esther Rabbah* and *Targum Esther* 3:8. Carey Moore (*Anchor Bible 7B: Esther* [New York: Doubleday, 1971], p. 39) translates *mefuzzar u-meforad* as "scattered, yet unassimilated." Hakham (on 3:8) suggests this possibility as well.

11. Mordecai is a variant of "Merodakh" (= Marduk). See Jer. 50:2; cf. II Kings 25:27 (~Jer. 52:31); Isa. 39:1. See *Megillah* 12b; *Esther Rabbah* 6:3; *2 Panim Aherim* 62; *Pirkei D'Rabbi Eliezer* 50; 1 and 2 Targum Esther 2:5, for midrashic explications of Mordecai's name.

12. See *Megillah* 13a (several alternative midrashic etymologies of the name Esther are given there as well). Yaakov Klein, Mikhael Heltzer, and Yitzhak Avishur et al., *Olam HaTanakh: Megillot* (pp. 238–239) maintain that the name Esther derives from the Persian word "star" (meaning "star" in English as well). They reject the derivation from Ishtar, since a *shin* in a Babylonian word (I*sh*tar) would not be transformed into a *samekh* in the Hebrew (Esther).

13. Even if pagan names suggest assimilation, it is possible that their host rulers gave them these names, as with Daniel and his friends (Dan. 1:7). Cf. *Megillah* 13a: "the *nations of the world* called Esther this after Ishtar." At any rate, it is clear that Esther needed to conceal her Jewish identity, so her using the name Hadassah would have been unreasonable.

14. Cf. *Esther Rabbah* 2:11; *Pirkei D'Rabbi Eliezer* 48. Other midrashim look to other eras for theological causes of the Purim decree: *Esther Rabbah* 1:10 turns to the Jews' violation of Shabbat in the time of Nehemiah. *Esther Rabbah* 7:25 considers the threat in the Purim story retribution for the brothers' sale of Joseph; *Esther Rabbah* 8:1 blames Jacob's deception of Isaac.

15. See midrashim cited in *Torah Shelemah* I:52, 60, 61.

16. *Shir Rabbah* 7:8 concludes that even if only a few Jews participated in the party, all of Israel still could be held responsible because of the principle of *arevut*.

17. See, e.g., *Esther Rabbah* 6:2.

18. Cf. Josh. 7:6; I Sam. 7:6; Jer. 14:12; Joel 2:12; Jon. 3:8; Ez. 8:21–23; Neh. 9:1ff., which all combine fasting and praying.

19. For further discussion of the Septuagint additions, see Carey Moore, *Anchor Bible 44: Daniel, Esther and Jeremiah: The Additions* (New York: Doubleday, 1977), pp. 3-16; 153-262.

20. See Gen. 23:7; 27:29; 33:3; Gen. 42:6; I Sam. 24:8; II Sam. 14:4; I Kings 1:23. Amos Hakham notes that the terms *keri'ah* and *hishtahavayah* (in Est. 3:2, 5) are collocated exclusively in regard to God, or to pagan deities.

21. Mordecai is a hero in the Megillah, but it is less evident whether his actions always should be considered exemplary (majority opinion), or whether he should be considered a hero for reacting properly to a problem that he had created in the first place. See Rava's opinion in *Megillah* 12b–13a; *Panim Aherim* 2:3. One also could argue that Mordecai was willing to assume personal risk but did not anticipate a decree of genocide against his people.

22. See also *Esther Rabbah* 7:5; *Pirkei D'Rabbi Eliezer* 50; *Abba Gorion* 22; *Panim Aherim* 46; *Esther Rabbah* 2:5, 3:1–2; *Targum* 3:2; Josephus *Antiquities*, XI, 6.5 and 8; Ibn Ezra; Tosafot *Sanhedrin* 61b, s.v. Rava.

23. *Megillah* 10b, 19a; *Esther Rabbah* 7:8; Rashi. Cf. *Sanhedrin* 61b, with Tosafot ad loc., s.v. Rava.

24. R. Yitzhak Arama was perhaps the first to argue that the reasoning of idolatry is *derekh ha-derash*. See Barry Dov Walfish, *Esther in Medieval Garb: Jewish Interpretation of the Book of Esther in the Middle Ages* (Albany, NY: SUNY Press, 1993), p. 69. The closest implicit reference to pagan practices in the text is Haman's lottery.

25. R. David Henshke, "Megillat Esther: Literary Disguise" (Hebrew), in *Hadassah Hi Esther* (Alon Shevut: Tevunot, 1999), pp. 93–106.

26. Cf. *Esther Rabbah* 3:10: "Everywhere in the Megillah where it says, 'King Ahasuerus,' the text refers to Ahasuerus; every instance of 'the

king' has a dual holy-secular meaning" (i.e., it refers both to God and to Ahasuerus).

27. Earlier commentators also address the issue of why God's Name is not mentioned in the Megillah. Ibn Ezra opines that the Megillah would be translated for distribution throughout the Persian Empire; since pagan translators may substitute the name of a pagan deity for God's Name, the author of the Megillah deliberately avoided referring to God. Rama (*Yoreh De'ah* 276) suggests that there was doubt whether the Megillah would be canonized (cf. *Megillah* 7a); therefore, they omitted God's Name anticipating the possibility of rejection, which would lead to the mistreatment of the scrolls. For a more complete survey of medieval responses to this issue, see Barry Dov Walfish, *Esther in Medieval Garb*, pp. 76–79.

28. For a thorough analysis of the use of irony in the Megillah, see Moshe D. Simon, "'Many Thoughts in the Heart of Man...': Irony and Theology in the Book of Esther," *Tradition* 31:4 (Summer 1997), pp. 5–27.

29. *Megillah* 16a: "And Esther said, 'the adversary and enemy is this wicked Haman' (7:6)—R. Eliezer says: this teaches that Esther began to face Ahasuerus, and an angel came and forced her hand to point to Haman."

One should not overlook Esther's remark to the king (7:4): were she and her people to be sold into slavery, she wouldn't have protested, indicating that the king and his interests are too important to trouble for anything short of genocide! Cf. 8:1–4, where Ahasuerus turns Haman's wealth over to Mordecai and Esther but does nothing to address his diabolical decree. The king's priorities are depicted as incredibly perverse in these episodes. Compare *Megillah* 11a: "'He was Ahasuerus' (1:1)—he was wicked from beginning until his end." This Gemara penetrates beneath the king's ostensible benevolence toward the Jews at the end of the Megillah, remarking that he was no better than before.

30. Although Bigtan and Teresh failed in their efforts, King Xerxes was assassinated by other court officials within ten years of the Purim story (465). See Moore (*Esther*), p. 32.

31. R. Yaakov Medan, "Mordecai Would Not Kneel or Bow Low—Why?" (Hebrew), in *Hadassah Hi Esther*, pp. 151–170.

32. R. Yonatan Grossman demonstrates how the entire Megillah is

structured chiastically around the principle of *ve-nahafokh hu* (Yeshivat Har Etzion, Virtual Bet Midrash 2007 [http://vbm-torah.org/archive/ ester/01ester.htm]).

33. See R. Avraham Walfish, "An Ordinance of Equity and Honesty" (Hebrew), in *Hadassah Hi Esther,* pp. 107–140.

THE CONTRASTING LEADERSHIP MODELS OF EZRA AND NEHEMIAH*

The Book of Ezra-Nehemiah (viewed by Jewish tradition as a single book, to be called EN) chronicles some of the final episodes of the biblical era. The Return to Zion and the rebuilding of the Temple lie at the heart of the first period in EN (538–516 B.C.E.). Zerubbabel, the political leader; and Jeshua, the High Priest, lead the community in tandem. These men are generally mentioned together, and they both work closely with the people.

In contrast, the two great leaders of EN's second period (458–432 B.C.E.)—Ezra, the priest-sage; and Nehemiah, the political leader—model distinct leadership typologies in their attempts to guide their community to a more committed religious life.

EN introduces Ezra with an extended pedigree tracing all the way back to Aaron the Priest (Ezra 7:1–5). Ezra emigrates from Babylonia to Israel in 458 B.C.E., bearing a document from King Artaxerxes of Persia which accords him virtually unlimited authority over the people (Ezra 7:11–26). Given this remarkable introduction, one may expect Ezra to dominate the narrative and exert power over the people, both as a priest and as a sage. Yet the opposite proves to be the case.

The first half of Ezra 8 lists those who returned to Israel along with Ezra. Ezra involves others and gives them credit for their participation. At the conclusion of the roster, Ezra invites others to help bring Levites to Israel (Ezra 8:15–20). A certain Levite named Sherebiah

---

* This article appeared originally in *Conversations* 3 (Institute for Jewish Ideas and Ideals, Winter 2009), pp. 21-25. Reprinted here with minor modifications, with permission from the editor.

is a particular success story for Ezra. He remains prominent through-out EN after having been empowered by Ezra (see Ezra 8:18, 24; Neh. 8:7; 9:4–5; 10:13; 12:8, 24). Ezra similarly appoints twelve other priests—though he is one himself—to care for the Temple treasures (Ezra 8:24–30). Despite the immense power and authority granted to him by King Artaxerxes, Ezra is surrounded by name lists and involves others. These features of Ezra's leadership set the tone for his transferring most of his authority to the people.

Ezra's reaction to the scourge of intermarriage follows the same pattern. Upon learning of the problem, Ezra pulls his hair in grief and prays on behalf of his people. Members of the community spon-taneously join him:

> When I heard this, I rent my garment and robe, I tore hair out of my head and beard, and I sat desolate. Around me gathered all who were concerned over the words of the God of Israel because of the returning exiles' trespass. (Ezra 9:3–4)

> While Ezra was praying and making confession…a very great crowd of Israelites gathered about him…the people were weep-ing bitterly. (Ezra 10:1)

After the completion of this prayer, the people propose and implement the solution, with Ezra endorsing their plan (Ezra 10:2–4).

According to Ralbag (on Ezra 10:44), Ezra was a brilliant strate-gist. He realized that confrontational top-down rebuke would not be effective, and he therefore contrived an alternate plan to bring mem-bers of his community into the process. However, one could argue that Ezra believed in this model of leadership as the ideal. He was not an authoritarian leader. He wanted others to take active leader-ship and participatory roles. He also wanted to create a leadership that could perpetuate itself, rather than forcing the community to be-come entirely dependent on him. Ezra is an exemplar of the dictum attributed to the Men of the Great Assembly in the first Mishnah in *Avot*: *Ve-ha'amidu talmidim harbeh*— raise up many disciples.

Nehemiah also is a strong God-fearing leader, but he is characterized differently from Ezra. When Nehemiah comes from Babylonia
to Israel in 445 B.C.E., no other names are listed with him. Nehemiah
dominates the narrative and forcefully exerts his own power and
authority.

When Ezra had come to Israel thirteen years earlier, he declined a
military escort, since he wanted to sanctify God's Name to the king
of Persia:

I proclaimed a fast there by the Ahava River to afflict ourselves
before our God to beseech Him for a smooth journey for us and
for our children and for all our possessions; for I was ashamed to
ask the king for soldiers and horsemen to protect us against any
enemy on the way, since we had told the king, "The benevolent
care of our God is for all who seek Him, while His fierce anger
is against all who forsake Him." So we fasted and besought our
God for this, and He responded to our plea. (Ezra 8:21–23)

In contrast, Nehemiah accepted a military escort: "The king also
sent army officers and cavalry with me" (Neh. 2:9).

We have seen that Ezra pulled his hair in sorrow upon learning of
the intermarriage in his community. In contrast, Nehemiah threatens
and uses physical force against the people:

Also at that time, I saw that Jews had married Ashdodite, Ammonite, and Moabite women; a good number of their children
spoke the language of Ashdod and the language of those various peoples, and did not know how to speak Judean. I censured
them, cursed them, flogged them, tore out their hair, and adjured
them by God, saying, "You shall not give your daughters in marriage to their sons, or take any of their daughters for your sons or
yourselves." (Neh. 13:23–25)

Ezra tears out his own hair; Nehemiah tears out others' hair.

Another significant contrast between the two leaders arises during
the one occasion they are seen together: the religious revival and

covenant recorded in Nehemiah chapters 8–10. The people gather together and invite Ezra—their accepted teacher—to read from the Torah. Ezra is not the one who initiates the ceremony. Ezra is flanked by thirteen other people (Neh. 8:4), again highlighting his allowing others to initiate and share center stage in every aspect of his leadership. The people voluntarily turn to Ezra because they respect him as a teacher, not because he exerts his authority over them.

Despite the narrator's assertion that the people initiated the reformation and covenant (Neh. 8–10; cf. 12:44–47; 13:1–3), Nehemiah casts himself differently in his first-person report (Neh. 13). He repeatedly gives himself credit, almost as a poetic refrain:

O my God, remember me favorably for this, and do not blot out the devotion I showed toward the House of my God and its attendants. (v. 14)

This too, O my God, remember to my credit, and spare me in accord with your abundant faithfulness. (v. 22)

O my God, remember it to my credit! (v. 31)

And also:

O my God, remember to my credit all that I have done for this people! (Neh. 5:19)

Nehemiah's repeated stress on his personal accomplishments stands out starkly, especially after the narrative in EN which credits the people for their initiatives. Additionally, Nehemiah makes it appear that the religious state of the people was entirely dependent on him. He attributes the spiritual decline and other woes on the fact that he had left the community and returned to Babylonia (Neh. 13:6).

To summarize, Ezra was given immense authority—but deliberately moderated it. Instead, he raised new leaders and engaged the members of the community to take active roles in their spiritual development. He surrounded himself with people and shared or transferred authority to others. He raised many disciples, thereby broadening the base of the leadership and also ensuring continuity rather than dependence on him. In turn, the people voluntarily gravitated to him for guidance and teaching.

Nehemiah, on the other hand, tended to occupy center stage. He gave orders to others and often threatened them and used physical force to implement his goals. He credited himself for his accomplishments, even though the narrator credits the people for their initiatives. He portrayed himself as an indispensable leader whose community failed as soon as he left them.

Both Ezra and Nehemiah were God-fearing individuals dedicated to rebuilding Israel physically and spiritually, and both were effective to a large degree. There are no explicit evaluations of either Ezra or Nehemiah by the narrator, typical of biblical narrative. Several rabbinic traditions give clear preference to Ezra while showing ambivalence toward Nehemiah.

Rabbi Yosei said: Had Moses not preceded him, Ezra would have been worthy of receiving the Torah for Israel. (*Sanhedrin* 21b)

When [Hillel] died, they lamented over him, "Alas, the pious man! Alas, the humble man! Disciple of Ezra!" (*Sotah* 48b; cf. *Sanhedrin* 11a, *Sukkah* 20a)

By likening Ezra to Moses, and by using Ezra as a paradigm for their beloved Hillel, these Sages enshrine Ezra as one of the greatest biblical figures.

Working on the assumption that Ezra and Nehemiah co-authored EN, the Sages wondered why the book was called only "Ezra" (as they referred to it). One responded that Nehemiah was penalized for his self-aggrandizement by having his name excluded from the title of the book:

The whole subject matter of [the Book of] Ezra was narrated by Nehemiah the son of Hacaliah; why then was the book not called by his name? R. Jeremiah b. Abba said: Because he claimed merit for himself, as it is written (Neh. 5:19), "O my God, remember to my credit." (*Sanhedrin* 93b)

Another believed that Nehemiah viewed himself as indispensable while denigrating all other leaders as ineffective, though some of his predecessors certainly were righteous and competent:

R. Joseph said: Because he spoke disparagingly of his predecessors, as it is written (Neh. 5:15), "The former governors who preceded me laid heavy burdens on the people, and took from them bread and wine more than forty shekels of silver, etc." (*Sanhedrin* 93b)

It appears that the aforementioned Sages balanced Nehemiah's positive and negative traits when compared and contrasted with Ezra. These exceptional individuals from the biblical period, as interpreted in traditional rabbinic sources, have much to teach contemporary Jewish leaders about leadership.

For further study:
- Hayyim Angel, "The Literary Significance of the Name Lists in Ezra-Nehemiah," *Jewish Bible Quarterly* 35:3 (2007), pp. 143–152; reprinted in Angel, *Revealed Texts, Hidden Meanings: Finding the Religious Significance in Tanakh* (Jersey City, NJ: KTAV-Sephardic Publication Foundation, 2009), pp. 205-216.
- Tamara Cohn Eskenazi, *In an Age of Prose: A Literary Approach to Ezra-Nehemiah* (Atlanta: Scholars Press, 1988).

ENTERING THE HOLY OF HOLIES:
THE YOM KIPPUR EXPERIENCE IN TANAKH
AND LITURGY*

INTRODUCTION

Our religious experiences are shaped profoundly by the narratives and laws in Tanakh and subsequent rabbinic interpretation. Yom Kippur anchors the High Holiday season and transforms us as we reinvigorate our relationship with God and our communities. This essay will explore some of the key biblical texts underlying Yom Kippur and how they should impact our experience.

LEVITICUS 8–10: THE TABERNACLE DEDICATION

After months of building with raw materials such as gold, silver, bronze, wood, and fabric, the Tabernacle was transformed into the place where heaven meets earth. Chapter 8 describes the seven-day dedication of the Tabernacle and the priests. Chapter 9 relates the eighth-day closing ceremony, dramatically climaxed by a fire from heaven that consumed the offerings. Chapter 10 then reports the shocking and tragic deaths of Aaron's sons Nadab and Abihu after they offered alien incense.

Ramban (on Exod. 25:2) explains that the Tabernacle was built to re-enact the revelation at Sinai on a daily basis. Aside from the religious services that generated an ongoing encounter between God and humanity, the Tabernacle (and later the Temple) was divided into three realms: the Holy of Holies, where only the High Priest

---

* This article appeared originally in *High Holidays Reader* (New York: Tebah Educational Services, 2009), pp. 5–15. Reprinted here with minor modifications, with permission from the editors.

could enter; the Holy, where only Priests could enter; and the Court-
yard, where all people could congregate. These three realms are parallel to the revelation at Sinai. Only Moses could access the top of
Sinai; Aaron, Nadab, Abihu and seventy elders stood lower on the
mountain during the revelation (Exod. 24:9); and the people gathered at the base of Mount Sinai.

During the seven-day dedication, the entire nation gathered to
watch the ceremony—just like at Sinai. On the eighth day the people conducted a ceremony to inaugurate the Tabernacle. The Divine
Presence entered (Lev. 9:6). The *hattat* (purification offering[1]) was
offered on the outer altar and then burned outside the camp (9:11,
see Rashi, Hizkuni). At the conclusion of the ceremony, Moses and
Aaron blessed the people—perhaps using the Priestly Blessing (see
Torat Kohanim Shemini 30, Rashi, Ramban)—and then God's Presence appeared. Fire emerged to consume the offerings:

> Aaron lifted his hands toward the people and blessed them; and
> he stepped down after offering the sin offering, the burnt offer-
> ing, and the offering of well-being. Moses and Aaron then went
> inside the Tent of Meeting. When they came out, they blessed the
> people; and the Presence of the Lord appeared to all the people.
> Fire came forth from before the Lord and consumed the burnt
> offering and the fat parts on the altar. And all the people saw, and
> shouted, and fell on their faces. (Lev. 9:22–24)

Tragically, Nadab and Abihu then offered incense, meeting instant
death:

> Now Aaron's sons Nadab and Abihu each took his fire pan, put
> fire in it, and laid incense on it; and they offered before the Lord
> alien fire, which He had not enjoined upon them. And fire came
> forth from the Lord and consumed them; thus they died at the
> instance of the Lord. (Lev. 10:1–2)

Though they were religiously motivated, they died because they had
performed a service that was not commanded.

LEVITICUS 16: YOM KIPPUR

The Torah explicitly links the laws of Yom Kippur to the deaths of Nadab and Abihu:

The Lord spoke to Moses after the death of the two sons of Aaron who died when they drew too close to the presence of the Lord. The Lord said to Moses: Tell your brother Aaron that he is not to come at will into the Shrine behind the curtain, in front of the cover that is upon the ark, lest he die; for I appear in the cloud over the cover. (Lev. 16:1–2)

In chapter 10, the sin of Nadab and Abihu is cast in terms of their performing a service that was not commanded. In chapter 16, however, their sin is framed in terms of their having drawn too close to God's Presence. They met the fate of anyone who would touch Mount Sinai during the revelation (Exod. 19:12–13, 21–24). Ibn Ezra (on Lev. 16:1) infers from the beginning of chapter 16 that Nadab and Abihu must have attempted to enter the Holy of Holies.[2] God now teaches the people how they may approach Him in an appropriate manner. The intervening chapters 11–15 contain the laws of ritual purity and impurity, which govern when people must refrain from going to the Tabernacle and the procedures necessary in order to return (Ramban on Lev. 16:1).

The Yom Kippur ceremony addresses a primary concern of ancient Israelites and later readers: How can anyone approach God, Who is so powerful and potentially destructive? In this vein, the very last words reported of the first generation in the desert, in the wake of the Korah rebellion, also involved illegal incense and a fatal fire from heaven. The people feared that they never would be able to approach God:

But the Israelites said to Moses, "Lo, we perish! We are lost, all of us lost! Everyone who so much as ventures near the Lord's Tabernacle must die. Alas, we are doomed to perish!" (Num. 17:27–28)

Tying together these laws and narratives, Rabbi Yoel Bin-Nun[3] explains that the Holy of Holies is not simply quantitatively holier than the Holy; rather, it is an entirely different domain. The priests who represent the nation enter the Holy and light the candelabrum, offer incense, and arrange the showbread. The Holy is the human realm where people perform services to God. In the Holy of Holies—the Ark, Tablets, Torah, and several other items all are objects from God to the people. God speaks to the people from between the Cherubim. The Holy of Holies is God's realm. A curtain stands between the two domains, separating God's realm from the human realm.[4]

During the eighth-day dedication ceremony, nothing was brought into the Tabernacle, even in the Holy, where people normally can enter. The *hattat* needed to be burned outside the camp, the only time this ever occurred. God's Presence descended onto both sections of the Tabernacle. The fire to consume the offerings came from heaven. Aaron's very first day as the functioning High Priest did not include his performing the daily service in the Holy. For that one day, the Holy became a part of the Holy of Holies—the divine realm. Yom Kippur represents the opposite phenomenon, when people (represented by the High Priest) may enter the Holy of Holies.

Rabbi Bin-Nun explains that Nadab and Abihu blurred the two realms on the eighth day by bringing human fire. They confused God's revelation with human input (cf. Rashbam on Lev. 10:1). So how should people approach God, if He is so dangerous? The Yom Kippur ceremony addresses this dilemma. God temporarily "withdraws" from the Holy of Holies. The High Priest brings incense into the Holy of Holies—the antidote to Nadab and Abihu's error. A close relationship with God requires recognition of the boundaries between God's realm and the human realm. On Yom Kippur, God invites people behind the curtain, in order to repair and reenergize the connection. People then retreat to the Holy for the duration of the year.

Different aspects of the dynamics of the relationship between God and humanity are manifest in the Song of Songs and Isaiah's vision. We will now turn briefly to these components.

THE SONG OF SONGS

In the Song of Songs, the passionate relationship between the man and woman constantly renews itself and expands as the lovers pursue one another. Even in the final verse, the woman calls to her lover to flee like a deer (Song 8:14). Yehuda Feliks explains that when deer go into heat, they do not mate immediately. The males and females first seek each other and flee from one another. The abundant references to deer in the Song of Songs attest to this type of relationship. Their love is an ongoing story that will continue to develop even after the Song of Songs closes, rather than the fairy tale-esque "and they lived happily ever after."[5]

The loving relationship between God and Israel takes a similar form between the eighth-day Tabernacle ceremony and Yom Kippur. God and Israel pursue one another in order to constantly build their relationship while maintaining the proper boundaries between them.

ISAIAH'S VISION

The mechanism of purification on Yom Kippur introduces another dimension to the relationship between God and Israel. The High Priest first atones for himself and his family, and only then turns to the service for the people:

> When he has made expiation for himself and his household, and for the whole congregation of Israel… (Lev. 16:17)

This service is reflective of the dual role of the priesthood in general, as priests remain individual people but also represent the nation. The High Priest cannot represent others until he first atones for his own sins.[6] Aaron went through the same process on the eighth-day dedication as well (9:7). In addition to the *hattat* that purifies the

Tabernacle, the High Priest brings incense into the Holy of Holies, at least in part to create a cloud of smoke that prevents him from looking directly at the Ark (Hizkuni, Boleh[7]).

There are strong parallels between the Yom Kippur ceremony in the Torah and Isaiah's exalted vision:

In the year that King Uzziah died, I beheld my Lord seated on a high and lofty throne; and the skirts of His robe filled the Temple. Seraphs stood in attendance on Him....And one would call to the other, "Holy, holy, holy! The Lord of Hosts! His presence fills all the earth!" The doorposts would shake at the sound of the one who called, and the House kept filling with smoke.

I cried, "Woe is me; I am lost! For I am a man of unclean lips and I live among a people of unclean lips; yet my own eyes have beheld the King Lord of Hosts." Then one of the seraphs flew over to me with a live coal, which he had taken from the altar with a pair of tongs. He touched it to my lips and declared, "Now that this has touched your lips, your guilt shall depart and your sin be purged away."

Then I heard the voice of my Lord saying, "Whom shall I send? Who will go for us?" And I said, "Here am I; send me." (Isa. 6:1–8)

In his vision, the prophet stood in the Holy of Holies and perceived God and the angelic host. The room filled with smoke—as does the Holy of Holies from the incense of the High Priest. Isaiah's initial reaction was one of dread. He felt that his human shortcomings created an insurmountable barrier between him and God. He felt unworthy. Through this experience, though, he became purified and attained *kapparah*—atonement. Isaiah belonged in the company of angels precisely because he felt that he did not belong there. With profound humility, he understood the boundaries between God and humanity.[8]

Immediately after this process of purification, God asked the heavenly host: "Whom shall I send? Who will go for us?" Isaiah responded as though he were an angel himself, "Here am I; send me." Isaiah transformed from being one who felt unworthy to one who was purified and filled with a spirit of volunteerism.

OUR EXPERIENCE OF YOM KIPPUR

Our observances and liturgy of Yom Kippur draw inspiration from the aforementioned biblical precedents. For one day, we refrain from human experiences such as eating, drinking, washing, wearing leather shoes, and having marital relations. We enter the angelic arena, crossing symbolically into the Holy of Holies. We are exhilarated as we stand in God's Presence like angels, but also are filled with inadequacy and guilt as we feel unworthy to stand before God. It is precisely these feelings of inadequacy that purify us.

Our liturgy highlights these themes. Of course, liturgical customs differ widely, particularly when one is reciting medieval *piyyutim*. Our discussion will follow the Shearith Israel (Spanish and Portuguese) ritual, using Dr. David de Sola Pool's translations.

Rabbi Yehuda Halevi's introduction to the Nishmat makes us feel small and confined by our human desires:

> I know not how to approach Thee, how to worship or serve Thee....How can I serve my Creator while still I am slave to my passions and thrall of my evil desires?...Though my days and my nights may be sweet unto me, the stuff of my life they consume till I be consumed. (Shearith Israel Day of Atonement Prayer Book, p. 128)

Beginning with the Nishmat, we move into higher and higher realms until we join the angels in purity. This upward trend continues as we recite Barukh Shem Kevod aloud during the Shema.

The introductions to the Kedushah of Shaharit, composed by Rabbi Yosef ibn Abitur and Rabbi Yehudah Halevi respectively, bring us into the chorus of angels:

Angels robed in purity before God who abhors evil declare Him holy; His people on earth before Him who created the ends of the earth declare Him blessed. Angels shining in fire before God who forms them of fire declare Him holy; His people tested by fire and by water, twice daily proclaiming His unity declare Him holy and blessed. (Shearith Israel Day of Atonement Prayer Book, p. 147)

By the forms of His service He led [Israel] on to refine them even as the first realm of light, as ministering angels proclaiming His holiness and singing His praises in hallowing. With soul-cleansing entreaty of favor they declare the praises of God. Enwrapping themselves as Seraphim and Erelim, they become like unto angelic ministrants....Robing themselves in awe and humility, they gather resolved to serve Thee, revering and sanctifying Thee with triple "Holy," O God revered in the assembly of the holy. (Shearith Israel Day of Atonement Prayer Book, p. 154)

We then ask for forgiveness in the Amidah, and this reference to sin sets us off in a downward spiral until we reach the confession Viddui, where we feel unworthy even to ask for forgiveness:

I am not worthy to crave atonement, pardon and forgiveness. For what am I and what is my life?... (Shearith Israel Day of Atonement Prayer Book, p. 159)

We fluctuate throughout the day between feelings of angelic awe and power, and feelings of lowliness and unworthiness. As Isaiah experienced these emotions when crossing into the realm of the divine, so too we are humbled on Yom Kippur. Ideally, we are transformed through this encounter, so that by the end of the day we can truly say as did Isaiah, "Here I am! Send me!" Like the High Priest in Leviticus 16, we first address our own spiritual state and only then look outward toward becoming one with the community.

CONCLUSION

R. Simeon b. Gamaliel said: there never were in Israel greater days of joy than the fifteenth of Ab and the Day of Atonement. (Mishnah *Ta'anit* 26b)

I can understand the Day of Atonement, because it is a day of forgiveness and pardon and on it the second Tablets of the Law were given.[9] (Gemara *Ta'anit* 30b)

Yom Kippur is intended to be the most joyous day of the year. The attainment of authentic religious joy is a lifelong process, involving self-reflection, improvement, study, and acts on behalf of others. May we reflect on the meaning of our prayers and actions as we symbolically enter the Holy of Holies, and ultimately be transformed and energized into a higher spiritual realm in the year ahead and beyond.

NOTES

1. For discussion of the *hattat*, see Jacob Milgrom, *The JPS Torah Commentary: Numbers* (Philadelphia: Jewish Publication Society, 1989), pp. 444-447; Rabbi Eitan Mayer, Parsha Themes Tzav, at http://www.yu.edu/faculty/emayer/parsha_shiurim/26tzav.html.

2. Ramban (on 16:2) considers it inconceivable that Nadab and Abihu would deign to to enter the Holy of Holies; rather, their flaw was simply that they brought uncommanded incense, as per the formulation in chapter 10 (and in Num. 3:4; 26:61). However, his interpretation does not account for the language in chapter 16, which appears to present a different facet of the sin of Aaron's sons.

3. Rabbi Yoel Bin-Nun, "The Eighth Day and the Day of Atonement" (Hebrew), *Megadim* 8 (Sivan 5749-1989), pp. 9-34.

4. The idea of the two realms approaching one another without meeting is expressed poignantly in a talmudic passage: "It was stated, Rab, R. Hanina, R. Johanan, and R. Habiba learnt: the ark [of the covenant] was nine handbreadths high, and the ark cover one handbreadth, making a total

of ten handbreadths, and it is written, And there I will meet with you, and I will speak with you from above the ark-cover (Exod. 25:22). And it has been taught, R. Jose stated, Neither did the Shekhinah ever descend to earth, nor did Moses or Elijah ever ascend to Heaven, as it is written, 'The heavens are the heavens of the Lord, but the earth has He given to the sons of men' (Ps. 115:16). But did not the Shekhinah descend to earth? Is it not in fact written, And the Lord came down upon Mount Sinai? (Exod. 19:20). — That was above ten handbreadths [from the summit]." (*Sukkah* 4b–5a).

5. Introduction to *Da'at Mikra: The Song of Songs* (Hebrew) (Jerusalem: Mossad HaRav Kook, 1973), p. 16.

6. For a discussion of priesthood in the Torah, see Rabbi Eitan Mayer, Parsha Themes Tetzaveh, at http://www.yu.edu/faculty/emayer/parsha_shiurim/21tetzaveh.html.

7. Menahem Boleh, *Da'at Mikra: Leviticus vol. 2* (Hebrew) (Jerusalem: Mossad HaRav Kook, 1991), p. 10.

8. Prophecy and humility are intimately linked. Moses' superior prophecy and humility are joined in Numbers 12:3–8. One talmudic Sage builds on Isaiah's vision to highlight this correlation: "A Master has said: If one walks with a stiff bearing even for four cubits, it is as if he pushed against the heels of the Divine Presence, since it is written, The whole earth is full of His glory (Isa. 6:3)" (*Berakhot* 43b).

9. Soncino footnote: According to a tradition in *Seder Olam* 6, Moses spent three periods of forty days and forty nights in the Mount, beginning with the seventh of Sivan and ending on the tenth of Tishri, when he came down on earth with the Second Tablets.

OUR JOURNEY IN THE HAGGADAH:
HOW ITS NARRATIVES AND OBSERVANCES
ENABLE US TO EXPERIENCE THE EXODUS*

INTRODUCTION

Though many read the Haggadah as a unified text, it was not composed all at one time by a single author. Rather, it is a compilation of biblical, talmudic and midrashic texts, with several other passages being added over the centuries.[1] Despite its composite nature, the Haggadah in its current form may be understood as containing a fairly coherent structure. It creates a collective effect that enables us to experience the journey of our ancestors. As the Haggadah exhorts us, we must consider ourselves as though we left Egypt, actively identifying with our forebears rather than merely recounting ancient history. The exodus lies at the root of our eternal covenantal relationship with God.

The essential aspects of the Passover story are not taken from the primary account in the Book of Exodus. Rather they derive from other biblical texts and later rabbinic sources. The Haggadah expects that we have learned the Book of Exodus and laws of Passover as well.

The Haggadah merges laws with narrative. Its text and symbols take us on a journey that begins with freedom, then a descent into slavery, to the exodus, and on into the messianic age. Though we may feel free today, we are in exile as long as the Temple is not rebuilt. Many of our seder observances remind us of the Temple and our prayer for its rebuilding.

---

* This article appeared in *Pesah Reader* (New York: Tebah, 2010), pp. 17-29. Reprinted here with minor modifications, with permission from Tebah.

The Haggadah also presents an educational agenda. Although most traditions are passed from the older generation to the younger, the older generation must be open to learning from the younger. Often it is their innocent questions that remind us of how much we still must learn and explore.

This essay will use these axioms to outline the journey of the Haggadah, using the text and translation of Rabbi Marc D. Angel's *A Sephardic Passover Haggadah*.[2] This study is not an attempt to uncover the original historical meaning of the Passover symbols or to explain why certain passages were incorporated into the Haggadah. However, perhaps we will approach the inner logic of our current version of the Haggadah and its symbols as they came to be traditionally understood.

THE FIRST FOUR STAGES: FROM FREEDOM INTO SLAVERY

Kaddesh: Wine symbolizes festivity and happiness. Kiddush represents our sanctification of time, another sign of freedom.[3] We recline as we drink the wine, a sign of freedom from Roman times, when the core observances of the seder were codified by the rabbis of the Mishnah. Many also have the custom of having others pour the wine for them, which serves as another symbol of luxury and freedom. Thus the Haggadah begins by making us feel free and noble.

Rehatz (or Urhatz): We ritually wash our hands before dipping the *karpas* vegetable into salt water or vinegar. As with the pouring of the wine, many have the custom for others to wash their hands, symbolizing luxury and freedom. Rabbi Naftali Tzvi Yehudah Berlin (Netziv, 1817–1893, Lithuania) observes that many no longer follow this talmudic practice of washing hands before dipping any food into a liquid. Doing so at the seder serves as a reminder of our practices in Temple times. We thus remain in freedom mode for *rehatz*, but we begin to think about the absence of the Temple.

Karpas: Dipping an appetizer is another sign of freedom and nobility that comes to us from Roman times. However, we dip the vegetable into either salt water or vinegar, which came to be understood as symbolic of the tears of slavery. In addition, the technical ritual reason behind eating *karpas* resolves a halakhic debate over whether we are required to make a blessing of *Borei peri ha-adamah* over the maror later. On the one hand, we eat maror after matzah and therefore have already washed and recited the blessing of *ha-Motzi*. On the other hand, it is unclear whether the maror should be subsumed under the "dinner" covered by the matzah, since it is its own independent mitzvah. Consequently, the *ha-adamah* we recite over the *karpas* absolves us of this doubt, and we are required to keep the maror in mind for this blessing.[4] In symbolic terms, while we are dipping an appetizer as a sign of freedom and luxury, we experience the tears of slavery, and we think about the maror, which the Haggadah casts as a symbol of the bitterness of slavery.[5] Thus we are beginning our descent into slavery.

Yahatz: The Haggadah identifies two reasons for eating matzah. One is explicit in the Torah (Exod. 12:39), that our ancestors had to rush out of Egypt during the exodus. However, the Haggadah introduces another element: the Israelites ate matzah while they were yet slaves in Egypt. The Torah's expression *lehem 'oni* (Deut. 16:3; "bread of affliction") lends itself to this midrashic interpretation.

Yahatz focuses exclusively on this slavery aspect of matzah—poor people break their bread and save some for later, not knowing when they will next receive more food (see *Berakhot* 39b). By this point, then, we have descended into slavery. At the same time, the other half of this matzah will be used for the *tzafun-afikoman*, which represents the Passover offering and is part of the freedom section of the seder. Even as we descend into slavery with our ancestors, the Haggadah provides us with a glimpse of the redemption.

To summarize, *kaddesh* begins with our experiencing freedom and luxury. *Rehatz* also is a sign of freedom but raises the specter of there no longer being a Temple. *Karpas* continues the trend of freedom but more overtly gives us a taste of slavery by reminding us of tears and bitterness. *Yahatz* completes the descent into slavery. Even before we begin the *maggid*, then, the Haggadah has enabled us to experience the freedom and nobility of the Patriarchs, the descent to Egypt with Joseph and his brothers, and the enslavement of their descendants.

MAGGID: FROM SLAVERY TO FREEDOM
A. EDUCATIONAL FRAMEWORK

At this point in our journey, we are slaves. We begin the primary component of the Haggadah—*maggid*—from this state of slavery.

Ha Lahma Anya: We employ the "bread of affliction" imagery of the matzah, since we are slaves now. This opening passage of *maggid* also connects us to our ancestors: "This is the bread of affliction which our ancestors ate in the land of Egypt....Now we are here enslaved." The Haggadah is an experience of our journey and connection to our past and our future. The passage begins our experience by identifying with the slavery of our ancestors, then moves into our own exile and desire for redemption.

Mah Nishtanah–The Four Children: Before continuing our journey, we shift our focus to education. The Haggadah prizes the spirit of questioning. The wise of the four children does not necessarily know more than his less appealing counterparts. His wisdom is found in his questioning: "What are the testimonies, statutes, and laws which the Lord our God has commanded you?" To create a society of wise children, the Haggadah challenges us to explore and live our traditions. Rabbi Barukh Epstein (1860–1941, Lithuania) observes that the opposite of the wicked child is not a *tzaddik*, or "righteous" child. Some might define a righteous person as one who uncritically observes commandments. Therefore, the Haggadah teaches that the ideal wise child asks, challenges, and thinks as he grows in his commitment to the Torah.

Avadim Hayinu: The Haggadah sets the educational agenda for our observances in general: we are not simply recounting ancient history; we are a living part of that memory and connect to our ancestors through an acknowledgement that all later generations are indebted to God for the original exodus. "If the Holy One blessed be He had not brought out our ancestors from Egypt, we and our children and grandchildren would yet be enslaved to Pharaoh in Egypt."

Ma'aseh Be-Ribbi Eliezer: The five rabbis who stayed up all night in B'nei B'rak inspire us to realize that the more knowledgeable one is, the more exciting this learning becomes. These rabbis allowed their conversation to take flight, losing track of time as they experienced the exodus and actively connected to our texts and traditions.[6] This passage thus venerates our teachers.

Amar Ribbi Elazar: As a complement to the previous paragraph, this passage reminds us that the lesser scholar Ben Zoma had something valuable to teach the greatest Sages of his generation. Learning moves in both directions, and everyone has something important to contribute to the conversation.

Yakhol Me-Rosh Hodesh: The Haggadah again stresses the value of combining education and experience. "The commandment [to discuss the exodus from Egypt] applies specifically to the time when matzah and maror are set before you." To recount the story of the exodus meaningfully, we must observe the rituals alongside it.

B. THE JOURNEY RESUMES

Now that we have established a proper educational framework, we can return to our journey. At the last checkpoint, we were slaves pointing to our bread of affliction, longing for redemption. Each passage in this section of the Haggadah moves us a little further ahead in the journey.

Mi-Tehillah Ovedei Avodah Zarah: Following the trend of *maggid*, we begin with the past but immediately shift into the relevance of this discussion to us: "In the beginning our ancestors were idolaters; but now, God has drawn us to His service." We quote from the covenant in the Book of Joshua:

In olden times, your forefathers—Terah, father of Abraham and father of Nahor—lived beyond the Euphrates and worshiped other gods. But I took your father Abraham from beyond the Eu-

in turn tell their children that they might put their confidence in God, and not forget God's great deeds, but observe His commandments, and not be like their fathers, a wayward and defiant generation, a generation whose heart was inconstant, whose spirit was not true to God. (Ps. 78:5–8)

Several midrashim on this Psalm magnify God's miracles even more than in the accounts in Tanakh, including the passage incorporated in the Haggadah that multiplies the plagues at the Red Sea. From this vantage point, our ancestors were even more ungrateful to God. The Haggadah then follows this excerpt with *dayyenu* to express gratitude over every step of the exodus process. The juxtaposition of these passages conveys the lesson that the Psalmist and the midrashic expansions wanted us to learn.

In addition to expressing proper gratitude for God's goodness, *dayyenu* carries our journey forward. It picks up with the plagues and exodus—precisely where the passage we read from Deuteronomy 26 had left off. It then takes us ahead to the reception of the Torah at Sinai, to the land of Israel, and finally to the Temple: "He gave us the Torah, He led us into the land of Israel, and He built for us the chosen Temple to atone for our sins."

Rabban Gamliel Hayah Omer: Now that we are in the land of Israel and standing at the Temple, we can observe the laws of Passover! We describe the Passover offering during Temple times, matzah and maror, and their significance. It also is noteworthy that the reason given for eating matzah is freedom—unlike the slavery section earlier that focused on bread of affliction (*yahatz-ha lahma anya*). "This matzah which we eat is…because the dough of our ancestors did not have time to leaven before the Holy One blessed be He…redeemed them suddenly."

Be-Khol Dor Va-Dor—Hallel: The primary purpose of the Haggadah is completely spelled out by now. "In each generation a person is obligated to see himself as though he went out of Egypt.… For not only did the Holy One blessed be He redeem our ancestors, but He also redeemed us along with them...." Since we have been redeemed along with our ancestors, we recite the first two chapters of the *Hallel* (Ps. 113–114). These Psalms likewise take us from the exodus to entry into Israel. R. Judah Loew of Prague (Maharal, c. 1520–1609) explains that we save the other half of *Hallel* (Ps. 115–118) for after the Grace after Meals, when we pray for our own redemption. Rabbi Joseph Soloveitchik adds that Psalms 113–114 consist of pure praise, befitting an account of the exodus from Egypt which already has occurred. Psalms 115–118 contain both praise and petition, relevant to our future redemption, for which we long.[8]

Asher Ge'alanu: Now that we have completed our journey and have chanted the *Hallel* thanking God for redeeming us, we conclude *maggid* with a blessing: "You are blessed, Lord our God... Who has redeemed us and redeemed our ancestors from Egypt and has brought us to this night to eat matzah and maror." For the first time in the Haggadah, we place ourselves before our ancestors, since our experience has become primary. As we express gratitude to God for bringing us to this point and for giving us the commandments, we also petition for the rebuilding of the Temple and ultimate redemption.

THE REMAINDER OF THE SEDER: CELEBRATORY OBSERVANCE IN FREEDOM AND YEARNING FOR THE MESSIANIC REDEMPTION

At this point we observe the laws of Passover. Though there is no Passover offering, we eat the matzah and maror and then the festive meal (*shulhan orekh*). Our eating of the *korekh* (Hillel's wrap of matzah, maror, and haroset together) reenacts a Temple observance (*Pesahim* 115a). Similarly, we pretend that the final piece of matzah (*tzafun*) is the Passover offering, the last taste we should have in our mouths (*Pesahim* 119b).[9] By consuming the second half of the matzah from *yahatz*, we take from the slavery matzah and transform its other half into a symbol of freedom.

After the Grace after Meals (*barekh*), we pray for salvation from our enemies and ultimately for the messianic era. By reading the verses "pour out Your wrath" (*shefokh hamatekha*, Ps. 79:6–7), we express the truism that we cannot fully praise God in *Hallel* until we sigh from enemy oppression and recognize contemporary suffering.[10] Many communities customarily open the door at this point for Elijah the Prophet, also expressing hope for redemption. We then recite the remainder of the *Hallel* which focuses on our redemption, as discussed above. Some of the later songs added to *nirtzah* likewise express these themes of festive singing and redemption.

CONCLUSION

The Haggadah is a composite text that expanded and evolved over the centuries. The symbols, along with traditional explanations for their meanings, similarly developed over time. In its current form, our Haggadah—with its core some 1,000 years old—takes us on a remarkable journey that combines narrative and observance into an intellectual and experiential event for people of all ages and backgrounds. In this manner, we travel alongside our ancestors from freedom to slavery to redemption. We are left with a conscious recognition that though we are free and we bless God for that fact, we long for the Temple in Jerusalem. *La-shanah ha-ba'ah be-Yerushalayim, Amen.*

NOTES

1. Shemuel and Ze'ev Safrai write that most of the core of our Haggadah, including the *Kiddush*, the Four Questions, the Four Children, the midrashic readings, Rabban Gamliel, and the blessing at the end of *maggid* originated in the time of the Mishnah and were set by the ninth century. "This is the bread of affliction" (*ha lahma anya*) and "In each generation" (*be-khol dor va-dor*) hail from the ninth to tenth centuries. Components such as the story of the five rabbis at B'nei B'rak and R. Elazar; the Midrash about the number of plagues at the Red Sea; *Hallel HaGadol* and *Nishmat*;

all existed as earlier texts before their incorporation into the Haggadah. "Pour out Your wrath" (*shefokh hamatekha*) and the custom of hiding the *afikoman* are later additions. All of the above was set by the eleventh century. The only significant additions after the eleventh century are the songs at the end (*Haggadat Hazal* [Jerusalem: Karta, 1998], pp. 70–71).

2. *A Sephardic Passover Haggadah*, with translation and commentary prepared by Rabbi Marc D. Angel (Hoboken, NJ: KTAV, 1988).

3. See, for example, Seforno on Exodus 12:2.

4. See *Pesahim* 114b; *Shulhan Arukh: Orah Hayyim* 473:6; 475:2.

5. The symbol of the maror underwent an evolution. Joseph Tabory notes that during the Roman meal, the dipping of lettuce as a first course was the most common appetizer. By the fourth century, the Talmud ruled that the appetizer must be a different vegetable (*karpas*) so that the maror could be eaten for the first time as a mitzvah with a blessing (*The JPS Commentary on the Haggadah: Historical Introduction, Translation, and Commentary* [Philadelphia: Jewish Publication Society, 2008], pp. 23–24).

In *Pesahim* 39a, one Sage explains that we use *hasa* (romaine lettuce, the talmudically preferred maror, even though five different vegetables are suitable) since God pitied (*has*) our ancestors. Another Sage derives additional meaning from the fact that romaine lettuce begins by tasting sweet but then leaves a bitter aftertaste. This sensory process parallels our ancestors' coming to Egypt as nobles and their subsequent enslavement.

6. Unlike most other rabbinic passages in the Haggadah which are excerpted from the Talmud and midrashic collections, this paragraph is unattested in rabbinic literature outside the Haggadah. See Joseph Tabory, *JPS Commentary on the Haggadah*, p. 38, for discussion of a parallel in the Tosefta.

7. Cf. Joseph Tabory, *JPS Commentary on the Haggadah*, p. 33.

8. Rabbi Joseph B. Soloveitchik, *Festival of Freedom: Essays on Passover and the Haggadah*, Joel B. Wolowelsky and Reuven Ziegler (eds.) (New York: The Toras Horav Foundation, by KTAV, 2006), p. 105.

9. The word *afikoman* derives from the Greek, referring to anything done at the end of a meal, such as eating dessert or playing music or revelry. This was a common after-dinner feature at Greco-Roman meals (cf. J. T. *Pesahim* 37d). The Sages of the Talmud understood that people needed to retain the taste of the Passover offering in their mouths. It was only in the

thirteenth century that the matzah we eat at the end of the meal was called the *afikoman* (Joseph Tabory, *JPS Commentary on the Haggadah*, p. 15).

10. Shemuel and Ze'ev Safrai enumerate longer lists of related verses that some medieval communities added (*Haggadat Hazal*, pp. 174–175).